WHEN THE BOUGH BREAKS

Abortion and the Rest of Us

WHEN THE BOUGH BREAKS

Abortion and the Rest of Us

Katie Reid

"Do you think because I am poor, obscure, plain, and little, I am soulless and heartless? - You think wrong! - I have as much soul as you, - and full as much heart!"

– <u>Jane Eyre</u>, Charlotte Brontë

Copyright 2009 Katie Reid

ISBN 978-0-557-20517-2

"Conventionality is not morality. Self-righteousness is not religion. To attack the first is not to assail the last. To pluck the mask from the face of the Pharisee, is not to lift an impious hand to the Crown of Thorns.

These things and deeds are diametrically opposed: they are as distinct as vice is from virtue. Men too often confound them; they should not be confounded: appearance should not be mistaken for truth; narrow human doctrines, that only tend to elate and magnify a few, should not be substituted for the world-redeeming creed of Christ. There is- I repeat it- a difference; and it is a good, and not a bad action to mark broadly and clearly the line of separation between them.

The world may not like to see these ideas dissevered, for it has been accustomed to blend them; finding it convenient to make external show pass for sterling worth- to let whitewashed walls vouch for clean shrines. It may hate him who dares to scrutinize and expose- to raise the gilding, and show base metal under it- to penetrate the sepulcher, and reveal charnel relics: but hate as it will, it is indebted to him."

– Charlotte Brontë, 1847

"For our Lord has surnamed Himself Truth, not custom."

– Tertullian

ACKNOWLEDGMENTS

To Karen and Randy for your faith, generosity, and friendship.

To Dr. Raymond Dennehy for your wisdom, words, and decades of courage.

To Dr. Steve Brown for all your cussin', spittin', prayin', and believin' and "the soft sound of sandaled feet."

To Michael Clancy for your picture that proves my thousand words.

To Sarah, Nancy, Donna, Kerri, Jennifer, Laura, Dianne, Andrea, Jody, and the many friends whom I lean on, delight in, and find joy with.

To Aunt Susie for all your editing, encouragement, and loving kindness – you have always been love personified.

To my family, you hold my heart.

To my Savior, who for some reason unknown to me loves me.

And to the five beautiful human beings who call me 'Mommy', the best name ever.

May this book speak truth and bring good... and of course, more babies, the second greatest good there is.

INTRODUCTION

"When a man steals to satisfy hunger, we may safely conclude that there is something wrong in society – so when a woman destroys the life of her unborn child, it is an evidence that either by education or circumstances she has been greatly wronged."

— Mattie Brinkerhoff, <u>The Revolution</u>, September 2, 1869

I was sixteen and it was almost seven a.m. I was in a bit of a rush, wanting to hurry inside and meet my friends at Shoney's for a brief laugh and a breakfast buffet before school started. I looked forward to the fun as much as the French toast. But as I passed by the newsstand outside, a headline caught my eye, and without thought my legs stopped in mid-stride and I stood frozen at what I saw. Could it be true? It didn't seem possible. But there it was in black and white, a scene so unreal and yet so good that my mind raced to verify. How could *that* be? How could the world have changed so completely, so drastically, so suddenly, so dramatically while half the world was asleep? Was it really possible to wake up to a world I had never known, had never thought possible, had never even dreamed? My heart pounded as I took it all in. But it was true. The wall that divided and defined the world as it is, as I and so many had always known it, was gone. The world's current oppressive reality was finally *history*. It seemed too good to be true, but it was. Change, victory, good finally triumphing, it overwhelmed me. For the first time in my life, I realized all the good I believed in and hoped for was truly possible. It wasn't just an ideal, it was something that could actually happen. The more I thought about it, the more I stared at that crumbling, graffitied wall, the more I realized why the wall had died. It was a lie. The lie had to end because it was a lie, and good had to prevail because it was true. Right there in that moment outside a breakfast buffet in South Georgia, I saw what hope can conquer when people care enough to <u>not stop</u> until things are as they should be.

    None of the things I am going to say are easy to hear. And I fear because they are so painful and so true that we won't have the courage to face the truth and right our wrongs. The truth is, we all have a part in this, this ugly thing called abortion. This gruesome lie makes women think that survival requires the death of their child inside them, and this is the lie which must be undone. It must be replaced with hope and opportunity for all. Until now women have born the shame, accusations, and burdens that come from the self-righteousness of the safe, the indifference of many, the cruelty and usury of men, and the humiliation of families, as well as their own fears and insecurities. The depths of ruins in their hearts are deep. They have hidden the truth, the ache, the guilt, the hardness, and the dreams behind smiles. Smiles are their front, their rear, their only guard, which is why they are so good at them. After all, can you talk about this awful truth to someone who is smiling? Isn't perception reality? Doesn't everything seem to be just fine? What the smile doesn't tell us is what this is really all about. Abortion is really about motherhood, how women, mothers, and children are treated. And yet I can't, hard as I might, think of a more important part of society or one that is more crucial and intertwined in the health, well-being, future, and prosperity of an entire nation. It all starts at home, not Congress, not court, HOME—the one where the girl came from and the new one she will build or run from. Home. What goes on there, what we learn, and what we love; it defines us all, good and bad.

So how do we make these homes, which we know to be so fundamental to... everything? How can women build them when they are surrounded by the wreckage of their lives? What are they to use? Where is their choice, their liberty, their life? How do they make a home when they are all alone and *mothers* aren't allowed inside the world they find themselves in? You can't buy one at a store or get one on a monthly payment plan. The one who has an equal share in wrecking a girl's life, well, you can't make him stay or pay, you can't make him do the right thing, you can't make him love, you can't force him to help you build this home. So how is a young woman to build this most basic necessity by herself when doing so requires more than what one person is capable of? What are these women to do when they lack the building supplies, the capital, the resources, the knowledge, the labor, and the ability to be in two places doing two things at once?

It makes me nauseous and angry when I think of the many, many men—and women as well—who preach with a haughty sneer "personal responsibility" and then turn their backs and look down their noses at the object of their disgust. They must be descended from those important people with important lives who walked by on the other side of the road. Arrogance, that's at the heart of it. The reality is that anyone can find themselves needing other people at some point in their life. Do we lecture on bootstraps and the American work ethic to those who lose everything in a fire, in a tornado, in a flood? Do we tell people who get old or sick and need to be cared for that they must summon the strength to care for themselves or die? Why not? Isn't it for the obvious reason that something has happened to derail their lives, and they need our help to set things right, to find a way to keep living? Isn't that enough for us to put aside our own personal judgments and prejudices and obligate ourselves with the messy business of loving our neighbors? Isn't it responsible and wise and good to help others find a way to become the self-sufficient, independent, taxpaying citizens we prize? Don't they have a much better chance of achieving such a worthwhile goal if we confront their fear with hope, their despair with love, and their problems with practical, workable solutions? So wouldn't the best, the right answer to this wrong, include that we make certain that women have the best chance to make good homes for themselves and their children, by insuring all the ingredients, the opportunity of the full blessings of liberty are possible for all?

When I began writing this book, I knew what I was coming up against. I know well the hostility and the emotional, heartbreaking stories women tell to justify what they have done when they felt choice was the one thing they didn't have. I know the tongue-tied expressions of women who know it is wrong but say nothing to other women, frightened into silence. Fear keeps those who should defend the helpless from saying what they believe or asking the unasked question of a friend. Many are simply afraid to say something that will hurt this person they know and care for. Even more are afraid of being branded the worst of labels, judgmental or intolerant, rather than daring to say killing babies is wrong. I know in writing this I am fighting fear, indifference, and arrogance—three of the most effective weapons to sustain injustice. As one young person told me, "It's not that it's not wrong, it is. But I don't want to know about it because I just don't want to care."

I know the arguments, I know the attacks, I know the rules of the game. I know the One who has the greatest interest, the Maker of these children killed so often and so efficiently has been barred entrance into court. And I know if you *show* the truth of what happens to these little babies, you are barraged with name-calling and cries of rule breaking and derision. Although honestly, this point in particular has always baffled me since that is exactly how cases are tried; evidence, however ghastly, is presented and truth is revealed. But it is these rules, this refusal to confront truth, which has polarized the greatest human loss of life in history into a firebrand of clichés and sound bites meant to protect any real discussion of truth and life for fear of the obvious wrong that will be exposed, the wrong women feel they need to declare as a right in order to protect and control their existence.

I also know from the many stories I have studied on fighting injustice that the ones who have the most power to make a case for the injustice done to them are the ones to whom the wrong was done, the power of personal testimony. But babies are killed before they have a chance to state their case, tell their tale, and the world doesn't want to see the evidence of how they die or look upon their torn bodies. It is too true, too real, too damning. And yet they still have a story, a testimony that we need to hear.

These human beings, killed before they could testify, needed someone to speak on their behalf. These humans needed an advocate. Somehow, I would have to argue for the babies, be their voice, share their stories. It seemed that the best way to stay true to what was happening and not to delve into fantasy, which is something I am not gifted in anyway, was to take stories I read, researched, or know personally and become the baby in that story. Empathy became my tool, my inspiration, my muse, and my pen. Armed with the stories of what was going on around these babies' lives, I imagined what I would feel, what I would say if I was the baby. I tried to think how would I feel if this was done to me, what would I say if this was going to happen to me, and how I would plead for my own life. Of course, I wept. When you put yourself in someone's shoes, especially someone innocent and helpless who doesn't know or understand why this awful thing is being done to them, you either cry or get angry. I have done both, and I have tried to do both honestly and appropriately, always remembering it is them I speak for first, but wanting to love their scared mothers as well. So I wrote to mommies, daddies, grandparents, even to the institutions which have helped maintain and defend this great wrong. I wrote these letters from the babies and became their voice. Some are long. Some are about big things that babies don't know about. Some are frighteningly honest about what was done to these babies and why. If you can, when you think to yourself, "A baby wouldn't say that," please remember that a broken human would, and in fact they have, and keep reading for their sake and for truth.

Harriet Beecher Stowe's *Uncle Tom's Cabin* gave me the best picture of how to speak truth when no one wants to hear it, how to show the humanity of those whom the privileged considered to have no real feelings, and how to speak both truth and grace when everyone plays a part in the madness. Her work, her courage, gave me the confidence to tell the whole truth, ugly and all, even if it hurt, even if it exposed, even if it judged. She also justified and confirmed my belief that God has a say in this. My thinking went like this, if it was acceptable, tolerable, in fact necessary for her to share God's truth, however "unfashionable" the old book was, in order to expose slavery for the evil that is was, then I do not need to be afraid to think on and thread His "unfashionable" truth into today's great evil, this present wrong.

Of course, I found many of her words rang as true and poignant today as they did when she wrote them over 158 years ago, which is why I used them throughout the babies' letters. That must be because there is a standard, a way of treating and valuing human beings that is constant, a truth about their worth and their nature which remains true despite all the efforts of men to control and contrive, diminish and destroy their value, including their consistent efforts to make humanity disposable and negotiable. It is this truth I write for, the truth that these babies and their mothers deserve all that we can give to help them make a life and a home for the simple reason that they are both human beings and need one.

"Abortion is the ultimate exploitation of women."
  – Alice Paul, author of the original Equal Rights Amendment, 1923

FOREWORD

"Open your mouth for the speechless, in the cause of all who are appointed to die."
Proverbs 31:8 (NKJV)

I was born that year, the year it became dangerous to make your dwelling place in a womb. Five months and seven days after Roe v. Wade, my parents got to meet me and hold me in their arms for the first time. I always found it remarkable that the first four months I was alive I was a person, and then, in the stroke of a pen, some strangers declared that for the next five months my personhood no longer existed, not even three fifths remained. One day I was precious, the next day I was disposable, the property of my mother to do with as she wished. How could I be a person one day, lose it the next, and yet still be alive, still living, still growing? How could I, as I got older, as I began to kick, grasp, grow nails, and move around, how did I lose the rights I previously held? I never could make sense of it, but I was one of the fortunate ones, I got to be born, I got to meet the world. Four years later my baby brother or baby sister was not so blessed. I wish I had been old enough to understand what was going on around me. I wish someone had cared or maybe dared to know what a child thought, or even just bothered to ask me, but they didn't. It's not the kind of question you ask a four-year-old. Certainly, if my mother had asked me if I wanted a baby brother or sister, as so many parents often do, I would have been wide-eyed and happy and full of dreams at such a wonderful thought. But a mother can't ask her daughter if she should kill the baby that is in fact her little girl's sibling.

So, no one asked or even told me until years later, and my mother paid a doctor to end that tiny life. His or maybe her body was tossed into a medical waste container, lost among other babies whose lives were taken, sharing a common fate and grave. And that is it; that is the story of that one little life, the one I should have been a big sister to. I remember feeling very helpless when I found out about that baby. My stomach hurt, and I wanted to cry. I wanted so badly to go back in time and say, "No! Don't! Stop! I'll help! I'll play with her, I'll hold her. I'll do anything you need me to do. Please! Just don't take her!" I wanted to scream, "Why?" And even though I knew the answer, it seemed so puny when I thought about that baby. My little brother or baby sister never knew a tender kiss, no gentle caress let them know they were loved; no one swaddled them, cuddled them, nuzzled their nose up to their soft cheek, or sang softly as they slept. There was just a beginning and a sudden, poisonous end.

As for me, because I was already where others knew I existed, I got to grow up in the mess that was left, the one she had tried to make less messy and complicated by ending that little life. But I still have so many questions. I wonder, little one, if you were a boy or a girl, or if we shared the blue eyes of our mother. I wonder, if you had gotten to live if she would have stayed instead of killing you and abandoning me so she could pursue her dreams. Not that I mind her dreams, just her leaving. I wonder what and who you might have loved. I wonder if you would have lived in books like me. I wonder if we would have stayed close through the years. I wonder what your name would have been, and what dreams you would have. I wonder what we might have laughed and cried about together. There is just so much to wonder about, quite simply one whole life. But I am left to wonder in shadows, the shadows of the disappeared.

My wondering has made me ponder every argument for and against abortion. I have poured over the different reasons why women abort, the pressures put on them by society, family, and economic realities, as well as the effects abortion, adoption, and parenting your unplanned child have on women. I have studied prenatal development and abortion procedures. I have seen the bodies of these babies and the awful ways they die. I have not shied away from anything that I came across that might bring light and understanding to the issue. One of the things I noticed and one that bothers me deeply is that nearly all the pro-life, anti-abortion arguments have been written by men and conversely the pro-choice, pro-abortion stance has largely been penned by women. I found well thought-out, logical arguments defending life compared to impassioned stories of why women chose to terminate their pregnancies and arguments defending the rights of women. To add to the frustration is the reality that when I look at the world around me, it is women—*women*—I find caring for, sacrificing, and giving up their dreams to raise children, and it is women who come to the aid of other women. As well, there are voices who never get to have a say, never get to tell their story, never get a chance to be heard—the babies whose lives are taken.

Apparently the choice given to America, the line conservatives and liberals have divided themselves on, is simply this: either choose to save and protect women or babies. Loving both, I find this option ludicrous. How could I possibly choose? I know intimately what it is like to be with child and without hope, engulfed and swallowed up by my circumstances. And then there are these children, held captive by our choices, full of life and of value, but defenseless. But it is not just me who knows and struggles. It is as if the nation has been immersed in Sophie's nightmare, and whatever Sophie or we choose offers only loss or guilt or both. But for so many women one thing is most assuredly gone forever, the blissful daydream of what life would have been like if only....

So because I love and admire all that women are and do, and because I cherish every little life because it has purpose and dignity and infinite value, this is my choice. I choose to fight for both of them, to defend both lives, to recognize the value and dreams of both mother and child.

*And I feel like I'm naked in front of the crowd
Cause these words are my diary, screaming out loud
And I know that you'll use them, however you want to*

*But you can't jump the track, we're like cars on a cable,
And life's like an hourglass, glued to the table
No one can find the rewind button now...*

– Anna Nalick (Breathe 2 a.m.)

MY STORY

"It's not always rainbows and butterflies; it's compromise that moves us along."[1]

"Boys will be boys. And even that wouldn't matter if we could only prevent girls from being girls."

—Anne Frank

Before I begin I must make certain you know this about me. I am not good. I have never had the luxury of, nor the predisposition towards, self-righteousness. My life is and has pretty much always been a mess, partly by my own doing, partly by the cruelty and selfishness of others, and partly by those burdens which no one thinks will ever happen to them. But maybe because I have been the frightened, pregnant young woman with no good options and a future that leads nowhere I want to go, maybe I can say the things that need to be said, and maybe all of us can put down our guards and listen. I do not want this to be about my story, but I want to tell enough of it so you will trust me enough to keep reading.

I was happy to leave home at eighteen despite being scared and penniless. There were far more bad memories than good there. I discarded goodness and ignored the God of my youth during college in favor of independence and reckless abandon. Like so many young people it was a time of countless mistakes but a steady self discovery. I had the sense during these years that my virginity was a burden I didn't want to carry. It's not that I desired to be bad; it's just that being good didn't work. With the exception of only a precious few, every relationship was just a battle to get into my pants, and "no" and "stop" simply didn't have any power at all. Every attempt at tender affection and intimacy with anyone I liked or cared about turned into a wrestling match. "Getting some" was all any of the boys seemed to want, and they were relentless.

If you tried to be stern or strongly resist a boy, he would call you the names that women find so particularly cruel. I wonder if all the purveyors of innocence and abstinence know just how bad boys can be and just how badly girls want to be wanted, especially when they haven't

---

[1] Maroon 5 *She Will Be Loved*

been loved at home. After a while I would just give in because I got tired of choosing between harassment, fighting them off, or my other favorite, getting dumped. Maybe you'll think to call me a name right now or wonder at my convictions or will power, but I already explained—I'm not good. My thought was if purity was my responsibility to maintain, somehow the power to physically resist, by sheer strength or sheer will or the power to make your "No" mean something, had somehow been lost. When I talked to other girls it seemed a loss of innocence was quite normal. Despite mine and all of my friends' fairytale dreams, childlike desires, and inadequate efforts to stay pure, the truth was that if you wanted to be loved by a boy, then you'd better go ahead and let him have what he wanted.

I know society wants to believe that it isn't true, that we have raised our boys better than that, that it is those girls who throw themselves at our boys, that equal rights means equal blame. But our not wanting something to be true should never allow us to close our eyes and deny its reality. It hurts to think that the boys and men we love could be capable of using, mistreating, and discarding young women. Yet it is our responsibility to look at the evidence and listen to the stories of these women and hear how these unwanted pregnancies came to be. We have to hold men responsible for their behavior instead of throwing *all* of the blame, shame, guilt, responsibility, and burden on women and then turning our backs on them so decency might be upheld.

I, like so many women, know what it is to have your manager grope you in a back room and the sick, helpless feeling that envelops you. I know what it is to have something put in your drink and wake up terrified at what you *don't know* happened. I know what it is like to care for a boy and think he cares for you and then wake to find yourself completely exposed to the hoots and hollers of his fraternity brothers. I know vulnerability and shame all too well. I know how far a boy will go to dazzle you and woo you, and frankly, how much he will lie to get his way with you. I know what it feels like to realize you are a stupid, gullible girl.

I remember joining a church as I attempted to tiptoe back to God, and the very kind, gentle pastor gave me the verse, "Be holy because I am holy." The irony was that a few short weeks later at a Christmas gathering this pastor's son, who was engaged at the time, suddenly put his hand on my breast as we stood there talking and laughing in his father's backyard the second after my friend walked away to get a refill. He quietly whispered, "You know you want it." Actually, I didn't, and I stood there petrified. I couldn't think of a single word to say. Who would believe me? But what could I do but push his hand away and walk back to the party, my heart pounding with humiliation, my stomach churning.

My first fear of pregnancy came when I was living with my boyfriend. I remember the lump in my throat when he sneered at the possibility of a baby and with a sinister gleam threatened, "That's nothing a few kicks in your gut won't take care of." I wasn't pregnant, but I didn't leave because I wasn't making enough money to get my own place. It took a few more nightmares before I left.

My next pregnancy scare was a few years later and real, but it was most notably marked by consistent, repeated denial. Although I had tried to take birth control pills, I had repeated complications, and I realized after several trials that I would have to rely on more traditional methods. But apparently, they didn't work. I honestly thought during that month that seemed to never end that eventually I would get my period and I shouldn't bother worrying about it. When that didn't happen, I took a pregnancy test at the insistence of my then unfaithful boyfriend. Despite the fact that the little blue line nearly burst into the small window, I refused to believe it. A week later I bought two more tests, with the same results of course. Finally I went to the school clinic where a doctor confirmed that yes, I was in fact pregnant, despite my concerted and consistent denial. Apparently, my not wanting something to be true didn't change the fact that it was. And somehow during that time the person I *was* quietly vanished, and someone new began... I felt the truth of those words: "A single event can awaken within us a stranger totally unknown to us. To live is to slowly be born."[2] But I was as clueless and helpless as any child in a strange new world. What was I going to do? The thought sickened me. I knew my family wouldn't help, I knew my boyfriend was grasping for a way out, and I knew there was no possible way to support myself, finish school, and raise a baby.

---

[2] Antoine de St. Exupery

This part of the story hurts to tell, but it is true and important. My solution to a life spinning out of my control was this. I decided I would just not eat. If I didn't eat, then the little blue line would surely go away, so I thought. So for about twenty-four hours I didn't. I don't think I can adequately describe the hunger that came over me during those hours. I know it doesn't seem like much, just one day, but that hunger consumed me. It was if my entire body, and maybe that little body inside me too, were battling my heart and my will. I didn't want to eat because eating meant accepting this, eating meant everything I was going to be would now be gone, eating meant becoming a mom when I didn't want to be. It was my last effort at denial, my last hope to make it all not true. But like I said, it was a force of hunger I have never experienced before or since. It occurred to me that this was not going to work, and this baby was not going anywhere. So I gave up, or gave in, and ate, fearfully taking those first willful bites. I remember thinking at that moment, "I guess I'm going to have a baby," and a lump stuck in my throat. I am fully aware that my not eating was my effort to make my baby die. And while by the grace and mercy of God, He did not let me continue, I am still just as much to blame as anyone who did have an abortion.

The next two months were spent hiding my secret, and hiding myself. Only a few people knew, and I made myself as scarce as possible. I simply disappeared except for work and class. Even then I kept my nose in a book or on the computer and only spoke when I was spoken to. I wore baggy shirts and baby-doll dresses. I hardly even made eye contact with anyone. My boyfriend dumped me for the other girl after letting me know he just wanted us to raise this baby as friends. He did briefly try to persuade me to give the baby up for adoption, but I would not even entertain the idea. I knew enough about myself to know that once I had acknowledged the inevitable, that acknowledgement was the first moment I loved this little person inside me. Of course, it was not the first moment she was real or precious, she was always that, but it was the first moment I had shaken off selfish for the awesome envelopment of motherhood. My heart had not been baby-proofed. Once that love opened my heart, I couldn't snuff it out or ignore it. I couldn't even conceive of the idea of giving my child away. This baby, for better or worse, had been given to me to love, and that was what I would do. I knew intensely that this little life deserved that and much, much more.

When I could not hide my secret any longer I began to tell the adults in my life. I was twenty-one at the time. What should have been a chorus of joy for a new life had my circumstances been different or acceptable was instead an unrelenting echo of anger, blame, and shame. I was not allowed the privilege of expecting or experiencing joy. That was reserved for good girls. These were just some of the responses: "You have ruined your life! You are such a stupid idiot! If you don't give that baby up for adoption, we will NEVER lift a finger to help you! You'll never get a dime from us! (Although I never *had* received one of those dimes.) You and that baby can starve for all I care! How could you? You had better marry him!" As well as lots of screaming and quite a bit of profanity that I will spare you. "You'll have to find some other place to stay. You just can't stay here. I'm sorry." This particular statement was from the very generous family that I had become close to during those years. They were the only family I had for quite some time. After my roommate had abruptly cancelled our lease because she and her boyfriend wanted to get their own place, they had let me stay in a spare bedroom, and my pregnancy was just too much for them. I knew they were so disappointed in me. My best friend said she just couldn't continue with our plans to share an apartment with me expecting a child. I really understood why she felt this way. Not only is a baby not the kind of housemate you want when you are twenty-one, but you don't even want to think about that future possibility.

My pregnancy had a plague-like effect on my life. The snickering and gossiping by other students and former friends were relentless, and the whispers were not so whispered. I just wanted the earth to open up and swallow me. I wanted to run away, to hide, to have never existed. Almost immediately after my humiliating condition became public knowledge, I found myself completely alone—abandoned. There was also this mounting impatient pressure that made me feel I had no right to even show myself among decent folk, and I knew I had better come up with a plan soon. The fact that a pregnancy center never even crossed my mind shows just how few or unadvertised they were. A home for unwed mothers was synonymous with adoption in my mind, and I didn't know of one anyway. Besides, I couldn't leave school, as it was all I had. Even my doctor could not contain his annoyance at having to care for a stupid, foolish girl.

My options were almost nonexistent. I remember in desperation calling my ex-boyfriend and telling him I had nowhere to live and could we please just be roommates and nothing more until I could support myself and the baby. That time was like living through a fog so thick I couldn't even take a full breath. Every moment was just a gasp to get you to the next. I waited a few days for his answer. I wish I could have known how his response was going to change my life, but I didn't and I was desperate. His proposal was this, his parents would help us get a place and get started, but only if we got married. I tried to explain to him why this was a bad idea for so many different reasons, but his parents had made up his mind for him. And so because I had decided this baby and I would eat, not just that one day, but every day, and because I wanted this baby of mine to not be homeless and hungry, I agreed, and we got married.

I remember having to force myself to walk up to that altar and forcing myself to smile. The dress I didn't care for and didn't want to be wearing, pulled tightly across my swelling abdomen. "At least I only have to wear this once," I thought and smiled meekly to myself. I remember making vows I knew I would keep, vows I knew he wouldn't. I was so frightened, so terrified, and yet I forced myself against every rational thought, everything I had ever dreamed all for the sake of this little one inside me. I knew what I desired and what I was sacrificing. I was giving up all of me for this tiny person that needed me for a lifetime.

I also remember wondering at the hypocrisy all around me. Everyone I knew was having sex and having it frequently, and the boys seemed to battle for the most partners. I knew I wasn't even the first to get pregnant, just the first in that circle to go through the humiliation of having the baby. I couldn't understand the punitive treatment I received not for having sex, but for getting caught. Apparently, pregnancy was the crime to be punished for, the scarlet letter to bear. And pregnancy was synonymous with stupidity. Smart girls were the ones who didn't get pregnant or didn't let anyone find out. Not bad grades, not laziness, not drunkenness or drug use, not deceit or theft, not even violence, nothing seemed quite so heinous or deserving of social shunning and disgrace as a young girl pregnant and unmarried. I also marveled at the genius of men, not one of whom has ever been so stupid as to get themselves knocked up. What gene made them so responsible, so smart, so uniquely adept at removing themselves from this common but life wrecking quandary?

As we stood there posing for our wedding-day picture, no one seemed to notice the very large bright red EXIT sign above our heads, captured forever in a three-by-five glossy. "How ironic," I think every time I see that photo. "That is exactly what we both wanted to do." He wasted no time getting right back into bed with the one girl and then many others. And I had a baby girl and fell in love.

> *You're just too good to be true*
> *Can't take me eyes off of you*
> *You'd be like heaven to touch*
> *I wanna hold you so much*
> *At long last love has arrived*
> *And I thank God I'm alive*
> *You're just too good to be true*
> *Can't take my eyes off of you...*[3]

No one can prepare you for that moment when you meet your first child. I just remember pushing and pushing and then opening my eyes to catch my breath, and there were the most beautiful sapphire eyes staring back at me from between my legs. I burst into tears. I had heard of people weeping for joy, but when it enveloped me it was like nothing I had ever known. How unearthly beautiful and wonderful and good! There, before me, was my baby girl, and nothing could be as sweet as that face at that moment. I remember being shocked because I hadn't thought or dreamed of what this baby would look like. I had been so busy being scared it hadn't occurred to me that anything so breathtaking and precious could come from me. Forgotten for that moment was all my shame and loneliness, forgotten was all my hurt and fear. All I could feel was love and joy and hope. As I nestled her close to me and kissed her soft cheek, she became my everything, and I couldn't help but think, "How could a baby be anything but a good thing?" So a mother and a daughter were born.

After Morgan was born I still worked hard to finish school, but it seemed so secondary, like a necessary afterthought. When I was with her, I wasn't that stupid girl who got herself pregnant, I was Mommy,

---
[3] Frankie Valli *Can't Take My Eyes Off Of You*

I was love, I was warmth and a full belly, I was kisses and hugs and caresses, I was smiles and sweet lullabies. Everything was somehow going to be all right because she was in my arms. I loved holding her and watching her tiny hand wrap itself around my fingers. I loved her blue eyes and the sweet sounds she made. I loved watching for every new thing she would do. I loved the smell of her sweet soft skin; breathing it in was like taking a breath of happiness. She made me forget I was supposed to be ashamed. But of course, I could always count on others to remind me.

I can't even begin to come up with a number to tell you just how many polite women, particularly at church, who would say, "What a beautiful baby," followed immediately by, "and how long have you been married?" with a smile that could not hide the judgment they seemed too eager to bestow. Since I had obviously been stupid enough to get pregnant, I must have also been too stupid to deduce the intentions of their less than subtle but polite inquiries. Certainly, they must have felt a civic and even divine duty to squash any dignity or joy I had the audacity to show and to make certain I knew how much I didn't belong. Girls like me must be reminded of their place, the outline of the letter retraced on our chests lest we dare forget. I remember wondering if they realized other girls were watching how they treated me. Didn't they know boys would treat those girls the same way they treated me? Didn't they know those girls had the same fears, desires, and nature I did? Didn't they know their judgment meant other young girls would rid themselves of the same burden to avoid a similar loss of dignity and ridicule? Didn't they know that babies die because they insist unwed mothers wear shame for life? Although I remained respectful and polite, there was something inside me that wouldn't let them take the joy that came from my baby girl. I guarded that joy like I guarded her. I had already given up my identity and put my dreams aside once, and I just couldn't let anyone take away the one good thing I had gained through all of that loss. I also realized I was good at being her mommy.

Although not always unspoken, I sensed that I was being watched and critiqued beyond what was reasonable; there was a scrutiny to every detail of my mothering. There was an eagerness to see me flounder and fail, a desire for me to give up on this idea of motherhood, an anxiousness to say, "I told you so." Before she was born, I knew they thought this baby would be better with someone else, but I knew there was nowhere better, nowhere she could possibly be loved and cared for more than with me, where inside she had first come to be. The reason was simple, she was part of me, lived inside of me, and belonged with me. One woman told me how selfish she thought these young women were who dared to keep their own children when there were plenty of families who deserved these babies. Somehow the right to parent your own child had, in the minds of many, become an exclusive right only for those who were married. Married couples deserved babies, stupid girls did not.

When I questioned this woman she based her opinions on the idea that one parent was insufficient and that these young women drain their families' energies by keeping their children. I was stunned and couldn't speak for a moment. There were so many thoughts racing through my head and so many emotions racing through my heart that I was afraid to open my mouth for what might come out of it. So biased and antagonistic she was that I doubted if even logic might persuade her. I asked if she could ever conceive of giving one of her children away at birth. She was aghast at the thought. I asked why she thought these girls should feel differently about their own child that grew and moved within them. Their hearts were not exempt from love just because their finger was exempt a ring. Their bodies responded with the same overflow of devotion that awakes and erupts from any womb. I asked if she thought it was unreasonable to take a child away from a father if the mother died during childbirth. This too was an inconceivable thought for her. The variables began to race through my mind, what about a widow, what about a woman abandoned? Would these women need to be stripped of their children too? It is just one parent, and one parent is insufficient you said! Why, all of these people would drain their families and communities! Who, who and how few can both parent a child and support themselves solely on their own? Are children only a privilege for those with a middle-class income or more? Don't we eagerly help a new mother who is married? We bring gifts and food and drop by to give the new mother a rest. Why is this much-needed helping hand a joy to offer if the new mother is married, but an unwelcome, unwanted, resented burden or duty if she is not? Why is one new life of more value or more reason to rejoice than another? Should we only rejoice over those children who are planned? Is this part of my punishment, the never-ending penalty for my fertile stupidity? Am I not entitled to my child?

Am I to be robbed of the joy that she brings? Am I to be treated as if I am selfishly stealing someone else's child because I dare to do the insensible selfish thing, because I dare to love and care for my own baby? Forget my body! This is my BABY! My identity, my purpose became clearer than ever before. No matter what anyone else thought or said, or how I was treated, loving this sweet child of mine, while it was not all I wanted to do, it was what I wanted to do the most.

When my little Morgan was still very little, five and a half months old in fact, I stopped nursing so I could do my internship, and before I could arrange a doctor's appointment I became pregnant again. This time was so different. I wasted not one moment in denial. I had so much joy from Morgan that I literally leaped in the air when I took that test. I couldn't wait to have another baby.

The raised eyebrows, disapproving looks, and comments such as "Already?" and "Again?" were still thrown about plenty, and not surprisingly still stung. But I didn't care quite as much. I wanted to please these babies and make them smile. Although we never knew anything but broke during those years, I threw myself into making a simple, but happy home. I read all the books I could get my hands on and took classes taught by wise, God-fearing women. During this time I also ran back to my God, who had never stopped loving me, never stopped beckoning me to Him, even when I ran from Him. It was so good to be close to Him and seek Him again.

Then one day as I blissfully played with Morgan, the phone rang and my life was never the same. Some memories are so clear you can relive them over and over, even if you don't want to. This was one of them. It was the one nurse at that doctor's office who had never judged me, never given me a funny look, never acted as though my pregnancies were anything but a complete delight. I am grateful it was her that called and told me what no parent ever wants to hear, and really what no parent ever expects to hear—that something is wrong and they're not sure what it is. "*One of the blood tests showed something is not as it should be and more tests are needed. It might be nothing you know. There are lots of false positives that turn out to be nothing. Oh honey, don't you worry...*" She must have heard me stop breathing. I couldn't even think. My end was silent, stunned with fear. Something wrong... something wrong... had honestly never even crossed my mind. There was so much else wrong, how could more wrong be added? And I didn't even know what "this" was. It wasn't like fearing the unknown, it was knowing there was an unknown that you should and would fear. At that moment though, "this" was threatening my baby, and I could do absolutely nothing about it.

As I hung up I really couldn't catch my breath. Fear constricted my airwaves and that familiar lump rose in my throat. I don't remember answering the phone again, or how much time passed, but I must have because my next memory was me telling someone else. She must have asked what was wrong. My panic sputtered out in short, breathless gasps to a woman I didn't care for at all. To be honest, I knew her well, and I feared and hated her because of the countless cruel things she did to me. "Why am I telling her?" I thought, as if my panic now had a voice all its own. Silence had always been my greatest defense, but before I could process my words or thoughts, she said something. She said the words that evoked something in me, turning my fear into repulsed indignation, and my indignation into strength and purpose. What she said was this: "I would completely understand if you aborted this baby. After all, you need to consider your quality of life." For the second time that day my lungs seemed to stop taking in air. *My what! My quality of life!* My emotions raced to find words, but all I remember gasping was, "No, I can't."

I was too stunned, too angry to be eloquent. Where were my words when I needed them? How often I have wished to go back and ask, and to defend my defenseless child. So if my child requires more help, more love, more patience, more money, more worry, and more of my time, I should simply get rid of this child? If my life were to be difficult, my dreams of normalcy or fairytale thwarted, then is it simply okay to kill my child? Shall I choose peaceful or pleasant over the life of my child? Shall I willfully choose to throw my own child in the trash so I don't have to be bothered to care for a little life that requires so much more than most? Shall I choose me over you, little babe of mine? Shall I choose a pretty little life I can control and predict, full of glossy pictures and lovely vacation spots over a life that journeys through the shadows and valleys of hopelessness, just so this baby and I might reach a place of peace that is as vast as the sea and know the exuberance and gratitude that can come when only the tiniest of miraculous milestones is reached, the ones most people never even notice? Shall I choose "problem-free" and miss the unfathomable joy that comes simply from glimpsing the great, great good that has come as a direct result of this pain, this loss, this baby, this unwanted journey, that I DID NOT SIGN UP FOR! What is quality compared to life itself? Is quality more valuable than a life, than my own child's life? Without knowing what would happen, I knew this was my child, and that answered all the other questions. Just like Morgan and without my planning, a life had been given to me to love. His name is Jacob.

The doctors could not find "the something that was wrong" in the many tests and ultrasounds they pored over. So my fear quieted, and I waited. When he was born I fell in love again, and everything seemed to be fine. He was so happy and full of life, all boy and all smiles. It was such a short time like this, and I want my baby back the way he was before he was taken from us. When I see his old smiles and his beautiful bright eyes, my stomach twists with what we have lost.

When he was eight months old he had a series of vaccines. Five days later he broke out in a few little red freckles. I thought it was odd, but I didn't want to overreact. He didn't have a fever and his activity was normal. I was slowly introducing him to each new jarred baby food. The next day there were more of those strange freckles, lots more. He was covered in red freckles, so I called the doctor, quite certain he would know what it was and tell me not to worry. He said to drop what I was doing and come in immediately. I did.

When he examined Jacob he told me he had already admitted him to Arnold Palmer Hospital and asked if we wanted to have an ambulance take us there. "Tests," that is all I was told when I asked, "Why?" When I arrived at the hospital the nurses took my beautiful, strong baby boy, and a hematologist stepped into the room. She spoke about the possibilities—leukemia, or ITP.

I was numb. I felt like I was watching it all happen. The old fear gnawed at my gut, but I somehow managed to drown out almost any feeling. Everyone said how strong and full of faith I was, but that wasn't true. I think when I handed Jacob to those nurses, I handed over my heart too. I was just waiting to hear the diagnosis to know what to feel.

It was ITP. Jacob's body did not respond properly to his immunizations and had started killing off his own blood platelets. I was relieved it was not leukemia, and we followed the treatment protocol. But the nurse's phone call from when I was pregnant was never far from my mind. Was this the something that was wrong? How would it affect him long-term? Should I let him get more vaccines since his body obviously did not respond appropriately? Was there more to come? The old fear slowly, stealthily crept over my heart. I fought it with denial and a thousand reasons why not to fear. Hope and diversion became my shield from heartache and reality, though I used them more as blinders. Besides, I thought to myself, I didn't have time for worry, I had morning sickness.

   I was happy because I knew babies made me happy, but it was a guarded happiness. I couldn't allow my heart to be quite so deliciously happy as before. It was too risky. Now I knew something could go wrong. Happiness came in the same sweet package that fear did. I waited as long as I could before I told anyone about this new baby because I knew what everyone would say, and of course, they said it. But this time I was angry. I had never asked for anyone's help. Who were they to judge how many children I should have? I had taken care of these babies without much help from my husband. He worked and went out with his friends most nights. There was never much money left over for us. Being a mommy was my life, my job. I loved these children and loved being their mother. The audacity of their judgmental arrogance and their lack of kindness and compassion only served to make me more determined to exceed their efforts at parenthood. I worked harder than anyone I knew with only the smiles and kisses of my babies as compensation. But the smiles and kisses of Jacob became fewer and fewer, and very quietly he left us.

   I don't know exactly when it happened. I do remember asking our pediatrician if he was certain the vaccines were safe for Jacob after what had happened before. He reassured me Jacob would be fine. Oh, how I wished I had listened to that gnawing resistance in my gut. But you do what the doctor says, especially when you are a young mother. And then you hope it will all be okay. But it wasn't. There wasn't one day that it happened, but it was if every day there was a little less of my perfectly precious baby boy. It was a long time before we got the diagnosis and there were many reasons for that.

   We sold everything we had and moved to Colorado, where I had a beautiful baby girl, Reagan, who had the face of an angel, and the biggest blue eyes I have ever seen. As I tried to care for my newborn and play with Morgan and Jacob, Jacob wouldn't play with us. No matter where we were, he was trying to run away. I couldn't reach him, I couldn't teach him. It was as if he had slipped into a world all his own.

I thought he was deaf and took him for more tests, but he wasn't. I knew something was wrong, but I didn't know what it was. I knew he didn't look at me or at anyone else. He wasn't interested in people. I can't tell you what it is like to be rejected by your one-year-old, for your one-year-old to refuse to be held, refuse to look at you, and put his hands over his ears when you try to talk to him. I can't describe how it feels to have your one-year-old run from you at every possible opportunity and to not even let you hold him to read him a story. There just aren't words for that feeling. It resembles failure, but I could not for the life of me figure out how or why. So I just carried the hurt and kept trying, simply because I didn't know what else to do. Even though I was wrapped up with all of this, I had more than just this peculiar behavior of my baby to worry about; there was a two-year-old, a newborn, and another move, this time to Atlanta.

I realized during this time that I was strong, and I was not a girl anymore. I was a woman who knew how to work hard and how to serve. I knew how to love, how to turn the other cheek, and how to be gracious and merciful. I knew the art of kindness and friendship. I knew how to be a good wife and mother, even when I wasn't treated like one. I knew how to put my trust in my Savior, who loved me and had promised that "all things work together for good and for those who love God and are called according to His purpose." So I set about making friends again and another place, a home.

Jacob didn't seem to notice or care about anything except running and bodies of water. He would throw himself into streams, ponds, fountains, pools, and tubs. It seemed there was no safe place to play. Water, danger, and escape were everywhere. Every environment I took my children to for them to simply play and enjoy the delights of childhood offered two children joy and another child the opportunity to nearly kill himself. There I was with an infant on my hip dragging a three-year-old, and chasing a two-year-old to prevent another water rescue. Eventually I realized I had to stay home, that going anywhere was just too dangerous. But at home all he did was eat, drink, and constantly run in circles. He couldn't stop, he was never satisfied. The noises he made all day were awful and ear piercing. I got to the point where I would never let go of him, and he would strain and pull, trying to free himself to run his relentless pursuit toward whatever was most dangerous. I didn't know what to do and every day my heart broke.

It was during this time that Jacob's bowel movements became grotesque. To call it chronic diarrhea doesn't come close to describing what came out of him. It was massive and smelled like something had died. It would go up his back and down to his knees five to eight times a day. It was so acidic it would make his bottom bleed. The pediatricians didn't care and didn't think any tests were necessary. "Just keep his bottom covered up with ointment," they suggested. And my baby would scream and reel in pain when I cleaned and covered his raw bottom. But the worst part about the poop was that Jacob would smear this foul, filthy feces on everything. He smeared it in carpets, rugs, walls, toys, books, sheets, blankets, clothes, the TV, even the ceiling, and of course, all over himself. He would pee on everything. Every morning, every afternoon, every day, every night there was another awful poopy mess to clean. I can't remember how many times I ran to turn the alarm off in the middle of the night after Jacob had set the motion detectors off; I would then run to find my little boy in the dark and would slip and fall or step in my son's shit or urine. He could scale any gate we put up to corral him, and he rarely slept.

I still remember the first time that happened. He had climbed out of his crib during his nap and had smeared feces all over the three-day-old down comforter I had painstakingly saved up for over several months. I remember looking up at the water stained ceiling of our tiny apartment where the water heater from the apartment above had flooded our home and saying to my God, "You want me to thank you for this?" But I was strong and had such faith and said, "If you can bring good out of fleas and lice in a concentration camp for Corrie Ten Boom, you can bring good out of this." And I trusted Him and His goodness.

Some of you may have already guessed, but it was hard for me to let the fear become reality. As crazy as it seems, there was somehow safety in denial. As long as I pretended the monster had not taken my son, I could hang on to my dreams, even if they were increasingly a fairy tale. As long as I pretended this was all normal, I could outrun grief and loss. As long as I closed my eyes I could keep that pain at bay. I struggled with the idea of accepting yet another uncertain future. I didn't want to let go again, especially to a future that stole my joy, my hope, and my child. But no matter how long I kept my eyes tightly shut, the ugly monster was still there… autism.

I once heard a father describe autism like this: "It is as if someone came in the night and stole your child and left this bewildered body." The unknown fear finally had a name, but the name was like death. It stole and ravaged everything. That is what makes loss so hard; you can't get back what you love. It's just gone. And you are left with a hole in your heart and in your life that won't stop aching.

I researched everything I could find because the doctors would not help me at all. They treated me and my children as if we had a communicable disease. Their apathy was palpable, arrogant, and infuriating. I tried to care about the things all young mothers care about, preschool, playdates, picture taking, playdough, and potty training. But we couldn't do anything normal. Every day was filled with the horrors of autism and the stench of my son's feces. Every day I would research articles, medical journals, the Internet, desperately searching for information, for a treatment, for a doctor that knew what to do, for a cure, for any word or hope to keep me believing there might be an end to this horror that had stolen my son. The remainder of my days was spent scrubbing shit, crying, trying to reach my little boy, and giving my girls the mommy they needed. I tried to be a loving, serving wife to a man who was cold, drunk, cruel, and selfish. I prayed and begged my Savior to help me and heal my son and give me peace in this nightmare.

I was so distracted and hurting. I became pregnant again. I don't even know what I felt. Every day was survival and a struggle for hope. I spent most days crying and nauseous, trying not to be sick as I scrubbed that dead-smelling shit off every surface my son could think to smear it on. I spent a lot of time finding or traveling to therapists. It was all such a tearful blur. And then it was time to have a baby. Very indicative of that period, I didn't have time to make it to the right hospital. It just happened so fast, and I got to experience natural childbirth, which is just awful. I am quite astonished more women don't die during childbirth. Still to this day I am taken aback when women who have had natural childbirth and not almost died act arrogantly and self-righteously about their birth experiences, as if the millions of women who have died giving birth throughout generations where just weak, lazy, or lacked will power and stamina. Those people, those attitudes, leave me speechless. When my son was born they took him away because they were working on me. I remember being surprised I was still alive and wondering why there was so much blood. Apparently, I almost didn't make it. I wept. I hurt so badly and I couldn't stop shaking. I was in shock. But there was a new baby to love, so I tried to be happy because that's what mommies are supposed to be.

Paul was and is the most loving, kind, beautiful boy. He has dimples that would put Brad Pitt's to shame. Of all the things in this world that speak of God, I think my son's dimples do more to show His love, His hand in making each human being uniquely wonderful, and His joy in His children than any natural wonder in this world. There is no reason for those delightful dimples, no evolutionary purpose, no gene I am aware of; yet every time he even grins, you can't help but fill with joy and smile at such a beautiful sight. I think Jesus knew how much I needed to see His love and to know His presence so He gave me a beautiful baby with dimples to remind me there is goodness and joy beyond this monster that ate up our lives.

The monster continued to devour. When Paul was five weeks old, Jacob ran away again after the front door was left unlocked. Five minutes passed. He was three and a half and was struck by a truck. Miraculously, he lived and there were no internal injuries. He looked awful, almost like he had been burned. But I thanked God he was alive.

I think that is when it happened. I was so tired and spent. I just couldn't see how God could work any good from all of this. My faith, which had once been so strong, had come face to face with my ugly reality and failed. Then my doubt snowballed, and I began to wonder if He even loved me at all. I told my God He was wrong, that this was more than I could bear, that this yoke was not light at all. I feared a season that would never end and imagined each day being surrounded by shit, but being less and less able to cope with it. My faith, once my firm foundation, was gone. My life seemed hopelessly helpless, and I wanted to die, or just go to sleep and not wake up. But those babies needed me, and somehow for them I kept going. One thing I knew, though, I couldn't take any more. I campaigned and cajoled and finally persuaded my husband to have a vasectomy. I was done having babies.

My husband's vasectomy was scheduled for a particular Wednesday. That weekend a familiar nausea came over me. Monday I slipped out to the store and bought a pregnancy test. In my bathroom I held my breath, closed my eyes, and counted. When I opened my eyes, there it was, the little blue line. I cried. I couldn't do it, not another baby. I shrunk to the floor, cradled my knees and sobbed. I wept because I knew what would happen. I would love this little one, and there would be nothing left of me. I would love this baby with the same fierce devotion I loved my other children. Loving these children and living with autism, domestic abuse, and infidelity was already too much. I was all used up, my youth and joy were gone, my heart was in pieces, my body exhausted and old. I also found myself consumed by a guilt I had known once before. The truth about my selfish, scared heart was this: I didn't want to be pregnant and to have another baby. I knew how the love of a child binds you and takes possession of your heart. I knew how vulnerable it makes you to love a child. I didn't want that hold on me again. I didn't know how I could love another baby like they need to be loved and survive myself. I was terrified. This one would most certainly kill me. The fear of another natural childbirth gripped me as well; the pain was still so vivid it made me cry. My husband was delighted, and I was devastated. I remember thinking callously, "He must know this will kill me." I was so ashamed that I was not happy, and I was too rundown to fake it.

Sometimes God uses the strangest things to get us out of the pits we find ourselves in. An old acquaintance had recently announced with great joy that she was expecting her first baby. I had kept my news quiet and did so for four months. But her husband visited, and my husband delightfully shared the news of our fifth baby. The congratulatory phone call came shortly thereafter. I didn't say too much, just answered her questions. Then I heard a familiar disdain and arrogance. "Well, you really need to find a better form of birth control! Ha! Ha! Ha!" Sometimes the audacity of people is truly astounding. I was too stunned and offended to respond.

It took another phone call before I had climbed out of my depression enough to defend my motherhood and my child. Even with my heart filled with fear, I was able to ask, "Why do you think my child number five or even more is not of just as much value and reason to rejoice as your first child?" Does a child's value decrease based on birth order or number of siblings? Does cost of living determine the value of a single life? While these thoughts did not take away my doubt, they sustained me through those months and the ones that followed.

Then Benjamin was born. Mercifully he was a full breach, so as soon as I went into labor there was a cesarean and I didn't die like

I thought I might. I was still so tired and distraught over raising these babies and living with Jacob's autism, but here was this baby, and he was not easy. He wanted to be held all the time. He would scream just to hear himself scream. He seemed to love the sound of his own screech. Yet he was so delightfully, willfully mischievous that you could never truly be upset with him. Breathtaking, he was that too. He would look at you with those big eyes and pout and my heart would melt. He had his sister's angelic face. He was also the gift I had not known I needed, the gift that brought my heart joy. Despite how hard it all is, I am grateful that I get to love and know these amazing human beings, and I feel wise to recognize that the greatest thing I will ever achieve is the simple name *Mommy*.

I know I don't deserve all of these precious wonderful children with such a selfish heart. I really have no defense, and it wasn't even the end of such thoughts. But they were my babies and I loved them. There was also my Savior's mercy, which knows no bounds. I don't know why or how He can love a heart like mine, but He does, and the truth is by His grace and gift, I love Him right back. I rest in His love and boast in His mercy and trust in His goodness, even more when I see how little goodness is in me. He has loved me when there was nothing lovely in me. Even when I couldn't believe Him or His promises He let me be a mommy to these five precious miracles. And despite all the tears, I am so grateful.

I won't lie to you, though, motherhood is not for sissies. The thing about being a mother is that it is the most impossible kind of love. When you give birth, it is as if your heart leaves you and is no longer your own. This tiny creature now carries your heart as it toddles carelessly through life, giving little heed to your worry, and you are left hopelessly bound, with no choice but to love. Not loving, not caring is simply not possible for most. It is a love that commands selflessness, but guarantees your heart no protection or security or even reciprocity. It is a love so consuming that the fear of your heart breaking, of losing that little loved one and living without them is always a heartbeat away. It is a love that never fades but must somehow be tempered as they become their own person and walk out in a world where you are not there to protect them. The fact that they jeopardize your fragile, fearful heart with every foolish step seems of no concern to them. And what can you do but teach, love, warn, beg, threaten, and ultimately watch and pray?

It was fear and grief that filled my days. Jacob's autism created an intense loss, not just for him, not just for me, but for all my children. I loved him so much, but I hated the autism, and I couldn't rescue my little boy. It was as if there was a death I couldn't mourn because my son was still here. At some point I began to start wondering about what my life would have been like if all this hadn't happened. What would I have become? Where would my dreams have taken me? What had I given up? The old dreams I had laid aside stirred within me. I wanted to be more and do more than just be a mommy. I wanted to be mommy plus something else. I wanted my life to count for something beyond cleaning up poop. All those years of dying to self and sacrificing had left me dying to live. But I couldn't, I had to be a mommy and desperately wanted to stay being a mommy. I just needed being a mommy to not hurt so bad, take so much, and be so so hard. I needed more joy, more hope to make it through the many, many dark days. I needed the *Occupation* line on every form to be filled to not leave me searching for words, feeling like a failure with my insides nauseatingly empty, not because I thought what I did was nothing, but because I knew that is how others with better titles viewed me. While I would tell myself not to care what others thought, I could see that none of us mothers, who only nurtured for a living, could escape the condescending looks or comments of the better employed.

A battle raged within me that was so ugly and awful I didn't dare share my thoughts. I wanted to be free, to only have to think of me, and I hated myself for feeling that way. I knew it was wrong. I even thought maybe all I needed was a vacation. Maybe that would fix all that was wrong inside me. While all of this was going on in my heart, my husband couldn't have cared less. He was so cruel, so callous and uncaring, so unwilling to help me with the children, and so selfishly attendant to his own desires and whims that I began to break. I just couldn't handle the kids, the autism, and my husband's abuse anymore. This was just no way to live and no way to raise children. But the truth is the financial reality I lived in kept me trapped. All my dreams could do nothing to pay the bills or finance childcare. I was dreaming of two different lives, and only one was possible. There was no answer to my problem, just the knowledge that I had to persevere and make the best of a bad situation. It's like C.S. Lewis says, it's "very much like an honest man who pays his taxes. He pays them alright, but he does hope that there will be enough left over for him to live on."[4]

Society is really no help at all. Women are educated to be professionals, and the ones who achieve this are honored and paid accordingly. Yet women are also reared to be selfless and loving, caregivers and homemakers. We give up ourselves to do just that, all because of that impossible love that envelops our hearts. In doing so we become vulnerable not just to that little loved one, but to the financial reality they represent. A child must be cared for all hours of the day and provided for as well. But how can one person do both, unless the pay and benefits are exceptional, the hours flexible, the childcare excellent, and the workload manageable? How can a young woman in high school or college or just starting out make it on her own with a baby? How can a woman who has lost years of job experience jump into the workforce with a childcare bill equal to her entire paycheck? This emotional and financial reality is what traps women into destructive abusive marriages and relationships because they literally cannot afford to feed and provide for themselves and their children on their own. Like I said, who, who and how few can both parent a child and support themselves solely on their own?

Working mothers are made to feel they are abandoning their children to daycare, and that they don't love like a mother should. Stay-at-home mothers, well, they are viewed as lazy, not contributing to society, a bloodsucking leech (actual words used towards a mother of five by her alcoholic husband), lacking ambition or skill despite what degree they might hold, housekeepers, not deserving of any respect. One friend described it this way: "No one thinks much of you at all." There is an air of condescension and pathetic pity toward stay-at-home mothers, as if your worth is solely determined by your ability to be financially self-sufficient. I remember going to court to get a Temporary Protective Order, and as I held my feverish, sleeping two-year-old on my shoulder and my three-year-old's hand, the judge looked down at me with annoyance and asked accusingly, "Do you have a *job?*" I didn't know what to say.

It is as if being pregnant, being a mother, especially to more than the acceptable nuclear number, is criminal, dirty, negligent, and wrong,

---
[4] C.S. Lewis, <u>Mere Christianity</u>

and society and its laws only exist to protect those who have already proven their worth with an acceptable, notable annual W-2. And while being a mother, guiding, teaching, correcting, loving, serving, giving, and making a home require all one's time and energy, it is work that does not produce a paycheck. In fact, what you give up in being a mom, is not just the money you would have made, but the independence, the fulfillment, the career that protects you from being vulnerable and forcing you to choose between poverty, abuse, or closing your eyes to the infidelity and addictions of your spouse. As well, how many women give all for decades and then find themselves discarded and abandoned like a used dishrag and replaced by a newer model, with those years forever gone, completely irreplaceable? What is a woman to do? She seems forced to choose between herself and her children, and someone is going to lose.

At this point it seems necessary to discuss what I don't want to share. But to ignore this reality and pretend it does not have any effect on a woman is to only tell a chapter in a story and then to tell the ending. The reality is this: the men so many women live with are not good or kind. They are Dr. Jekyll to the world and Mr. Hyde at home. They are selfish, controlling, often deceptive and manipulative, creating an environment where their wife is utterly dependent on them with little to no freedom, where the wives are belittled, threatened, and crushed until they are a shell of a human being. Often women's names are left off every important financial document and they are told they don't have a right to anything, they didn't earn a dime. They are nothing. Many times the very children she has so completely and selflessly poured her life into are manipulated against her or the threats of a custody battle are held over her head when she has no way to pay for legal representation.

The very real nightmare many women find themselves in is one where the country, the culture, and the courts do not acknowledge the time, energy, and labor she has invested in raising her children as *work*. A basic understanding of economics reveals that he who holds the capital gets to determine the value of the labor being performed. Because mothering does not produce a profit, mothering has been viewed as having no economic value or monetary contribution. Without capital, mothers are without the power to declare and protect their labor and their worth. This has allowed society to view those doing the labor of mothering as having little to no value, despite the very real and significant contribution of rearing and raising a human being. Fear, loss, love, an enormous lack of opportunities, power, and recognized worth are coupled with monumental responsibilities, leaving many women entrapped in a life that robs and wrecks. They are left with little to hang on to but the love they have poured into their children and the faith knowing there is purpose in this pain and goodness in tomorrow. Despair becomes common, and one has to wonder what makes women persevere.

Quite simply it is love. And as much as this love takes, it gives in ways nothing else can. It is love, that love for those little ones that started it all that has kept so many women going and has remained the bedrock of a mother's perseverance and devotion. It is this love that keeps moving us despite all that moves against us. It is this love that creates hope, and in time heals. And even though the anguish remains very real, it is distant. It is this love that takes a defeated soul and gives it new dreams of peace and freedom and fulfillment. It is in knowing the love of your child and in loving that a woman, however scarred, can triumph in both the joy of her children and the joy of chasing her own dreams.

As for me, you might want to know how my story ends, but the truth is I don't know. No one really does. Despite all of our best efforts to control and predict our existence, much of what happens to us and often defines us is beyond us. I cannot tell you a pretty fairy tale where everyone lives happily ever after, but I can tell you the truth, and the truth is this... Nothing I have gone through or will go through changes this one fact: these babies that grew within me were human then and are human now. They were my children then, and they are my children now. They are today the same human beings with the same genetic structure and the same parents that they had when they were at their tiniest, when they were only one cell. What has changed is their clothing size and their ability to talk back, both of which have expanded exponentially. But their size and skill does not define their worth or their humanity, just as it does not define mine. Their value was given to them when they were made in the image of the One who made them, value that we all believe is given to every person equally and cannot be separated from them based on any manner of things by which man finds to discriminate against, "unalienable" is the word we use; do you remember it? None of the things *I* was feeling or feared changed any part of who or what *they* were. Being thrilled over one baby or fearful over another didn't make one baby human and another one not. They were all equal and deserved the same rights I did for the very same reason, because we are all human beings. Not my shame, my dreams, my fears, my pain, or even my utter exhaustion and despair could do anything to undo or diminish the miracle of life within me. It is that miracle that remains my story, a miracle that keeps unfolding, and one that I will always fight for because these precious little people and their amazing mothers are worth the fight.

One other word, this life has been hard and so many times I have wondered if I could ever believe that God could work any good through all this mess, but He has and continues to. Even Jacob has given me reason to hope, and more than anything God has used my little boy to show me what truly matters in life, from the pointless pursuit of possessions to the unfathomable power of love. In loving my son, I have learned the futility of fancy things and the joy of loving someone who needs you so very much. I have also learned that although I will *always* be a mommy, it is not *all* that I will be. For even though a life can be wrecked, the wonder of it is that every one of those lives can be rebuilt. So I remain in awe of the One who is the giver of both life and faith and in His promise that "If we are faithless, He remains faithful; for He cannot deny Himself" 2 Timothy 2:13 (NKJV).

THEIR STORIES

"It is only with the heart that one can see rightly; What is essential is invisible to the eye."

– Antoine de St. Exupery

Dear Mama,

I'm scared. I'm scared for a lot of reasons. I'm scared you'll be angry at me. I'm scared you won't care. I'm scared you won't listen. I'm scared you'll be so scared of me judging you or of the guilt you have buried that you won't read what I and the others so desperately need to say. I'm scared you'll lie or believe the lies and clichés of others. I'm scared you'll blame me and that will make you feel justified in what you chose to do to me. I'm scared you'll say I was and am nothing. I'm scared that you'll look at your present, pleasant circumstances and coolly say to my cries, "The end justifies the means." I'm scared you'll think forgiveness isn't possible. I'm scared that I might not even cross your mind. I'm scared you'll pretend it didn't happen—pretend *I* didn't happen. I'm scared you lack the courage to face all these possibilities and me.

But despite all my fears, I can't keep quiet any longer. Maybe it's the brave heart that emerges from standing with so many just like me. Maybe these words are bursting out of us because we've kept quiet for so long. Maybe it's the indifference to us that makes us cry, "Listen, just listen to me! Let me speak!" Or maybe, it's just the right time. Hopefully, these will be just the right words, words that can break the stalemate, end the hostility, heal the resentment and hearts of so many, and maybe even bring about the change necessary to ensure the value, hope, safety, and dreams of both women and children, whatever their plight may be.

So Mama, I ask for you to hear from us all, even if it hurts. It's time for someone to tell you what you need to hear instead of what you want to hear. It's time for us to tell you the truth. You might find yourself surprised at the compassion, or interested in our ideas. But please, let us tell you our hearts, and take the time to listen long enough to care.

The Babies Who Disappeared

"Who would ever think so much went on in the soul of a young girl?"

– Anne Frank

Dear Diary,

Most days it seems as if my entire being waits for dusk. Just to be able to move about our cramped quarters without fearing every step, just to walk, wear shoes, make noise, it is the freest feeling my feet have known for years. Every day I wake longing for those people who work below us to *leave already* so that for a few brief hours I can remember that I am alive. How silly to wish for something so small. I don't think people can understand who don't live every day hiding the fact they are alive. Isn't it strange that to keep living, to keep existing, to keep from dying I have to hide more than a mouse might? Isn't it amazing to think I am hidden here in plain sight, and the world doesn't know?

Sometimes I wonder how many others are hiding like us, how many friends are keeping their secret. Secrets are funny things. Some I think are wonderful to have, they can make you smile inside with just a thought or keep you warm in your dreams. Some secrets I think are good to keep, and they make you better and stronger for holding them. But I think some secrets hurt more than you can ever tell, and they change you without you wanting to change. And other secrets, like us, were never meant to *be* secrets! How can a living being pretend not to be? I simply can't stop growing or learning or thinking or dreaming just because I am confined to this hidden corner. People just aren't meant to work that way. We don't stop being people because others don't want us. I guess I'm like the truth, the kind of secret that is bursting for the moment when it can break free into the world and *be* again.

Out there is danger and fear and hate, but in here we are just waiting to live again. I still think "The best remedy for those who are afraid, lonely or unhappy is to go outside, somewhere where they can be quiet, alone with the heavens, nature and God. Because only then does one feel that all is as it should be."[5] It sounds so good, but so far away.

But today and for all the tomorrows I can see, I have to hide in my hiding place, do nothing, and stay quiet just to live another day. I have so much time to think, and I think about so many things, big things for

---

[5] Anne Frank, Diary of a Young Girl

little girls. I wonder if there would ever be a day when other children would be in danger because they weren't seen, or be unreal because they couldn't be heard, or couldn't do things. How funny to think that what saves my life, could be the very thing that endangers theirs. I just don't see what is so dangerous about a child. It's sad really. When will the world realize how much possibility is in each life, and how what is essential isn't the stuff that's always visible? I love knowing what so many seem to live never seeing, that "Everyone has inside of him a piece of good news. The good news is that you don't know how great you can be! How much you can love! What you can accomplish! And what your potential is!"

Maybe one day they will. Maybe one day no one will need a hiding place, and every life will matter.

Love,
A Young Girl

Dear Mommy,

I'm scared.

Being inside you is all I know.

What's going to happen to me?

Am I going to be all right?

Is anything bad going to happen?

Will you stay with me?

Will you be there to hold me?

Where am I going?

I'm scared.

You are all I know.

Love

For Always,

Your

Baby

Girl

Julie

Who's to say the darkened clouds must lead to rain?
Who's to say the problems should just go away?
Who's to point a finger at what's not understood?
— Natasha Bedingfield

Dear Mommy,

I know why you don't want me, and who could really blame you. It's not selfishness, convenience, freedom, money, or any of the other things women are accused of. It's also not privacy or women's health or reproductive rights. It's me, and the awful images, fright, and sickening helplessness that rise within you every time you have a wave of nausea or I move inside you or you see yourself growing larger with me. There I am, the evidence of the violence and humiliation done to you. My presence inside you confirms the brutality; refusing you the comfort of pretending it was only a bad dream. It all seems so raw, so real, so wrong. How could this be happening? Panic grips your heart. And yet despite decency or sanctity I am here, buried within you, constantly reminding you of the evil done to you and the horror you lived through. If only the scrubbing would wash me away.

I know you hate the thought of me and I make you cry. The very idea of knowing me, or worse yet that in meeting me you might helplessly and hopelessly love me, paralyzes you. How can I possibly make a case for my worth and my right to exist when my very conception is the result of all that you have been robbed and raped of? How can I say you owe me a chance at life when yours was ripped from you? How can I claim I am as important as you? How do I demand anything from you when no one ever gave you a choice in how I happened to you?

At the same time, I don't believe this is between you and your doctor, he's just a number in the yellow pages, and of course, the one who did this to you has no say at all. As for you and your God, you know what He would say and right now you may not believe in Him, especially after what happened to you. One day I pray you do know His love and see His goodness, even through this awful agony. But that will take time, time you don't have. Every day makes me more real, more frightening, more life-altering than the day before. Two choices, two paths, both of which you can't help but resent, both of which wreck your life and steal your dreams and force you to become someone you did not want to be. So I guess that leaves this between you and me, and I am so very small. You can't even see me. How can I possibly matter at all?

What if I were to tell you that one day you would miss me and wonder about me? I know that is hard to believe considering how sharp and painful those memories are today. What if I told you I could make you smile and laugh? What if I told you that I, the hurt and shame inside you, would one day be your joy? What if you just held on to me, knowing there would be a day you would be so grateful to be my mommy? What if I could show you how amazing God is at bringing good out of bad? Would you want me then? Could you carry me with only the hope of something good?

Of course, there is that other possibility, the one that terrifies you. What if I only reminded you of what was stolen from you? What if I only sifted the embers of resentment in your heart? What if my being here took away your chance at your dreams for good? I guess just the possibility of this combined with the anguish and shame you carry along with me is enough to make you end me before either one of us can see how the story ends.

But, Mommy, I am asking for a chance at my life, despite how I came to be. There is no scarlet *R* or *I* on my tiny chest, only a small steady heartbeat within it, each tiny thump beating with life, hope, and humanity. You see, Mommy, I don't know that I cause you pain; I only hear your voice. I don't know that I'm not supposed to exist, I just grow. I don't know that you have every reason to be repulsed by me and not want me. All I know is that I began here, inside you, am a part of you, and I am made to love you. That might be asking too much today, so I guess I just want a chance to love someone, a chance to be the good that came from bad.

I know we do not usually make decisions based only on the hope of something good, and too often we decide based on what is the easiest or hurts the least right now or leaves us the most control for the future. But would it be too much to ask to make such a decision based on what is right now and always? For it is always right to protect your child. It is always right to love me. Letting me have a glimpse of all that life in this world is giving me a chance at life, and even simply loving me is not heroic, it is human. A lot of good can come from a little one's love you know, and one little life can change the world. A baby is a good thing.

And as much as I think my life should be protected and cherished and allowed to flourish, so should yours. Your heart, hurt so badly, should be given every opportunity to heal and love and dream and know the satisfaction of realizing your longings. I guess I just think we both matter and that life for one does not have to be the end for the other.

I realize though, for you this decision is really about your pain and you wanting what happened to be a memory as soon as possible, in your past forever, instead of a present reality, confronting you again and again, refusing to let you forget. But because I am the one whose life is taken, I need to ask you, is my worth determined by my conception? Is my worth determined by who my parents are? Is my worth determined by their deeds, by his deeds, by yours? Is my worth determined by who wants me or if anyone wants me? Do I need your consent to be valuable? By ending my life, aren't you saying I don't matter? Is it okay to punish me, kill me for what that rapist did? Isn't that an injustice? Isn't there another way to right this wrong, some way where I don't have to die? No human being should be treated differently because of how they are conceived. Just as people have equal rights no matter their size, race, religion, sex, economic or social status, their worth rests solely on this sheer and single fact, that they are human beings, and all human beings, all of us, even the tiniest most unwanted and unplanned among us, are endowed with equal rights. These rights are no more dependent on my location than the color of my skin. Wherever a human exists, value, worth, and dignity are present. Mommy, my personhood, my humanity is not increased or decreased by the manner in which I came to be. I live and I grow and I am human, a small one for sure, but completely and uniquely worthy of life.

But there is the anguish again, eating away at you, rushing you, pushing you, gnawing at you to make it stop. "Hurry, hurry and get rid of the baby," it cries. The pain is excruciating, and the bad so big you can't imagine any good coming from it. My humanity seems so incomparably insignificant when placed beside the ache inside you, even though you know I am here. For you, for now, good simply does not exist. In fact, this belief consumes you—hope and good are gone. You struggle to discern the path that will set things right again. The world tells you, "Sometimes you have to break some rules to set things right." And you want to believe that is true. But deep, deep within you, you know that a baby dying, *your* baby dying—me dying—can't be the thing that will bring you justice or peace. My death will not undo what was done; it will only get rid of the evidence. Even the immediate relief of knowing you don't have to deal with me, even that, for some reason brings its own guilt, guilt for feeling relief, and a guilt you instinctively know will grow. Of course, me living means you, as you are now, will never be the same. So I guess the real question is instead of you breaking rules to right the wrong that happened, will you trust God to take a broken you and make it all better, bring good from bad, and give you the gift of new life and a new love? And don't scoff because I mention the One who made us both. "For it is no slight thing when those who are so fresh from God love us."[6]

I won't lie to you; the right thing is often the most difficult. You will need courage, hope, and a friend would help so much. You probably can't find these within you or near you, but they are there, and they will carry you as you carry me. And one day, the pain will be a memory, but you will have my love for always.

Love,
Your Baby Girl

---

[6] Charles Dickens

"Even a child is known by his actions, by whether his conduct is pure and right."
Proverbs 20:10 (NIV)

"All children must look after their own upbringing. Parents can only give good advice or put them on right paths, but the final forming of a person's character lies in their own hands."
– Anne Frank

Dear Mommy,

I know you didn't think it could happen to you, just to the bad girls, the loose ones, and to the characters in some faraway script made for a TV movie. How could you be having a baby at fourteen? I mean you didn't even know what was happening when you were cuddled up watching movies in the basement. All you know was he made you feel loved and wanted when he wrapped his arms around you. The kissing and holding and his warm breath were like a dream—a wonderful dream. You put up with the other stuff just not to be without him, just to keep him there wanting to be with you, just to stay in his arms. And then it happened. You felt he had somehow taken a piece of you that you didn't know could be taken, leaving you vulnerable, missing something, and yet also knowing something you shouldn't. After that when you were with him you were scared but wouldn't or couldn't stop him. Was it fear of him abandoning you or your heart breaking or maybe fear of losing forever that something you knew was now gone? If you lost him, giving up your purity would be lost for nothing. Maybe it was the thought that if you kept doing *it*, all those feelings would drift away. They didn't. But a baby, well that fear, however biologically real, didn't ever penetrate into the abyss of your emotions. All that mattered to you was your heart and that desire you just couldn't shake, no matter how cool you played it, that need to be wanted and loved by that boy.

When you told him about me, he did everything you were afraid he would do. He was distant, unaffectionate, and blamed you. He accused you of trapping him, and then your biggest fear, he was cruel. You tried everything a girl could do to prevent the inevitable, but inevitable it was, and he broke up and broke your heart, leaving you at fourteen to handle this on your own. "I have my whole life ahead of me! I'm not going to let some leech try to hold me down and trap me. I don't even know if it's mine! I've seen the way you look at other guys.

You make me sick! How dare you try to put this on me! What kind of a whore has sex at fourteen anyway?" His words thundered in your heart. You didn't even know how to begin to defend yourself. It seems as if all you know lies crumpled around you, and you don't know how to move. You want to cry out, "But you said... But it was you that took... I'm almost fifteen... I am not a..." But silence strangles you, those words choking you as you swallow them back, letting them echo within you. Nothing seems adequate to those verbal daggers, and you stand there soundly beaten and abandoned.

Things like child support and paternity suits don't occur to you, looking into the hole where your future was once. I know that all you see, Mommy, is the end, and all you can think is how to get things back the way they were before, and what can possibly be done to make this nightmare untrue. Panic rules... Too young, too young, you are just too young to have your life suddenly be over. You try to ignore the awful truth, wishing and praying for me to vanish. It's hard to even think of me as a child, as a baby, as your baby. To you, I'm more like a plague, a cancer trying to overtake you. I can understand why you feel that way. But that is only the fear talking. What I really am is something very different.

I know having a baby so young must paralyze you. If only you could run away from it all. I know you are terrified of what your parents will say, of what your parents will do. And your friends are sure to disappear. Everyone will talk and whisper and laugh and scoff and blame. Your love will join them. Shame, betrayal, fear, and loneliness flood your body so much that even I sense the stress and nausea that envelop you. No wonder you think there's no hope. No wonder you can't think of me. No wonder you find yourself here at one of those clinics looking down at the tile floor, blinking back tears with only the hum of the fluorescent lights above you. Today, you are here to get rid of this problem, to get rid of me before your world crashes around you. At least right now it is only your heart, but tomorrow the damage includes me—my body and my life. If only I could say something to make you change your mind, something to show you how much I matter.

You see, Mommy, I know you think you are too young to have a baby, but I am too young to be thrown away. Who at any age deserves that for a destiny? I am just not ready to die. And when I think about it,

I can't think of an age where it is justifiable to take your child's life even if you are a child. Despite your youth, you know I am alive inside you. You know this abortion would kill me, so your fears don't become reality. But you are scared, you tell yourself, very, very scared. If I knew what you had planned for me, wouldn't I be terrified? Wouldn't I hide myself inside you, wrap myself around your heart and cling to you? If I could just latch on to your finger, my tiny fist would grip you, and you would know there was someone else to consider and something else besides fear to move you. But now all I can reach is your womb, my home, and maybe, just maybe your heart. One day I hope to grow big enough to clench your finger and stare into your eyes and you will know... you will know right at that moment that you chose right, you chose well. But that means today and for months and more to come you have to hope in a future that is hidden from you now. Choosing me means living with the ridicule and the messed-up life. It means losing your plans and having to dream new dreams. Why should you have to go through all that anguish, you tell yourself, attempting to silence that gnawing voice, my voice. "Why do I owe some stranger my whole life, however small? I didn't plan for this baby, so why should I be forced to carry it? It's not like it could live..." But I could and you know it.

The thoughts of what I might be one day startle you. Competing futures mingle as you ponder what could happen if there were no fear, no humiliation, just you and a baby. Hope and love, a new story, a new beginning, your imagination nurtures a few glimpses of possibilities, but just as quickly fear blurs and devours the picture, and you are left staring at the same cold floor, thinking I could ruin your life, and therefore I must die. Right or wrong, you command yourself, you have to get rid of me so you might live every day pretending I was never here.

But that is a lie and one that will haunt you. Never mind, though, I have something important to tell you. I understand you wanting and needing to have some say in the matter, some choice in the course your life will take. But you need to know that you don't have to terminate me to rescue your life. You can choose to love me or let someone else experience the wonder of loving a child, and this is why. Because despite time and circumstance, I am your precious baby, distinctly made from you and in you and as dependent on you as any baby or any human that has ever lived is, as they grow big enough to meet the world. The truth about me is that I will change your life, not ruin it. You will grow and mature in some ways sooner than you would have, and you will develop a much deeper compassion and appreciation for what is truly valuable in your life. You will endure much, but it will make you strong. You will struggle, but it will give you a dignity independent of the trappings and shallow fluff of the spoiled and self-absorbed. You will meet people you never would have known, and you will experience a love so rich it will define a part of you that you didn't know was there and give you a depth you cannot imagine. You will dream dreams for two, and know the fierce love that flows from devotion. I would never ask you to stop living or growing yourself, just as I would never ask you to stop my growth or my life. The devotion I speak of is one which never stops seeking the best in you or the best in me. Dream chasers make great mommies because they show their little ones in the way children learn best, that people can fly, dreams will come true, and that growing up happens best when you are fulfilling the joys and abilities you have been blessed with. Plus, if you decide to remain my mommy, you will get all my hugs and kisses, and I will make you laugh with a joy you have yet to know. I will give you memories that will make you smile unaware every time you get lost in them, and peace amidst the mayhem. This is no little reward, for in this sweet innocent affection is much of what makes life good.

Certainly, things will change and there will be loss. But in reality they already have changed, and killing me won't change that. For every life, once it has begun must be dealt with. It is far better to experience the hope and joy of a tiny life and your own new one, even with its heartache and setbacks, than to only know the loss. The fear and hurt will not last forever, and your future will not replace the void my death will leave. If anything it will make your career lack the luster of before, whereas if you keep me and your dreams, you will experience triumph, joy, and wonder. Your life will not exist for the sole purpose of blessing yourself, but you will know the incomprehensible joy of being a blessing to another. But, Mommy, the best thing about doing the hard thing and the right thing is being able to wrap your arms around love, cradle me tight to your chest, look at my sleeping face and know that I am worth every tear you have cried.

Love,
Your Baby Boy

"We think some severely afflicted infants should be killed."
— Should the Baby Live? *Helga Kuhse and Peter Singer 1985*

Dear Mommy,

Is something wrong? It's just that I can feel you crying, and it scares me. I love the sound of your voice and your laugh. They are music to me, and I want to twirl and tumble or sleep peacefully to the melody I hear all around me that is you. But this is a new sound, and I can feel your stomach churning. Is it me?

I wonder if it's because something strange entered my world today and took some of my tiny world with it. I didn't know what to think of it, but now that I hear you crying I wonder if it's me that makes you cry so. Did you learn something about me that saddens you or scares you? What is it?

I've closed and opened my fists, I've sucked my thumb, I've curled my toes, and hugged my knees. I can't see what could be wrong. But it must be me, what else could it be? Is it possible I didn't grow as I should? Is it possible I will be so very different? Is it possible that being a mommy to me will be too difficult and loving me, taking care of me, will make you cry more than a mommy should?

Oh, Mommy, I wish I knew what it was. I wish I could fix me; I want you to want me and be so very proud of me. I don't want you to cry when you think of me or think of how things should be. I guess I need you to know why being a mommy to me would be wonderful. I need you to know why I'm not a mistake, despite what the tests or the doctors say. I need you to know I matter even if I'm not like most babies, and that I'm worth all the trouble. But I'm just a baby, and I don't know how to tell you all that a mother learns in a lifetime. How do I explain to you that every single life has purpose, even when you can't see it, even when you never see it? Maybe I can't. Maybe you'll never understand. But does that mean that because you're scared and a normal life seems impossible with me in the picture that somehow you're justified in ending my little life before I have a chance to have a story, before I have a chance to love you and a thousand other things that most people forget to cherish?

I know I don't understand too much. But I know I'm here, and if I'm here, then God made me, and if God made me, He has a reason, a purpose, a whole plan for me. Maybe you might think less of God or less of me because I don't look or act like all the other kids, and you won't be able to have the same dreams and memories as other parents. But how is different the same as less? How is my life worthless? Why am I disposable? Why don't I deserve a chance to love you, Mommy? How else could God work miracles in the hearts of those who will meet me and know what it is to care for a child like me? How else could God create compassion and selflessness in the hearts that only knew how to seek their own gain? How else would God ignite a love like His own that would never stop giving even if the love was never returned? How else might God open eyes to prejudice and injustice if He didn't open your hearts first to love the not quite as lovely, or the not so easy, or the totally defenseless? But how can your hearts change into something so beautiful, so wonderful, so honorable, so lovely if you never know me or love me? How can such a miracle happen in your life if my life is thrown in the trash with all the other unwanted, imperfect babies? How will you ever know all that truly matters in life if you get rid of the problems, all the inconveniences, all the things that prevent perfection and force you to rethink your world?

But maybe you think there is no God, so these possibilities of change in a human heart are of no concern to you. Or maybe you think you have your own plans and purposes and don't want to be burdened with loving a baby like me. Maybe you think it's just too hard and you don't have the strength. Of course, most of us don't see the change we need, how we should want something so much bigger than what we presently desire. We think we're just fine as we are right now, that the little things we strive after are big things, or that such an enormous change isn't possible or wise. *We are like ignorant children satisfied making mud pies in a slum because we cannot possibly imagine what is meant by the offering of a holiday at sea.*[7] Suffering and sacrifice is something few of us ever eagerly run to, and character development is something we hope will happen after reading a book or attending a seminar, but never too much character, only enough to make us look wise and well-learned, not enough to make us want something different. That kind of character is only pretension and makes little difference in you or the world. What

---

[7] C.S. Lewis, The Weight of Glory, originally published in Theology, 1941.

I am talking about is a change rooted in love. Yes, I am sure of it. That must be what the world needs, what you need, Mommy.

Whether you believe in God or not, whether you want to be affected or not, you have no right or reason to kill me because I don't measure up to all you think a life should be. A defect in form is not a defect in character or a default in my humanity. An extra chromosome, a fragile one, a body with missing parts, or a soul locked in a body that won't move; these are not the things that define me. It is not my abilities or lack of them that measure my worth. It is not the cost of my existence that determines my value. I am more than my thoughts or senses, more than my dreams, more than my IQ or abilities, more than my potential, and certainly more than my skin, bones, and tissue. What makes up me is the same that makes up you, the same wondrous spark of humanity that cannot be summed up with an equation or formula, an essay or a song, a resume, trophy, or plaque. It can maybe only be fully known by the most selfless acts of generosity, courage, honor, and tender loving kindness. Whether we give it or receive it, being a part of it, being kin to it, capable of it, desiring it, rejoicing in it, desperately needing and longing it, or surviving to seek it someday, these are just how our stories are told. This is how we all become a part of the great human story; how we participate and interact with all those whose image we share in God's great love affair with us.

Just because my story is different does not take away its importance or value. I remain just as significant despite what the world sees as my shortcomings. Poor eyesight has never kept a person from having vision or foresight, and the biggest brawn does not guarantee a heart of courage. A pretty face might cover a cruel heart, and the brightest dreams might flourish in the weakest body. I like to think the world will continue to see the equality of all people. Did you ever hear what one great man said? I wonder how he might have said those words if it was me he was defending, me he saw value in, me he struggled for...

> You say A, is normal, and B, is not. It is *normalcy*, then; the one whom there are more of having the right to dispose of those who are not the same, who do not meet the same standards? Take care. By this rule you are to be disposed by the first group whose standards you do not meet.
>
> You do not mean *normal* exactly?—You mean normal people are the *intellectual superiors* of those with handicaps and disabilities, and therefore can

dispose of those people who do not have the same intellect or the same abilities as normal people?

Take care again. By this rule, you are to be considered rubbish to the first you meet, with an intellect or ability superior to your own.

Well, genetics is the issue, a genetic disorder creates a natural disorder in the value of a human being, you say, and these individuals can therefore, be discarded because they are of lesser value.

Take care. By this rule, any genetic difference can be seen as a disorder, and you can be rounded up and gotten rid of by anyone who views your genetic differences with disgust.

This could never happen you say, but... didn't it, just half a century ago? Wasn't there a science to the rating of human beings?

But, you say, it is a question of interest; and, if you can make it your *interest*, you have the right to kill another, especially if they would trouble you, cost you, need you. Very well. And if that person, can make it his interest, then he can kill you.[8]

Of course you object to such strong words. You say it's your body, your right to privacy, that you can do what you want. But you don't die, I do. You think because I grow inside you that you own me, that I am your property to do with as you wish? Mommy, no one has the right to do wrong to another! And don't forget, the great man's words spoke of viewing other people as property, of the incomprehensible hypocrisy of demanding the right to enslave and own another person. Isn't killing a person, your child, because I don't measure up just as wrong? Isn't getting rid of people and only letting the perfect people, people like yourself, live a wrong that has enabled some to stand by and watch millions die? If it is wrong when it happens to many, isn't it wrong when it happens just once? Isn't it wrong when it happens to me? Aren't I real? Don't I matter? Isn't a wrong done to me the same as a wrong done to anyone? The wrong is the same no matter whom the wrong is done to, no matter what the reason.

But raising a baby like me will be too hard and you just aren't willing to give that much of yourself. I don't deny I will probably be an awful lot of work and cause an awful lot of tears to fall. But I am not less human because I am more work. And if you just can't do it, give me to someone who doesn't mind the imperfections, give me to someone

---

[8] Abraham Lincoln: adapted from quote in Hadley Arkes, First Things: An Inquiry Into The First Principles of Morals and Justice (Princeton, NJ: Princeton University Press, 1986) pp. 24-25, 43-44.

so I can love and be loved. Let me keep growing, let me keep living, let me be the blessing I was made to be, please.

Love,
Your Imperfect Baby Girl

In October 1939, Hitler himself initiated a decree which empowered physicians to grant a "mercy death" to "patients considered incurable according to the best available human judgment of their state of health." The intent of the so-called "euthanasia" program, however, was not to relieve the suffering of the chronically ill. The Nazi regime used the term as a euphemism: its aim was to exterminate the mentally ill and the handicapped, thus "cleansing" the Aryan race of persons considered genetically defective and a financial burden to society... Popular films such as Das Erbe ("Inheritance") helped build public support for government policies by stigmatizing the mentally ill and the handicapped and highlighting the costs of care. School mathematics books posed such questions as: "The construction of a lunatic asylum costs 6 million marks. How many houses at 15,000 marks each could have been built for that amount?" The idea of killing the incurably ill was posed well before 1939. In the 1920's, debate on this issue centered on a book coauthored by Alfred Hoche, a noted psychiatrist, and Karl Binding, a prominent scholar of criminal law. They argued that economic savings justified the killing of "useless lives" ("idiots" and "congenitally crippled").

In the spring and summer months of 1939, a number of planners began to organize a secret killing operation targeting disabled children. Beginning in October 1939, children with disabilities, brought to a number of specially designated pediatric clinics throughout Germany and Austria, were murdered by lethal overdoses of medication or by starvation. Some 5,000 disabled German infants, toddlers, and juveniles are estimated to have been killed by war's end. Euthanasia planners quickly envisioned extending the killing program to adult disabled patients living in institutional settings. In the autumn of 1939, Hitler signed a secret authorization in order to protect participating physicians, medical staff, and administrators from prosecution, code-named T-4, where patients were sentenced to death after a review of a questionnaire about their state of health, with a "+" in red pencil, meaning death, or a "-" in blue pencil meaning life, or "?" for cases needing additional assessment. These psychiatrists rarely examined their patients and were expected to process large numbers of forms. The Euthanasia Program instituted the use of gas chambers, complete with showerheads to deceive victims—prototypes of the killing center facilities built in occupied Poland later in the war, and crematoria for systematic murder. The doomed were bussed to killing centers, mostly former psychiatric hospitals. In the town of Hadamar, school pupils threatened each other with the taunt, "You'll end up in the Hadamar ovens!" The thick smoke from the incinerator was said to be visible every day over Hadamar (where in midsummer 1941, the staff celebrated the cremation of their 10,000th patient with beer and wine served in the crematorium). The personnel who participated in the Euthanasia Program were instrumental in establishing and operating the extermination camps Belzec, Sobibor, and Treblinka, later used to implement the "Final Solution."[9]

"From May to November 1988 I worked for an abortionist. He specializes in third trimester killings. I witnessed evidence of the brutal, cold-blooded murder of over 600 viable, healthy babies at seven, eight, and nine months gestation... One day Dr. Tiller came up from the stairs from the basement, where mothers were in labor. He was carrying a large cardboard box and ducked into the employees only area so that he wouldn't have to walk through the waiting room. He called out for me to come help him. So I unlocked the door for him, and pushing the door open I saw very clearly the gleaming metal of the crematorium, a full-sized crematorium, just like the one's used in funeral homes. I went back to my computer. I could hear Dr. Tiller firing up the gas oven. A few minutes later I could smell burning human flesh."[10]

---

[9] Excerpts from the United States Holocaust Memorial Museum and the Holocaust Teacher Resource Center.
[10] Luhra Tivir quoted in Celebrate Life Sept/Oct 1994 **When is the Violence Real?**

"This is a very great adventure, and no danger seems to me so great as that of knowing... I left a mystery behind me through fear."

– C.S. Lewis

Dear Mama,

I know you don't have much of a memory of those weeks. Who knows what influence you were under, Jim Beam or an assortment of pills of unknown origin. But whatever it was that blurred and erased those days, it took with it the memory of who my father might be.

You have told yourself because you can't remember I must not really exist. Besides a baby conceived under those circumstances, who will never know their father, isn't really the same as a baby with parents, especially sober ones. But, Mama, don't worry. I'm a baby, a good one, and I'm growing peacefully inside you. I have a Father too, and He won't ever leave me. He knows me, He made me, He was there. He planned my life, even though you didn't. Amazing, huh? He even planned your mistakes to bring about me, the good, from them. I know I don't seem like the good right now, more like evidence of the bad. But you don't have to see the good right now to know that there will be some one day.

If you are scared of me having problems because of the things you were drinking and doing, I understand, but I can work through it. I'm tough, even though I'm small and it takes me longer to do what others do easily. You'll see. I love to hear somebody tell me I can't, it's all the ammunition I need. I have a will of steel, Mama. You'll be amazed at all the things I'll be able to do, even the things I can do right now inside you, things people will tell you aren't possible for somebody like me. Some people think only the kids from perfect homes with perfect parents can make something of their life. But my Father has a much bigger plan for me. He's all I need, Mama, just Him and a chance to chase my own story.

Some people will look down and sneer at you, at me, at the audacity of you bringing a bastard into this world. But I don't know what that is. I don't have a clue that I should somehow be ashamed of how I came to be because the truth is I shouldn't be ashamed, and I won't be. I know every baby came from the same place for the same reason, from and for Him. I don't have to worry about their disdain.

But yours, well, yours scares me. I am afraid your shame will lead to my end. I am afraid you will believe their crazy idea that some lives are more valuable than others, that some human beings should be rejoiced over and others should be destroyed. They will tell you to rescue your life instead of mine. But, Mama, you can do both. I can't imagine giving me away would be easy, but it would be better, better than throwing me in the trash like yesterday's garbage. Leave the bottle of Jim Beam there, leave the pills, but not me. Keep me, cherish me, love me, or at least give me my chance to break out into this world and be somebody you can be proud of. I'm a little baby that will grow to be a part of something so much bigger and more wonderful than you ever thought could come to be from what was once only a mistake.

Love,
Your Princess

"There is, actually, nothing to protect the slave's (or child's) life, but the **character** of the master (or mother)."

– Stowe[11]

Dear Mommy,

I can't understand something I heard you say. It just doesn't make sense to me. I heard you tell someone that "unless my baby's father sits on the Supreme Court, then no justice has a say in what I choose to do with my baby or my body." I guess I'm confused. Why would you say that about me? Are you planning on doing something to me? Do you not want me to grow inside you? Why? I don't know where else to grow big enough for you to cradle and cuddle me. Do you just not want me, is that it? What does that have to do with my daddy? What does that have to do with the court? Does my daddy want me and you don't? Does the Supreme Court want me? Why would you mock someone who would defend me and dare to give a child who can't defend themselves a voice? Why would you demonize a brave heart who thinks I shouldn't have to die just because you apparently don't want to be my mommy right now? Does somebody have to want me before they can or will or should protect me? Can someone else protect me if you want to kill me or rip me from your womb, from your body? Can my daddy? If you don't want me, does that mean I don't matter? It can't be that I don't exist, that's one thing I'm sure of. I'm living and growing and you and daddy are my parents. Besides, if I didn't exist, your pants would fit a lot better than they do right now. What else could I be but a very small, very real human child, growing exactly in the spot that every human child begins and grows?

So I guess that leads me back to my other question. If you don't want me, does that mean I don't matter? Does that mean I shouldn't be saved, shouldn't get to keep growing, keep living? How can that be? Has anyone ever not wanted you or maybe some other human being? Homeless people, diseased people, deranged people, they're not wanted either, right? Do people get to kill them too? Can the courts speak for them even if they're not wanted? Can Daddy speak for them, or does Daddy have to be on the court? Does Daddy have a right to speak for

---

[11] Harriet Beecher Stowe, <u>Uncle Tom's Cabin</u>; p. 457

me? Does being my mommy or daddy mean you get to say if I live or die? Why is that? Isn't mine a separate life from yours and Daddy's? If I was torn from inside you and my body ripped to pieces, wouldn't you go on living even if I were dead? Do you think you own me? You don't. I'm yours to love, not possess. Do you think I'm some piece of property to be tossed in the garbage if YOU don't want me? I might be your child, but being someone's child is not about privacy and ownership and title, it is not about property rights and trespassing, it is not about timing and convenience. Being your child, Mommy, is something beyond these very base ideas, for no one can own another person, and no person can ever qualify as property to be adjudicated with the luggage and cartons and cattle. Being your child is more than being *your* baby, it is the vast distance that lies between belonging *to* someone and being *with* someone. It is the difference between being a *thing* and a *person*, and how we treat these persons who have not developed the lung capacity to scream, "STOP!!!" or the muscles to restrain the knives, scissors, and forceps sent to dismember them.

Since this is *my* life, I will tell you where I belong; I belong with the one who will love me and protect me, who will not kill me. I don't need you to grant me permission to be a human person. I already am whether you want me to be or not. I just need you to not disregard my humanity in order to protect yourself from having to carry me or parent me.

Is the person who will love me you? Is it Daddy? Or will the court speak for me since my voice is too small to be heard? Who will fight for me and let me know I belong with them and that they will love me? *"When and where I find the country, the courts, the family, the arms that embrace me, the laws that protect me and recognize that I am a living, bleeding, human being and worthy of the rights endowed to me, not because you say I have these rights but because these rights are self-evident and given to me by the One who made me; wherever that place is, that will be my home, that is where I belong."*[12]

– *Joshua*

---

[12] Harriet Beecher Stowe, Uncle Tom's Cabin, p. 117

DID YOU KNOW?...[13]

By five weeks, my brain has already begun to bulge, and my heartbeat began at three weeks. During my first month of existence I grew 10,000 times my original size.

I have all my body systems by eight weeks and my forty muscle sets are moving by impulses through my central nervous system.

By nine weeks I can hiccup, bend my body, move my arms, breathe amniotic fluid, open my jaw, stretch, and react to loud noises. Before my first three months of life is over (what doctors call a trimester), I yawn, suck, swallow, feel, smell, and respond, I also have fingernails, toenails, and a unique set of fingerprints. By the end of my second trimester I can hear.

Just as adults do, I experience the rapid eye movement (REM) sleep of dreams.

I savor my mother's meals, first picking up the food tastes of a culture in her womb.

Among my other mental feats, I can distinguish between the voice of my mommy and that of a stranger and respond to a familiar story it is read to me, which is evidence of my cognitive recognition and memory.

My behavior develops in the womb and correlates to my behavior and activity levels after birth. I move fifty times or more each hour, flexing and extending my body, moving my head, face, and limbs and exploring my warm wet compartment by touch.

Heidelise Als, Ph.D. a developmental psychologist at Harvard Medical School is fascinated by the amount of tactile stimulation I give myself. *I touch my hand to my face, one hand to the other, clasp my feet, touch my foot to my leg, my hand to my umbilical cord,* she reports.

Odder activities I do include licking the uterine wall, bouncing up and down on my head, and pushing off the uterine wall with my feet, all caught on camera of course.

---

[13] Information gathered from several sources, most notably and including quotes: Janet L. Hopson; *Fetal Psychology*; Psychology Today; Sep/Oct 98. Other sources: Alexander Tsiaras and Barry Werth; From Conception to Birth a Life Unfolds. (Doubleday, New York, 2002) and *Abortion: A Woman's Right to Know* booklet developed by the Georgia Department of Human Resources to comply with the Georgia "Woman's Right to Know Act" of 2005.

"Birth may be a grand occasion," says the Johns Hopkins University psychologist (Janet DiPetro), "but it is a trivial event in the development. Nothing neurologically interesting happens."

At thirty-two weeks of gestation, two months before I am considered fully prepared for the world—or "at term"—I behave almost exactly like a newborn. And continue to do so for the next twelve weeks.

"It's pretty generally understood that men don't aspire after the absolute right, but only to do about as well as the rest of the world."

– Stowe[14]

"It's a free country, sir; the [child's] **mine,** *and I do what I please with him—that's it!"*

– Stowe[15]

Dear Mama,

It must be strange to try to think of somebody else when there really hasn't been much reason for you to ever have to do that before. Our presence inside you must surely be a surprise. Yes, that's right. There are two of us. It's doubtful you were expecting two little people to show up after that very hot night with that guy you hardly know, but here we are, right where you don't want anyone to be for now, and maybe for years. It's all just too foreign. I mean one day you only have to think about you, and then the next day you're supposed to suddenly grow a heart and conscience, suddenly care and let your entire life be radically altered just because you had sex? Please! Putting us out of your mind for now seems like the most expedient thing to do. Maybe it's just a mistake... that happens, you know. Well, Mama, unlike the hangover, we're not going away even after the Advil. Of course, it was a night you just want to let pass by, to put down to experience and walk away wiser, and as such, you can't see any reason why you should not get rid of some uninvited trespassers on your person, best removed, discarded, and forgotten as quickly as possible. Maybe you think that's your right, and since it's your life that would get screwed up, we should just be okay with dying because we weren't planned and aren't wanted because you have better things to do, bigger plans, better days to insure.

Well, we're not! Would you be? What if you were suddenly killed in some horrible accident? Would that be okay with you? What if someone intentionally plotted to get rid of you for their own reasons and you couldn't stop them? Would that be acceptable or justifiable or excusable or right? Or would it be wrong? Something breathtaking is happening in here, not just once, but twice; two miracles unfolding and

---

[14] Harriet Beecher Stowe, Uncle Tom's Cabin; p. 190
[15] Harriet Beecher Stowe, Uncle Tom's Cabin; p. 18

growing, intimately nurturing a bond that is beyond words. We aren't as big as you are and can't do all the things you can do yet, but we can do all the things babies are supposed to do when they are as big as we are. When our muscles grow big enough, we'll feel the ground beneath us and we'll scoot, then crawl, and one day walk. When faces surround us we'll look at them and love the face that goes with the voice we know so well that has calmed and comforted us since we first began, the voice we love over any other. But right now we're busy growing fingers, toes, eyelids, and napping, just like any baby. We can already bend, stretch, and breathe. That funny repetitive thump was one of us hiccupping. Yup, we hiccup. You can't possibly think that we are things, your belongings, your prerogative to rid yourself of just because we grow inside you. Where else should we get bigger? Do you know of better lodgings? Is this what humans do, destroy their unwanted? What if apple trees thrashed and ripped their branches to rid themselves of their sweet fruit, declaring their independence? *How dare you grow on me! These branches belong to me!* But I guess apple trees couldn't do anything like that. They are not made that way, with the ability to act against their nature, to violently strip themselves of their next generation. Mama, just because you're able to throw us away like a bad memory, just because you can does not make it right. How many bad things have been done because they could be without any regard to whether they should be?

Maybe you think because you've been around longer, or because you're bigger that you're more important, more real, that you matter more than us. Maybe you think motherhood isn't fit for you because it's inconvenient or embarrassing right now so we are suddenly not your children, not children at all. But, Mama, how can you think so flippantly about paying someone to vacuum out your own children so our bones break into a tangled mess? I know it sounds awful. It is.

Some people tell you we don't look like babies so therefore we're not, and it doesn't matter what you do to us. But that can't be, it doesn't make sense. Do you think it's acceptable to destroy us because we don't look like you imagine we should, because our appearance differs from yours? Isn't that what they said about those who had dark skin? Isn't that what they said about the people they didn't want around before that really big war where so many people were killed? Didn't all the doctors prove that they looked different, so they were different, and therefore they didn't matter and deserved to die? Do people still determine who is valuable and worth being protected based on how someone looks? Is that how truth and law, right and wrong, are determined, by the way things appear? If that's true, then I guess the world must still be flat; the earth must still be the center of the universe. And I guess young men will never grow old and die and the tiniest emerging bud on a rosebush will never perfume a spring morning. After all, none of this could ever happen, for it doesn't appear that way today. It's just so silly to think like that. Silly, and not smart. Wrong, and not right. Like a defiant child, you stomp your foot and say, "I can't see, I don't want to see it, so it won't be, it can't be."

You say it's about your body, and of course our bodies are connected, all three of us. We depend on you, we need you. That is just how life works, the smallest most helpless ones depending and clinging to the most nurturing, where the most love lies waiting to be woken. Our needing you to feed and sustain us does nothing to affect our identity. You are you, and we are me and me. Each of us is distinct, each of us unique, with different blood types, brainwaves, heartbeat, and DNA. One moment we were not here, and then in another, a miracle took place and two separate living persons began inside you. Mama, each of us is a separate individual human being worth nurturing and protecting. In fact, every baby, every human life that has ever lived has needed someone to care for that life when they were very much alive but too small to care for themselves. Needing other people, being connected to others is part of being human. You make it sound if we are robbing you if we dare to need you, that no child has any right to expect anything from their mother. Too many fathers have made that declaration, but they have appropriately been named scoundrel.

You say you should be able to do whatever you want with your body, that it's your private property and we're on your property. But certainly others don't let you do whatever you want with your body. Don't they stop people who try to end their lives? Aren't those people guarded and protected from themselves? Why should you be allowed to end our lives if no one would willingly allow you to end yours? And people aren't free to kill others just because they're on their property. Certainly doctors don't become the property of their patients if their hands enter into their patients' bodies. They are different people entirely. And no one should be able to own another human being or destroy another human being just because of where they live and grow.

But maybe it's really much more than that. Children do indeed tie a mother's shoes. You have often told yourself we're nothing to justify what you think you need to do to save your education, your career, your best-laid plans, to keep yourself from being tied down before you are ready, to keep your heart from loving something so fragile, so helpless, so connected to you. Maybe it's really motherhood that you're fighting so fiercely against, a job that will ensnare your affections for a lifetime. Somebody once said a long time ago, "*The law is reason free from passion.*"[16] Maybe so, but motherhood is most certainly not. Motherhood wraps you so tight around the little lives depending on you that you think the only option is to cut the heartstrings before they grow too long, too strong, and throw whatever is at the other end away before that love possesses you. Maybe, Mommy, it's not mothers who own children, but children who take possession of their mother's heart and make independence, ambition, and chasing dreams such a difficult proposition.

We know you demand the right to choose whether or not to have a child. We know you insist that motherhood is something that should never be forced on anyone. But what if you could still choose and not be forced into that role before you were ready? What if you could acknowledge the miracles growing inside you and act with tender compassion and choose to let someone else take on that enormous load of love with all its entanglements? Couldn't that be the choice, choosing to be our mommy or choosing for someone else to be? Can't you just take us dying off the list of options? Please, Mama, please, it's wrong for our small, growing bodies to be crushed for your sake. We shouldn't have to die to keep your world as you want it to be. No person should. Just as you have a right to decide if you want to be a mommy, we too have a right, a right to continue to be, a right to keep existing, keep living, keep growing. Your right should not eliminate our right or eliminate us, and our right should not entrap you. Both of our rights can and should be won. Would you, Mama, would you please keep us alive inside you till we grow big enough to grow up in someone else's arms? Your voice will always be the sweetest, most wonderful voice we know, please don't make it be the last.

Love,
Ben and Abigail

---

[16] Aristotle

"People tell me not to be mad, no one likes an angry girl; but they'll help me if I stay sad, it votes better in my world."

— Kim Hill

"The great difference is that the table and chair cannot feel, and the man can; for even a legal enactment that he shall be 'taken, reputed, adjudged in law to be [the property of]' cannot blot out his soul with its own private little world of memories, hopes, loves, fears, and desires."

— Stowe[17]

Dear Mama,

What am I supposed to say? I guess you expect me to just be slightly disappointed that I'm getting ready to be sucked out in pieces, a little bummed maybe, but generally understanding and encouraging to you, the person organizing the whole fateful, insidious plot. But there's a problem. I'm not ready to die. I don't want to die. Everything I've experienced just makes me want more of life, more feelings, more comfort, more delight, more wonder. I have a big life of tomorrows ahead of me, and tomorrows mean I can't end today. I've got dreams so big I can't wait to get started; that's why I do so much tumbling about in here. Like a wild horse rearing, I'm ready for the gate to be thrown wide. I clung on once when you tried to get rid of me, and I'll cling again. I'm not the only baby that has; killing us is not so easy you know. That's because we're alive. You say you don't want me, so I shouldn't be allowed to come into the world, but I'm already here, Mama! I'm already here! Even if you expel me I'll gulp air, I'll fight! This is my life! I want to live it!

If I were bigger, I could defend myself, I would scream, I would call for help. I think you call that survival. What did I do to deserve such a horrible cold end? What crime did I commit that you get to declare my death sentence? Where is my appeal? What about my sense of right and wrong, my desire to live and be loved, my desire to grow and dream and know this great big world, my desire to seek greatness?

You don't think anyone should force their morality on you. Aren't you forcing your lack of morality on me? If you don't want to be my mother, fine! But don't you dare throw me in the trash as if I'm some clump of lifeless tissue. I am not lifeless until after you pay the doctor.

---

[17] Harriet Beecher Stowe, Uncle Tom's Cabin; p. 347

I know how you think; I'm not the first of your babies to be tossed out. It's all just so heartless, thoughtless, careless. You throw me away, discard me, Kill ME, with less thought than you put into your wardrobe, as if getting rid of me were the same as cleaning out your closet, because I just don't suit your lifestyle right now. Don't you see, don't you understand how much just one little human life matters? I have a heart that beats the same as you. I have a mind that senses my world the same as you. I have hands that grasp, fingers that touch and reach to discover, a mouth that yawns, sucks, and swallows. Loud noises that scare you startle me. I recognize the familiar. I think you call that remembering. I can see and I dream. Yes, Mama, I dream, same as you.

You may think these feats small, and it's true I have much more to do before I can tackle the giants of my story. But it started here, I began here, I exist here. And existing here is the same as existing out there. I don't become some*thing* different because I'm some*where* different. But just as where I am does not determine who or what I am, all that I can do today is not all that I am or will be. However, it *is more* than enough to show the world that I'm really here, I'm really human, and like every person I really do matter.

My dreams, my hopes of freedom, my rights; what happens when they end so abruptly, so unjustly? What happens to liberty when some people, little ones in fact, are declared less than others? What happens to freedom when all lives are not equal, when some lives are seen as disposable? What happens to equality when one baby is rescued and rejoiced over in one room and another baby can be intentionally and violently killed in a room down the hall, babies the very same age? Where is the democracy when only *you* get to decide if I live or die? Why are only your interests of concern? Why is one life significant and another life not? Why does one life get a chance and another is damned? Why do you get to decide I'm not worth the trouble, not worthy of all that this amazing world promises? Not one person has ever petitioned for existence, and yet we are all here just the same. Our parents' desires do not determine our value, nor do their fears or constraints strip away our humanity. I'm here, Mama; that is what makes me worthy of the dream, worthy of the fight. I am alive and I am here!

Love,
Your Baby Girl

"God made man because God likes stories."
  – Elie Wiesel (Holocaust survivor, Nobel Peace Prize Winner, and author of <u>Night</u>)

Dear Mama,

There is no money and there hasn't been for a long time. You are hungry and so are my brothers and sisters, the little ones you already love, the little ones you are already responsible for. You are scared and so are they. You already know what to expect. You have already seen the suffering and hurt. You have already felt the hate. You have already wept and wiped away their tears. You know it will be the same and even more of it if there is one more life, one more mouth to feed, one more child to set off the monster, one more broken baby to grow up wounded. Right now you can just barely manage it all. There is not a single doubt about this. The one thing you do wonder is if he will leave and if you will be left to feed and provide for us all on your own. It must be too much, too much to think about, and most definitely impossible to actually do. The pain must stop, that is the only thing you know. The pain must never, never be allowed to grow.

Of course, only the most courageous willingly go to the place they know they will be hurt. It is the kind of job reserved for rescuers or soldiers. But even fewer willingly immerse themselves where they know they will be hated. I think hate must be worse. I guess you think of aborting me as a way to save me from the hate and the hurt. I am sure someone told you that you are being merciful to me. You must think it is merciful to you too. But I guess to believe that you have to think that no good can be found in a life that has been crushed, that a life that will experience pain or loss or fear or hunger should be snuffed out and not allowed the possibility of love either. But, Mama, I am a person, your child, not a horse or a cow that does not have the ability to reason and strive, devote and endure, create and love. The fact that I can see a wrong and right it or seek truth or struggle until I have risen beyond my circumstances is what makes humanity so beautiful, so different. Don't think there isn't hope. Don't believe my life is destined to be miserable. Don't convince yourself that my life is much better off never lived. That is what the pragmatists think—I just call them self-interested and lazy. They see any life that requires more than the usual amount of help a waste, but I see something else. I see a story.

I bet all the practical people with their budgets, degrees, and titles dripping with condescension make sure you know how difficult help will be to get, how much easier your life will be without *another mouth to feed and care for*, how much easier their job will be without me in their caseload, how much better the world will be without *another needy child*, how you can count on them confirming their disgust in your stupidity and neediness every time you dare to hold out your hand for help. Low, hopeless, a waste of resources that could certainly be used to build a lovely monument or raise a councilman's wages or pay for the new landscaping or new school computers; that is the palpable disdain that rushes toward you when you ask for help. They would have you believe that people exist for the benefit of their precious society instead of society existing for the benefit and betterment of the precious people. They tell you death is better than poverty, death is better than abuse, death is better than being a burden to your family, as if a human being only has the right to exist if they can make it without requiring anything of anyone else.

But, Mama, that's just not true. All that stuff makes life hard, but it also makes us work and fight. It gives us compassion for others because we know how it feels; it makes us stand up against those who crush others. It gives us the courage to right wrongs and live life for more than ourselves. It makes us love and fight for good instead of settling for easier. These are the things found in the hearts that make the world better, not worse.

You have certainly noted that not everyone in the business of helping is like that, but you can't escape the pressure of the values of the helper to whom you are assigned. Maybe some of the young ones care, but that ideal must fade with age, quickly replaced with the much more useful virtues of practicality and cost efficiency. You can see, feel, and hear them calculating the value of my life and reducing you and me to numbers. Quickly and without remorse they determine if a life is worthy of living based on the estimated cost of sustaining that life compared to the amount of assistance needed and the amount available based on the current budget allocations. In more ways than you can count the message is made clear. The poor should not be allowed to have children. Children are only for those people who have money. "They never say to you, 'What do you dream his voice will sound like? What games will he like? Do you think he will collect butterflies?' Instead they demand, 'How old is he? How many brothers does he have? How much does he weigh? How much does his father make?"[18] Yeah, that is what life is about for sure. How very sad.

Gee, if I had only known what a burden and drain on the family and the economy I was going to be, I would have stopped myself from beginning... I know I sound bitter. But, Mama, it makes me angry that they make you feel guilty for needing help, guilty for wanting me. It makes me angry that I might die because I am not in the budget. It makes me angry that my dad has robbed you of hope, so much so that you can't see a way out of all the awful stuff that is going on in your life right now, in our lives. That is the answer Mama, not me dying, but all of us leaving, starting over together, away from the hate and the hurt. Yes, yes, we all know how hard it is, but we could work together and make a new life. The thing that scares me is him, what he might do to us all if we leave. I know that paralyzing pit of fear you have been living in. I can feel it in everything you do, everything you can't say. But he could hurt you anyway, even if you didn't let me live. There is no hope in my death. But hope can be found another way, in another place, in a new home and a new job and a new beginning. Let me be the end of awful and be the start of a whole new life. Some of the most amazing people the world has ever been blessed with have risen up out of the dirty, small, poor holes they grew up in. Their beautiful lives show the world the value of a life is in the life, not in the circumstances, not in the bank accounts, not in the job descriptions, not in the pedigree. Those lives that triumph show us not how many people need to discarded and thrown away, but how much depth and beauty lies hidden in the rubble, hidden in the slums, waiting for a hand to help them step out into this wonderful world.

We need a hand like that, someone to help you as you love us. But somehow, I really believe that there are people out there who will help with love in their hearts, and give with the intention of making the goodness of God real to you and our family. Cry out to Him who made and loves us both. Cry out to Him. He will bring these people to you, or bring you to these people. He gives good gifts. He will not leave us. He will never forsake us. He will be in front of us. He will prepare our way. He will be our rearguard. His love, His goodness, they will be sufficient.

---

[18] Antione de St. Exupery

He wants me to live. He wants me to be with all of you. I am a part of this family, one of your children. I want to meet everyone else, the little voices that always seem so near to yours. I want to be there to smile and laugh and give you your joy back.

Don't get rid of me, Mama. There is more to our story. The best stories aren't the boring ones, where no one grows and no heroes are made. We have a much better tale to tell. The thing is, Mama, you gotta keep dancing, even if it hurts. Please... I will dance with you if you want. Actually, it would be wonderful, to do it together, all of us. You see, I want, no, I *need* to be a part of the remarkable story God is writing in your life. Your story is one that penetrates into other women's hearts and identifies with their failures, fears, and loss. Your story grips those who hear it and awakes their compassion. Your story makes them hate oppression and rise to defeat it. You make them desire much greater things than the shallow, self-centered lives they presently lead where a to-do list is their greatest accomplishment. Your story makes them grateful for the good in their lives and makes them want to give. Your story gives them hope when they don't have any, and eyes to see a purpose to the pain. Your story makes them gasp at the unmatchable goodness of God and the love of a Savior, love that perseveres and finds that a heroine has been born, but I call you 'Mama'.

Love,
Your Babe

"I don't think of all of the misery, but of the beauty that still remains."
– Anne Frank

"He will feed His flock like a shepherd; He will gather the lambs with His arm, and carry them in His bosom, and gently lead those who are with young."
Isaiah 40:11(NKJV)

"Every adult was once a child, it's just that most of them don't remember."
— Antoine de St. Exupery

"When I was a child, I spoke as a child, I understood as a child, I thought as a child; but when I became a man, I put away childish things. For we see in a mirror, dimly, but then face to face. Now I know in part, but then I shall know just as I also am known."
1 Corinthians 13:11

Dear Mommy,

I guess what hurts so bad is that you just don't care. I wish you were scared, then maybe I could understand how or why you could throw me away. It wouldn't make it any less wrong, but at least it wouldn't be so cold, casual, and callous. The thing is you're not scared; you're annoyed that I'm here inside you. You said you could do what you wanted with me because you're a life already being lived as opposed to a life not properly begun... Okay, this one stumps me. I just don't get it. It's honorable, charitable, and good for you to fight for the little girl in a village in Africa to have clean water to drink because she is already living, and my life is disposable, unworthy of the same honorable effort because I have not properly begun? Who gets to decide which is the life being lived and which isn't? Where is the list of criteria? Who makes the list? Is there some test I have to pass, some body part I have to grow? Does an arm make a person? Does a leg? Is it ears that are required to be real, or eyes? Which body part do I need to be human? Which body part do I need to appeal to your sense of human decency, morality, and compassion? Which one?

You say I don't look like a baby, but I have all the beginnings of all my body parts, and all of it has been here since my first moment. All that makes me *me* is written on every cell of my body. Even when all of me was only one amazing miraculous cell, I was all there. My parts well, they are just the right size for just this stage of my young life.

Is it because not everyone else can see me? That's as simple-minded as a toddler who thinks because Mommy is hiding under a blanket, she must have left. You might not be able to see me every moment, but you know I'm here. Your whole body tells you so. But I think not everyone else being able to see is actually the thing that you are using to make it okay to get rid of me. If no one can see, no one will know, no one will judge, and you can do whatever you have to do to keep things the way they were before. Besides, you could see me if you wanted to, and you have. I know you see my kicks and when I move from one side of your tummy to the other, it's just like kicking and rolling in a crib. Babies are seen every day inside their mommies. It's even where they get their first picture taken. I got mine taken too. The lady kept having to start over because I just couldn't keep still. I think you must have had coffee, Mommy. We were both pretty wiggly. Then I posed. I heard you gasp. I felt your tears well up within you and a gush of something wonderful flowed between us. You even got to see my most private little plaything; it's where my pee comes out. I heard you say, "Boy," in the sweetest voice, but then it was as if you pushed that swelling of love right out of your heart. But I'm still here, Mommy. Hmm... It really is amazing inside you. I wonder what the world must be like.

But anyway, back to my life not properly begun. So when does properly begun begin? It can't be when I'm born, I mean seriously, don't you know that is just when you and I meet face to face for the first time. Of course, first impressions, first loves, those are things that make life so mysterious and well, wonderful. But, Mommy, nothing developmentally significant happens at all. It's kind of like walking through a door from one room to the next. Being in one room doesn't make you one thing and being in another make you something else. The person you are doesn't change from one side to the other. Kind of like that boy in the striped pajamas that made everybody cry. He didn't become somebody different just because he was *somewhere* different. What was wrong on one side of the fence was wrong on the other side of the fence. It was just as wrong for one boy to die as it was for the other boy. But I guess some people have always thought some other people weren't people if they didn't want them. That, of course, has made it okay for them to dispose of unwanted people for whatever reason fitted them. They have always found some way to make it sound okay, but it isn't.

You know, I did begin properly. The first moment when I came to be there was an electric spark. I ignited into being. After that I grew like crazy, forming all the parts that make humans look and act like humans. Brainwaves, a heartbeat, growth, and responding to my world, all the things doctors use to measure the presence of life, I do them all. I do exactly what every human being has ever done when they are my age growing inside their very first home. But it wasn't doing those things that made me a person. I'm a person because I am a living, growing human being, not because of what I can or will do. I am a person because I have a soul, an essence mysteriously attached to my body. I can't really explain it, but I know without my soul, my body is just lifeless matter—lifeless. It is my soul that makes my body alive, makes it grow, breathe, hurt, love. If there were no soul, then well, there would be no life. They're connected and always have been. I think that's what that spark is all about.

Of course, I know you still want to find some way to justify disqualifying me from my own life. What are you going to choose? Is it what I look like? Or is it what I can't do yet? Is it because I can't walk up to you and kick you in the shins and say, "Don't do that, it hurts"? Do I need to submit a notarized request for the disillusionment of your parental authority? What is on the list of things I need to be able to do before I have your permission to join the human race? And how, might I ask, how can any person have that kind of authority and power over another?

I must tell you, none of it makes sense, none of it is consistent, and you don't have to think too hard to understand how crazy it all is. Just think about it, are girls not female because they don't have breasts? Is Miss America not beautiful because you looked at her awkward sixth-grade school photo and determined no beauty could possibly develop from that face? Are boys not male because they can't yet do the thing that makes men *men*? Don't all those things that will happen one day happen because of their nature, because of what they are, not what they *look* like or what they *can* do today? The abuse and killing of infants by their parents could never be acceptable simply because these infants could not express their pain with words. Does the inability to testify make my pain, my life, invalid? Don't all people express themselves with what skill they have developed? If you don't know another language, you can't use it, but that doesn't mean you aren't thinking or feeling appropriately for someone of your age and development. If I didn't know how to write yet, I would speak. If I didn't how to speak, I would point and gesture. If I didn't know how to point, I would scream or cry or laugh or smile or reach and touch you. Maybe I would even have different cries for different needs. If my lungs weren't strong enough to cry, I would still flinch in pain, my little heartbeat would still race.

Writing, speaking, pointing, crying, flinching, none of these things make me a person. They are just some of the many things people do because they are human. If you lost one of these abilities, you would not lose your humanity. So how can the fact that I have just not developed this skill, but will in time, possibly take away my humanity?

The smart people use big words to try to make this about something it's not. And babies don't have big words and count on bigger people to protect and defend them. But if I could borrow their big words and their big mouths, this is what I would say, "*Function does not determine worth, and body parts don't either.*" If I was talking about women you would say, "Here, Here!" If this is truth, true for humans, true for women, it should be true and right for me too. You act as if there is some secret password or ritual I have to perform before I'm worth being protected. Why isn't being alive enough? Oh yes, I know why. It's because me living requires something of you. How selfish of me, I guess I should have realized that I'm not real unless you're willing to take care of the bill.

You know, since you put so much emphasis on what I can't do yet, I bet you would believe me if I told you I don't know how to throw a ball. But did you know I already possess that ability in a way that is far beyond what most people can do? It's one of my gifts, one of my talents, but you can't see that right now. There's no sign of it yet, but it's there just the same. It makes me wonder. Should all the tee ball teams disband because not one of the little guys has hit a ball any respectable distance? Certainly tee ball is baseball not properly begun. I guess they should all be scrapped and never allowed on a diamond. There is simply no need to wait and see the hidden talent, the pregnant unmasked human potential awkwardly holding the glove in the wrong hand and never making contact with the ball. The fact is these little guys are not great today, are definitely not playing baseball as it should be played, and by your standards are therefore unworthy of the game. Since they don't know all they need to know to play the game today, they should never be allowed the opportunity to grow and learn. There is just no reason for them to experience the joy of discovering their own power, their own gifts, no need for them to practice and pursue to see just how good they really are, no need to be grateful to their Maker for making them this way. What would be good about that?

I guess that great swimmer should have been born with a tattoo, "The Greatest Olympian the World Has Ever Seen!" Then his gangliness, his shyness, his fidgetiness, would have been appreciated before he had yet developed the skill, the discipline, the perseverance, the hope, the greatness that was in him. The truth is though, they weren't. His greatness, his ability could not be seen. It took a mother believing in the wonder of her child, never losing hope, never ceasing to encourage, never letting him lose his dreams or believe any of the lies others told him. It took all of that for many, many years before the world got to see swimming as it should be swum, and winning as it should be won. But all of that ability was there at that first spark of life. Time was all that the world needed to see the potential that lay stored up at the beginning of that one spark of humanity.

Mommy, I am not a potential life. I am a life that has already begun with all the potential in the world.

Love,
Your Baby Boy

"Pain throws your heart to the ground, love turns the whole thing around, no it won't all turn out the way it should, but I know the heart of life is good."
– *John Mayer*

Dear Mommy,

With all this talk of lives and dreams and who all of us want to be, I realized that maybe you didn't know that I have a dream too. Maybe you don't know I can feel the weight of my own soul and it makes me imagine what will be. I think it's called possibility. It's not the kind of dream you know all at once, it's the kind that grows and gets bigger the more days you get through. I want to share my dream with you so you know what it is that lies in this little heart inside you. I want to share with you why I want to live, why I don't want to die. Dreams have the strangest possession over us, don't they? Having them births perseverance, courage, vision, and greatness. Losing them often means losing a part of ourselves, losing hope, settling for things we shouldn't settle for, becoming someone we don't know. This I know, Mommy. And I know you think you and your dreams will die if I don't. But maybe you could see that killing your baby is not the way to go about dream salvage. Maybe you could see there are ways to keep your dreams alive, and me and my little dreams too. Maybe when you meet me and look into my face you'll find a new dream, and we can chase dreams together. Because the thing no one tells you when you're drowning in the fear is the joy waiting for you, the joy of a child, the joy of watching someone you love that is so much a part of you grow and chase and catch one of those illusive, fluttering magnificent dancing stars, especially when you taught them how.

So this is my dream. I dream of wonder and magic and surprise, the kind that captures a child's heart on Christmas morning. I dream of heroes and adventures and the magical pictures in my mind's eye that capture my heart at story time and make me yearn for another day and another story. I want to feel Eskimo kisses and your arms holding me tight. The peace that comes from falling and waking to the same beautiful face, yours—I want to know that peace. I imagine splashing in puddles and playing with play dough. I long to make a friend and make her laugh, playing hide and seek, dress up, and pretend. I dream of my first day at school, and struggling to learn the things that are beyond me. I envision the exuberant joy that sets my feet dancing when I suddenly conquer what once seemed impossible. I can't wait to know the delight in discovering I'm good at something and determining to be even better. I wish to jump in heaps of crisp, colored leaves, and ride my bike down Dead Man's Curve, surviving—triumphant. I imagine what the crisp, cold silent kiss of snowflakes will feel like and the scent and sight of spring that will leave me breathless. I even dare to think I could win a race, and know the breathless joy that accompanies it. I dream of my heart-thumping first crush and first kiss. I even believe one day I'll make my own way in the world and begin again with the same awe and wonder and fear that captures a child's heart, but also with the hope and confidence of someone who has begun to discover who they are and who they want to become. I think I'll find more than I ever knew there could ever be.

One day, I dream of falling in love and having little people look at me like I want to look at you. I long to love them like I want to be loved. I hope to be a part of someone else's life for the simple reason that I love them, not for what I can get, but for what I can give. I believe I'll find more than I hoped for, or expected, and understand what love is really all about.

I imagine the beauty I'll see in simple things, and the extraordinary splendor that will captivate me and even surprise me. I dream of long, long runs and the grace that washes over me as a lone doe and I lock a long gaze, both of us overtaken in the sweet serenity of a kudzu-covered valley, breathing in a beautiful dusk, heady with honeysuckles and wisteria's last bloom—loveliness that can't be found in words, but a moment of goodness that will stay with me forever and a peace that makes me forget myself. I want to be stunned by God's goodness and love, and know what it is to be grateful so I can delight in beautiful, even when I can't see any.

Yet life isn't all pretty, even though nobody dreams of the bad stuff. Sometimes the ugly, the hole, the *hell* is somebody's whole world. After all, nobody dreams of screwing up. Nobody longs for things to go badly, for failure, or loss or hurt. Nobody desires shame. Nobody thinks they will play hide and seek from God. But not dreaming it doesn't stop any of it from happening. So I hope that when I fail I'll know to keep going. I pray that when my heart is lonely I'll have the wisdom to seek a friend by being one. I hope that when I'm cruel and cowardly I won't stay that way. I expect to have the courage and the humility to say, "I was wrong, I'm sorry." When I'm a fool and wrong seems so alluring and curiosity entices me, I hope for God's grace and enough good sense to run from my wrong instead of embracing it with pride. I want to know that I won't forget that God loves me when I am humiliated and abandoned and know what it is to rest in Him. I believe He will even help me learn and grow from failures, strive and hope in nothingness, love and forgive in betrayal, fight for what's right, and defend those with nobody to help them. I dream I will see His goodness in my life.

I hope I won't do wrong or hurt another because I'm afraid. And I even want to do the right things and fix the wrong ones. I dream that when Jesus confronts me with His love, I'll have the good sense to love Him back. I dream of the peace and pondering that will mystify me as I spend a lifetime trying to understand how big God's love must be, how He could love me, and why His Son would willingly die for all my screw-ups. I believe that God won't leave me a child but will grow the faith He gives, as only faith can, through the ugly awful trials and doubts and loneliness that are faith's fertile growing grounds. I hope to see the good, and trust it's still there when I don't. I dream I'll still love when it's not returned. I long to share my hope and my Savior's love. I dream of living in His light when my world is enveloped in darkness, and knowing the awe and love that will fill me when God answers the deepest cries of my heart. I dream of finding purpose in something far beyond myself or my accomplishments, and fighting the *impossible, the unwinnable, the unrightable*,[19] no matter how I look in the process.

What I dream of, Mommy, is simply this; I dream of something that is already true, that my life has a purpose that you can't see right now, and I long for the journey that will take me there. I dream of being able to seek the One I was made for, doing the things He designed me to do, discovering the things that lead me closer to Him. I dream of being able to see God's face and telling Him *thank you* for it all. Yes, all of it. It's waiting for you too, Mommy, the good, the bad, the dream, the journey, this too is *part* of it, not the *end* of it. But I need you, Mommy, I can't complete a journey, a destiny, I never get to start.

Love,
Your dream girl

---

[19] Adapted from Dr. Raymond Dennehy, Anti-Abortionist At-Large (Trafford Publishing, Victoria, B.C.; 2002) p. 12

"One should never direct people towards happiness, because happiness too is an idol of the market-place. One should direct them towards mutual affection. A beast gnawing at its prey can be happy too, but only human beings can feel affection for each other, and this is the highest achievement they can aspire to."
– Alexander Solzhenitsyn

Dear Mommy,

I guess the fun stops here, with me. I wasn't supposed to happen. Those stolen moments in someone else's arms were just supposed to be the relief from your dull life. The comfortable, well-stocked, uninteresting existence that you called your life needed some excitement, some reason for you to feel something different, something to look forward to. He was that something. You didn't love him, just the idea of him, or maybe even just the idea of an affair. It felt good, you felt young, and it all felt fun, until me.

I'll spoil it all. Everyone will know, the fun and fancy-free affair will end, divorce will certainly follow, and then you will have to start over with a not so comfortable existence, and... disgrace. You don't love my daddy, and you don't love me. The dull life you wanted to escape from suddenly seems worth saving, but that can only happen if I'm out of the way. Besides, you tell yourself, it's not like he wants to have to deal with a baby. This kid, *me*, is better off dead because *you're* better off with things just as they are. A baby would just complicate everything.

But, Mommy, when did it become okay to kill defenseless children who expose the secret sex taking place in the hidden corners of our country? Why do I have to die because of what you did? I don't need you to love me to be real. I'm real simply because I'm here. Killing me, well it's just wrong, totally and completely wrong, despite how desperate and deliberate you feel right now. I have a right to live, a right to be here, and you are not the guardian of that right! It is not your gift to me. It is mine, given to me by the One who made me. I think they say God *endowed* it to me, and that it is *unalienable* to me, and that means that no one, not even you, can take it from me. They also say that all of us, you and me, the wanted and the unwanted, the legitimate and illegitimate, all of us are equal. No one is of more value than another; no one has a greater claim to the rights of humans than others, which is why one person can NEVER claim to kill another person for their own interests, why you can't take my life to pursue your liberty and your happiness. Of these truths, Mommy, life comes first because you can't pursue happiness where there is no liberty, and there is no liberty to obtain if there is no life living, breathing, and being, needing to be free.

I know you let yourself believe the clichés, that freedom is choice and choice is being able to do what you want when you want and getting rid of the things that stand in the way of the choices, the plans you have made for yourself. But freedom and liberty are actually about *not* being oppressed, *not* being owned, *not* having a government forced on you with no say, *not* being unjustly punished, imprisoned, or put to death for no crime with no trial, it is about *not* being silenced. And yet that is the freedom and authority you demand to have over my life, to oppress me, own me, kill me, force your will on me, silence me. Liberty is not about doing anything you want, it is about the absence of oppression and abuse, and the opportunity to pursue a future. Motherhood doesn't eliminate futures, it molds new ones; it doesn't eliminate freedoms, it creates new patriots and new people to love. The choice should be between embracing the challenge and letting another person love a tiny, endowed life.

As for your disgrace and the hardship my existence brings on you, well, that is not a reason that makes it okay for you get to get rid of me. I can feel the pain and shame and fear that are swirling inside you. They are very real, but none of them is more important than a baby, than your baby. Killing me so you don't have to deal with me is NOT what our forefathers fought for; it isn't what the suffragists or abolitionists fought for either. They fought for life, for every life, because they all have infinite worth, infinite potential. Your embarrassment doesn't make me less human than your other children, my sisters. Your shame doesn't take away my uniqueness, or how precious I truly am. Yes, I know, me being here changes everything. But me being here has a purpose too. So let me be, Mommy, just let me be.

Love,
Your Son

"But what is liberty without wisdom, and without virtue? It is the greatest of all possible evils; for it is folly, vice, and madness without tuition or restraint."
– *Edmund Burke*

Dear Mommy I have a story to tell
It's a story about people
A story you know well
You may think you who know all that you should
At least all about people, or all that you would

But listen this time and see if you find,
Some people you thought didn't fit half the time
People who cost, people who smell
People who did not fit in that well
People who spoiled the fun we were having
People who it's easier to pick on than help

Women are people, men are people,
The poor are people, the old are people,
Infants are people, children are people,
Adolescents are people, the homeless are people,
The uneducated are people, the disabled are people,
The brilliant are people, the foreclosed on are people,
The unemployed are people, the rich are people,
The hungry are people, the slow are people,
The sick are people, the injured are people,
The deranged are people, addicts are people,
Foreigners are people too; and even people who don't look like we do,
People we don't want around don't stop being people no matter what reason we've found

An arm, a leg, an ear or an eye
An impressive intellect, or the talent to cry
Speed or beauty, and all the things we can see
These are not the things that define you and me
Without them we remain as human today, than if we had never started out that way

For people are more than a limb or a flaw, more than an inconvenience, more than a draw
People are worthy every last one
Because of who we were made for, not for what we have done

People of every color and creed
People of every thought and deed
People of every age and stage
People of every wage and sage

Old people and young people don't look quite the same
But people they are and people they remain
Sickness and poverty shame people for sure
But these are things to fight and things we can cure
I am a person despite what you see, despite what I need, despite who you might be

My hands are tiny, but human hands they still are
Small, but safely growing in my tiny little world
Despite my size and what challenges I bring
My humanity is not determined by the absence of a ring

I fail to see, looking at you and looking at me
Why I should die and you should be
I have not changed, nor have you
To become a non-person because of something I can or can't do

No one can own me, not you or my mother
And no one should be allowed to crush another
My form might be hidden, safe and inside
But my body still grows and my little mind still thrives

How can my life be determined by your joy?
Can someone's feelings or fears also make me a boy?

Choice is the claim you stake for my life
All must be done to keep you from strife
No matter that your choice robs me of everything
I am not supposed to care or feel; I am not a human being

You state so boldly, you make a demand
In case there is some reason, some pause in your plan

"*Only one life has precedence,*
Only one life matters,
Only one should be free, let women be,
Since I was here first, I am in charge, so it must certainly be me"

But please, Mama, please, why can't you see?
My life is not yours, it belongs to me
My life is special all on its own
Existing completely without need for you to condone

It is true I need you and your warm womb to grow
But that is the place that all babies know
All humans begin in a womb just as warm
For so long it has been a haven from harm

But now that you claim my body is yours
Somehow the safe place has become quite the curse
For only babies that are wanted you see
Can come out alive to meet their family

What do I tell you, what thing can I do
To show you my value, so you see what is true
Women they say, are more than a mother, more than a lover
More than a wife, more much more than someone to fix all the strife
They are it is true, more than what some people want to limit them to
Surely we must for all that is good let women discover all the things that they should
Let them know fully all they could be, see them chase dreams, see them be free

But if women are not just who they are today, but who they will be if give them a way
Why can't this reason be reason enough for the tiniest of humanity not yet big or tough,
Not yet able to draw or climb trees, but able to dream and able to bleed

Not one life is greater, not one life should suffer
Not at the expense of one life or other
But all people everywhere should treasure this life

Help one another, look out for what's right
Help the young and help the old
Help the young women who think their future's gone cold
Give them every opportunity to see
These unwanted babies as a beautiful blessing

When oh when will humanity see that we are all people, despite a different story
When oh when will people be every bit as special whether needy or mighty
When oh when will women believe that they don't have to kill to keep dreaming their dreams
When oh when will this country find a heart that treasures its people more than its bottom line.

– *Baby Zoe*

"Don't you believe the Lord made them of one blood with us?" said Miss Ophelia shortly... "Don't you believe they've got immortal souls" said Miss Ophelia with increasing indignation.

"O, well," said Marie yawning, "that, of course—nobody doubts that. But as to putting them on any sort of equality with us, you know, as if we could be compared, why it's impossible! There's no comparing in this way. (She) couldn't have the feelings that I should. It's a different thing altogether-of course, it is—and yet St. Clare pretends not to see it. And just as if (she) could love... as I love."

– Stowe[20]

To the Offended,

You will most certainly object to the descriptions of how we die. You will accuse of us of being inflammatory, of inciting anger, and overt emotionalism. But to proceed we all must accept that the nature of a human being as they live out their life is intertwined. Just as the *understanding* of the reality that a human life has begun inside a mother's *body* evokes an enormous *emotional* hold on a mother's *entire being*, likewise we are all made. When our bodies are hurt by another, it is our heart that aches the most. When our voice and mind are deemed worthless, it is our body that is suddenly in jeopardy. When the slurs and shameless attacks of others converge in our understanding, it is our emotions that call our bodies to stand and defend our humanity. Our mind, body, and spirit remain knit together by that wondrous, mysterious thing called life.

So when life is taken violently from a human being with no cause, no defense, it is wrong to then claim we should give no credence to that human being's feeling, no consideration to their understanding, no indignation to the destruction of their bodies simply because we don't like what they will say and all that it says about what we have allowed to be done to them.

We proceed knowing that what happens to these small human beings' bodies happens to their hearts and minds as well. For what happens to one part of a human happens to the whole person. For being human is all that is necessary to evoke the human nature with

---

[20] Harriet Beecher Stowe, <u>Uncle Tom's Cabin</u>; p. 180

human heart and human understanding that exists within the body, existing simply because the body is a human one. Being unwanted, being thought less important as another human can do nothing to untangle one's nature from one's body. And we will remain as we are, small but human all.

So to your offense, to your indignation, we offer our own, the indignation, the injustice, the wrong done to us. We dare to offer the facts, the evidence, and the impact of such on us. We cry out to you how a human being thinks and feels as they come face to face with their ruin. We will not apologize because the facts of our death offend you, for we reserve the right to be offended for what was done to us. We offer you our stories, and like offensive, harsh stories from the past that mired and convicted the conscience of a nation, we offer you current and *Select Incidents From a Lawful Trade*...[21]

The Children[22]

"I appeal to God Almighty I'm willing to go with the case to Him, and ask Him if I do wrong to seek my freedom."

– Stowe[23]

---

[21] Harriet Beecher Stowe, Uncle Tom's Cabin; Chapter Title p. 122
[22] Each story is based on documented accounts of abortions, the condition of these babies after being removed from their mother's womb are accurate to these accounts. While doctors argue about fetal pain, most experts recognize the brain functions which process pain are developed by 20 weeks; *The First Ache*, NY Times Magazine, February 10, 2008.
[23] Harriet Beecher Stowe, Uncle Tom's Cabin; p. 115

"Scenes of blood and cruelty are shocking to our ear and heart. What man has nerve to do, man has not nerve to hear. What brother-man must suffer, cannot be told us, even in our secret chamber it so harrows the soul! And yet, oh my country! These things are done under the shadow of the laws! O, Christ! Thy church sees them, almost in silence!"

– Stowe[24]

Dear Mommy,

This is how I died. You were nauseous and couldn't eat. I was hungry. I was moving around a lot because I had that empty feeling and wanted to feel full. I didn't know what was about to happen. I just knew you were lying down, and that is when I like to move the most.

Then I could see everything get brighter. Somebody squirted something on your tummy because you jumped a little. I wonder what it felt like. I could see the little round thing with someone's hand go in slow circles all over your tummy. I heard you talking; your voice was shaking a lot. Then somebody else was talking. You were shaking a lot. I thought I heard you cry. I wanted to know why you were so scared. What was wrong? Then it got quiet.

Then I saw this thing come into my world. It was terrifying. It was huge. It was bigger than me. It squeezed something into my home. Quite quickly, the something surrounded me. I couldn't get away from this strange foreign substance that seemed to engulf me.

Then it started to hurt... I had never felt this before. But something, something was wrong. I kicked and kicked and moved every way I could. *It was burning me, burning me!* **I, I, I... MOMMY! HELP ME!** It wouldn't stop. I tried to gulp more of my special air, but my lungs were burning too. The hurt took over all of me.

Then something pulled me out of my home, away from you. This, this was new air. I tried to gulp it, but everything burned and burned. It was too big an ache to tell you. I couldn't make a noise, but I kept trying to breathe. I kept trying to live. Something placed me on something cold, hard, and shiny. I kicked and kicked. But it got harder and harder. I breathed and breathed. But it burned and burned. My heart kept beating and I just lay there when I used up every bit of energy to keep

---

[24] Harriet Beecher Stowe, Uncle Tom's Cabin; pp. 427-428

kicking and breathing. Then it was over. Somebody threw my tiny burned body on top of other burned babies, bloody and lifeless like me.

Of course, here it is. Here is the mass of tissue always being talked about, the tiniest of arms, the most translucent of perfect fingers, the ever so small ribcages, and well, there they are, what do I call them but what they are, tiny heads of lifeless babies. Yes, the mass of tissue, the mass of chopped up babies.

So what was the reason that had to happen to me?

Your Baby Boy

78   When the Bough Breaks

"To him, it looked like something unutterably horrible and cruel, because, poor ignorant [fool!] he had not learned to generalize, and to take enlarged views. If he had only been instructed...he might have thought better of it, and seen in it an every-day incident of a lawful trade...His very soul bled within him for what seemed to him the wrongs of the poor suffering thing that lay like a crushed reed on the boxes; the feeling, living, bleeding, yet immortal thing, which American state law coolly classes with the bundles, and bales, and boxes, among which she is lying."

– Stowe[25]

Dear Mommy,

This is how I died. I was growing, just growing and being inside of you. I didn't know that day would be my last. I didn't know I would leave my home so suddenly when I really was not big enough to be alone in that big world outside of you. You are my home, Mama, you are almost all I know. I eat what you eat, and I hear every word you say. Your voice is the most wonderful sound; it quiets me like nothing else can. So I don't know that you don't want me, that today you have paid somebody several hundred dollars to kill me.

You are tense, very tense. I can sense something is different, but I don't know what it is. Then slowly, I feel you ease, maybe you are asleep. Time for me to play! But something else happens.

A hole begins to open. Light begins to come in, more light than I have ever seen. I am strangely in awe of that light, but I don't want to leave all that I know. But the hole keeps getting bigger and bigger. I begin to get a little scared. It doesn't take too long before the hole is bigger than my whole world. And I find myself unable to stay inside you, unable to stop falling, unable to hold on.

I'm gasping, gulping this new air. It's so hard to breathe. It's so hard to see. Everything is so bright. It's so much all at once. I need air. I need to hear you, Mommy. I kick and kick and wave my arms trying to take in more air. Where are you, Mommy? What is happening? Then I hear you. But not like I've ever heard you before. You are moaning and then you... you *shriek*. You keep shrieking. It scares me. I kick even more. I'm so scared, Mommy!

---

[25] Harriet Beecher Stowe, Uncle Tom's Cabin; pp. 135-136

Someone, not you, picks me up and places me somewhere dark and cold. I can't hear you anymore. I keep straining to move like when I was inside you. I try to kick and my chest goes up and down with each painful, labored breath. I keep breathing. I am alone. I am cold. I am not strong enough to make any noise, to cry out for help. I wait, for what I don't know.

Then I saw a light. Someone came close. They picked me up and held me. They wrapped me in something soft and warm. It wasn't as good as you, but it was better than no one. I tried to keep breathing. I tried to listen for you... but I couldn't do it forever. Every breath I took was shorter and harder. I opened my eyes again and tried to look at the face that was holding me. I wanted it to be you. It wasn't. Then I took my last, my very last breath.

You were given Valium. I was placed in a plastic bag.

So why did that have to happen to me? For what reason was I killed and torn from you and my home?

Your Baby Boy

"The magic of the real presence of distress—the imploring human eye, the frail, trembling hand, the despairing appeal of helpless agony—these he had never tried."

– Stowe [26]

Dear Mommy,

This is how I died. I was doing what I usually do. Floating, rolling, sucking my thumb, and listening to you. I felt you lie down. There was eeriness inside you. I could feel it, I just didn't know why. Something funny and round was going back and forth on top of me like it was watching me. I kicked it. It paused, hesitating for a moment. Then it moved again, more slowly.

Then I saw something, something I knew was wrong, frightening. It was sharp and long and came into my home; closer and closer it came to me. I tried to move away from it, but it followed me. Then it happened. I felt it pulling me, pulling me so hard. I tried with all my might to pull away and fight it. But, Mommy, it was so strong. I couldn't. I wanted to cry out to you to save me, to comfort me, to make it stop, to make it go away. But you couldn't hear me.

It pulled off my arm first. What sound do you make when you feel something so awful that you can't describe even if you were big enough for words, for sounds, for screams, for cursing, for wailing? What sound is that? All of my insides screamed with everything that can scream in a body. A piercing terror came over me as more of me was ripped from me, and my little heart still kept beating faster and faster, kept feeling, the hurt worse and worse with every beat. I couldn't make it stop. Then my chest was ripped from my neck. That was my last moment. My head had to be crushed because it wouldn't fit through the sucking pulling thing. It was pulled out separately from the rest of me.

My body was laid in pieces on a steel tray. Some person counted my body parts to make certain all of me was out of you. They whispered to the person who sucked me out of you that two fingers and a piece of my spine were missing. There was an awkward silence. Then the person smiled, suppressed a chuckle and told the doctor they were joking. Oh

---

[26] Harriet Beecher Stowe, Uncle Tom's Cabin; p. 85

yes, that's funny.[27] Your head was turned, and I don't know where your heart was...

Then I was thrown away with the parts of other babies. Trash. And I have to ask, why? Why was I killed and broken into bits? Why was I thrown in the trash?

Your Baby Girl

---

[27] "At least 80 percent of the women would try to look down at the end of the table, wondering if they could see anything which is why our doctor always went in with the scalpel first. Once the baby was already cut up, there was nothing but blood and torn up tissue for the woman to see. When a later abortion was performed, workers had to piece the baby back together, and every major part–head, torso, two legs, and two arms–had to be accounted for. One of our little jokes at the clinic was, 'If you ever want to humble a doctor, hide a leg so he thinks he has to go back in.' Please understand, these were not abnormal, uncaring women working with me at the clinic. We were just involved in a bloody, dehumanizing business, all of us for our own reasons. Whether we were justifying our past advocacy (as I was), justifying a previous abortion (as many were) or whatever, we were just trying to cope–and if we couldn't laugh at what was going on, I think our minds would have snapped. It's not an easy trying to confuse a conscience that will not stay dead." – Hearing on H.R. 4292, the "Born Alive Infant Protection Act of 2000."

> "It's just as much an act of murder to kill a sickly man it is to kill a healthy one; a poor man as a rich man; a black man as a white man; and just as much an act of murder to kill a human fetus as it is to kill a child or an adult."
>
> – Yves R. Simon

Dear Mama,

This is how I died. It is really so awful, so painful, I'm just not sure where to start. I want to start by screaming WHY! But I'm trying to tell my story, and that's just not the best beginning.

You had been scared for a while. At least that is what I think you call it. Your stomach was always upset and tense. You didn't seem to ever be hungry, even though I always was. I tried to move around a lot to make you laugh or rub your belly. I liked how your laugh would make my world jiggle, and I loved it when you would caress me so tenderly. I would watch your hands move over me, over my home. It was so peaceful. I felt so close to you. Sometimes it seemed like you were talking to me. Were you? I tried to show you how much I loved your touch by turning around and tapping your tummy with my feet. Could you tell?

But one day something happened that had never happened before. You lay down and there were bright lights all around. You were so tight and stiff. There was something very strange about the way you breathed. I didn't know what to think. I didn't know what would happen. I couldn't do anything. You didn't put your hand on me.

Something else, something that was not your hand was set on top of me. It went back and forth, up and down, again and again. Very suddenly it felt like something around my little world broke, and an opening I didn't know existed, a way to another place emerged. But I wanted to stay with you, Mama. I kept trying to move deeper into you, deeper into my home. Then I saw something emerge from that place, getting bigger and bigger, closer and closer. It opened wide like two thin arms as if it was reaching for me. I was trapped. I felt it grasp my leg. Quickly, before I knew what was happening, it twisted my leg in a way legs don't go and with one powerful yank, ripped my leg off. And it was gone. Gone, Mama, GONE! It was a pain that doesn't have words, a pain you can only make sounds for, pounding more, burning more, screaming with a feeling I didn't know more and more and more. My body SCREAMED! My heart was beating so fast. I was flailing, and the thing that took my leg reached and grabbed my arm. Twist, Yank, GONE! No sound comes out when I open my mouth. My lungs can't tell you how bad it hurts, Mama. But it won't stop. Please, Mama, please make it stop! Make it go away! Instinctively I do the only thing I know to comfort myself, I put my thumb in my mouth. Then I felt those terrifying arms grasp me hard and press together, squeezing. I thought I would be crushed. That's when the pain stopped, when I stopped.

My skull was crushed flat so the rest of my body could be pulled out of you with more easily. Then all the pieces of me were placed little limb by little limb in something you call a bedpan. Despite yourself, you kept trying to look. I hope you didn't see me like that, all in pieces. They were counting my body parts to make certain no trace of me, no trace of my home, was left inside you. Apparently, that's not good. But there in the bedpan, was me. My thumb was still in my mouth.

What was my crime? Mama, WHY was I killed, slaughtered like an animal?

Your Baby Girl

84   *When the Bough Breaks*

"But what needs tell the story, told too oft—every day told—of heartstrings rent and broken—the weak broken and torn for the profit and convenience of the strong!"

— Stowe[28]

Dear Daddy,

This is how I died. It's an ugly awful story. I can't even believe the violence and brutality of it, even though it was me, my body that experienced it. I can't tell Mommy. It's too hard, too ugly, too vile. Maybe you should hear what happened to me, your child.

    It was the third day in a row we'd gone back to this place. I could tell because Mommy got so sick and would cry so hard each time. I would get very still. I was scared. I remember some of the questions seemed to really bother her. Somebody even asked her if *you* were a big guy. My size impressed them. I didn't know what to think. I think it made Mommy upset. She wanted to think I was small and nothing.

    When Mommy lay down it got so very quiet. I wondered if she was sleeping. But she was so tense, almost like her heart was a burning stone. Of course, I didn't know what was about to happen. There was nothing I could do to stop it. My home was slashed open. I wasn't ready to come out yet. I had a lot more growing to do, but I was still a strong, wonderful, healthy baby boy. Then my leg was gripped powerfully. My heart raced like I'd never felt before as this thing pulled me somewhere I'd never been before. In a moment my entire body was outside, in your world, well, all of me except my head. As I grasped with my little hands and kicked in shock and fear, someone kept me as still as they could. They were so strong. Then I felt something so painful stick sharply into the back of my head. I had a sudden flood of panic and pain all mingled into some overwhelming flood of helpless instant agony, and my body jerked just like when a baby thinks it's going to fall. I guess in truth, I did.

    The next moment was when I died. A suction tube was quickly inserted where the scissors had been opened up to make a whole at the base of my skull. My brain was sucked out. My head fell limp. My body hung like a lifeless doll. But no doll can feel what I felt. No doll can feel

---

[28] Harriet Beecher Stowe, Uncle Tom's Cabin; pp. 130-131

terror. No doll can wait helplessly for their life to be sucked from them. No doll can desperately listen for his mother's voice. No doll has flesh and soul that has grown intimately over time. No doll can ever be loved like the affections that erupt from the birth of child. No doll can love with the devotion of a child who knows and rests in his mother's voice. I'm a living being, Daddy. Where were you, Daddy? Why was I murdered?

Your Son

"If there must be trouble, let it be in my day that my child may have peace, and this single reflection well applied is sufficient to wake every man to duty."

– Thomas Paine

Dear Daddy,

They say hindsight is 20/20, but sometimes it's a sight we'd rather not see; sometimes it shows a side of ourselves that's not quite as pretty as we thought it would be. But I was there. I know the story. And despite how much you don't want to hear it, I'm going to tell it. You see, it's my story.

I know you always had big dreams for yourself. You were on the "anything but ordinary" life plan, every day of which you've fought fiercely for well... *you*. You prided yourself on being a player and being great at it. The girls were just a bonus, something to make you feel good, something to boost your ego, a carousel of trophies to impress the guys. It's not your fault some of them didn't know or appreciate their status. You had to watch out for yourself, especially around girls. All they did was hold you back and hold you down. Get in and get out! That's the policy that has always worked so well for you. Their hearts were their problem. If they were smart, they'd see sex for what it is—fun. If they were stupid enough to get pregnant, the most they'll get from you is a disconnected number. You don't play that game. Besides, you've learned to beg them for their number in a way that never makes them think to ask for yours. You've learned to say what they want to hear for the night and have just enough charm to get out the door with little more than a devilish smile and a goodbye kiss. Your reputation precedes you. Not everyone can get the girls you get, or the sheer number of them, but then again, they're not you. Hey, you tell yourself, it's a free country, Thank God!

And then, along comes me. Not that you care, but I'm a girl. My mommy is a ballerina. You swept her away one night. She doesn't do that with guys. But she'd never heard one talk to her and look at her like you did. She doesn't know she's beautiful and elegant. She was awkward for too long to think much of her looks. All she's ever known of beauty is the joy that washes through her when she dances. She thought you'd call, but she doesn't know how your kind works. She doesn't get out much. She doesn't know that some people think far too much of themselves and far too little of everyone else.

Having me would ruin her. And yet strangely, she still wants me. To her I'm not disposable, I'm her baby. But she's so scared. The company is viciously competitive with an almost legendary thread of cruelty and professional treachery. If I survive, she won't, and she knows it. Dancing is all she knows, her whole life, everything has been to get to where she is today, and she has a gift, a beautiful gift. Despite all of that, right now she's looking for a way, looking for you to help her find a way to keep me. She doesn't have any family, or anyone she can turn to, just a player, just you, my daddy.

Remarkably she tracked you down. Quite the feat, and admittedly you were shocked and slightly impressed. For a moment you considered another round, but then you saw the fear in her eyes. Not good, she definitely wanted something. Okay, how to get out of what you knew was coming, you ran a few different strategies through your mind while she spilled her heart. She really was quite pretty. You even thought about showing compassion, but that's just not your style.

So you gave her a thousand dollars, more than enough to finish me off, solve *her* problem, save *her* life. You congratulated yourself on what a generous gentleman you were being. The fact that she was asking for your help in saving *my life* seemed to have escaped you. She should be grateful; you've never given anyone anything. You wrote her a check, kissed her forehead, and told her everything would be fine. It was her problem now. Quickly, you left, leaving my mommy weak-kneed with a runny nose and swollen eyes, unable to catch her breath. Yeah, Dad, you're a regular Clark Gable.

She sat there frozen, unable to stand. For a long time after you left she didn't move. Without looking at it she slowly fingered the check. I wish you could have felt what I felt her feel. I wish you could have read her thoughts, but you didn't even want to be bothered with the ones she shared with you. You didn't want to be bothered with her. You *definitely* didn't want to be bothered with me. And in the silent struggle it was as if a bottomless pit opened around her heart. Choosing.

The next day she saw the counselor at the clinic. She wanted to be sold on what the woman was selling. Again and again she insisted they tell her that I was just tissue, nothing to feel bad about, that she was doing the best thing she could do for herself. She didn't believe it, but she wanted to hold on to the lie long enough to get it over with. Over and over she told herself that it had to be done, must be done, there was no other option, almost chanting inside her head to flood out any other thought that would stop her from going through with killing the baby that she so desperately wanted to love.

She tried to be strong and sure. Later that day, I was dead. As she stood she couldn't shake the despair that mingled uneasily with relief. She couldn't shake the feeling that part of her was dead now too. The mantra that had carried her through, she suddenly couldn't recall. Empty, yes she felt empty. Do you know that feeling?

Dancing was all she had to fill the hole I left. So she danced. More and more, harder and harder, she threw herself into her choice, her identity, with a drive that consumed every moment. But something was missing. She didn't realize what it was at first. In fact it was years before she could name what was missing. It wasn't until she realized she no longer wanted to dance ever again that she knew the thing that was gone. It was the joy—killing me had killed her joy. She'd desperately hoped she'd get over me in time. But she didn't. The loss became bigger and ate up more of her heart. She began to hate dancing, hate herself. There was no dance, no matter how intense, that could give me back to her, give her joy back to her, give her heart back to her. So she walked away from it all. She couldn't help but think if she'd only been willing to walk away that other day she might have been able to make another start, a different start and live both dreams in a new way. But that was as impossible as mending her shattered self. She couldn't give the broken pieces of her heart to anyone, couldn't let herself love, she couldn't be trusted, didn't deserve the chance to love, especially a baby. At least these are the thoughts she told herself. Because once your baby is gone, your heart is never the same. Is your heart the same? Would you admit it if it wasn't?

Maybe you won't and maybe I'll always be your secret; but once you finally chose your trophy bride and she had your second baby, something happened in your heart. You didn't realize it until your little girl, my sister, called you "Dada" and held her short chubby arms up to you. And the thought you had at that precious moment was of me. Looking at that precious child in your arms you realized what you'd done. You choked back tears you didn't know you had for someone you'd never realized you cared for—me, your first baby girl. You found yourself *wondering* if she had gone through with it and looking intently at the faces of children my age, trying to see a resemblance, *wondering* what *was* the color of my mommy's eyes. You felt guilt for the first time, and regret. Feelings you'd never allowed yourself to feel before engulfed you with an intensity that made you want to drown them out. You found ways of coping. Over time, it became harder. Anger took over, intense anger where you would lash out at everyone except yourself. Of course, that always was your style. It makes me so sad. I wish I wasn't what made you angry. I wish it could have been different. I wish I could have been held by you and loved by you. I wish I could have kissed your nose and put my head on your shoulder. I wish you could have seen my smile.

But that didn't happen. Instead, because of the way you were and the way things were, I didn't get that chance, and now you can't escape me. I became the ache, the longing, the *what would have been*. Increasingly you grew more aware that despite your player ways, you were not exempt, that the rules of heartstrings apply to you, too. Regretfully, you realize you've treated women like they were things. More and more you realize how selfish, how cold, how cruel, how many lives you used and threw away like their only purpose was to satisfy your desires. The ugliness of it all overwhelms you. You wish you'd been different. Me too.

Desperate fury begins to rule your heart, which finds no calm but the sweet face of your child, a face that reminds you and unwittingly rekindles the rage it first subsides. Anger becomes your keeper because you're too much of a coward to admit you are one, and too terrified to accept blame. Is that bad of me to say that? It's true, we both know it. The anger is just a cover for the fear. What you really want is to run from it all like you used to. Escape, which used to be your rescue and relief, evades you because quite simply you can't; you're trapped, unable to flee the face you love and my unknown face that haunts you. Your hope is that if you lie to yourself for long enough, time will bring relief or extinguish the rage inside. But, Daddy, guilt doesn't go away, no matter how much anger you pour on top of it. It is only healed in the wonder of repentance and forgiveness.

I see it all. I see you so angry, so incapable of changing the past, so desperate for something to take away the hurt. Would it really be so difficult, Daddy, to be sorry for what you did to me? Would it really so hard to cry over me, to grieve me, to beg for forgiveness? I would you know, I would forgive you. But no one has asked. I would love. I would forgive. I want so badly to be missed, to be wept over, Daddy. I know you don't like how angry and judgmental I am. But I don't know what else to say when I just keep being ignored like I'm nothing! Please, Daddy! Please hear me! Please cry for me! Please! Would it really be so hard to stop lying to yourself, to accept the fact that you paid to have me killed, paid for a quick fix because you couldn't be bothered with your own child? I know it's awful to see what you did in words. I tried to tell it just like it happened. I'm not trying to make it worse; I'm trying to make it real. I'm trying with every harsh, true word to make ME real. If I'm not real to you, how can I be real to the world, how will any baby like me ever be real if everyone keeps closing their eyes and hearts? Are we just supposed to keep dying quietly? Is that the answer? Would it really be so hard to admit that what you did was so very wrong, especially when you know that if you'd just helped that young frightened woman, I'd be alive right now, calling you "Daddy", playing with dolls, reading Nancy Drew, and being a beautiful blessing—a beautiful, dancing angel just like my mommy. Would it really be so hard to just say "I am so sorry, my baby?" That's what I want, for you to call me your baby and mean it. I want you to be my daddy.

Love,
Your Baby Girl

"Violence can only be concealed by a lie, and the lie can only be maintained by violence. Any man who has once proclaimed violence as his method is inevitably forced to take the lie as his principle."

– Alexander Solzhenitsyn

Dear Daddy,

Taken care of, that's what you wanted. The other woman shut up, silenced, placated, paid, pacified, problem solved. You knew how to handle such things, such things like me. Whatever it took to keep your wife from finding out about your plaything on the side, you were willing to do. All that needed to be done was convince the little blond my death was in her best interest. And you *are* a salesman, one of the best. You just tell them what they want to hear, and then guide them along until they think they thought of it, that it was their idea.

She was trying to be casual about the whole baby thing—the *me* thing. She knew you ran at the first sign of neediness or clinging. She tried to be the exact opposite of what you told her your wife was like. She was experimental and let you do what you wanted with her. She never told you how it really makes a girl feel to be handled like that, because she was pretending to be different, cool, young. She would curse and drink right along with you and be coy and flirt with other men, just to make sure you were always enthralled, entranced, always chasing her. She knew how to get and keep a man. As far as the adultery, well, she wasn't taking anything that didn't want to be taken. Why put in all the poor years with someone her age when she could get some bored older man to give her everything she wanted? Homewrecker, golddigger, she didn't care, as long as she was rich and got her man. Of course they would have children, but not until the timing was perfect. She wanted the whole picture, the way it's supposed to be, in the right order, and *I* was ahead of her schedule. *I* would have to die, simply because I didn't show up at the appropriate time

Of course, you were the man to get, Daddy. Money, charm, and formerly quite handsome, despite the current extra pounds around the middle, what more did a man need to snag up a pretty little player? To be honest, when you have money and a good smile, you don't need much else. The girls are giving it away. You just have to make sure not to get caught. Child support and alimony cost a lot more than a girlfriend, even a spoiled one. She had no idea who she was dealing with. You knew what her idea was, but that *timing* was never going to happen, no matter what she did in bed.

Daddy, you were so professional, so businesslike. I had no idea that my murder could be such an efficient, emotionless event. I guess as I grew within the womb of my mother, I didn't know I had bad timing. I didn't know I was some*thing* to be taken care of quickly and quietly instead of some*one* to be taken care of tenderly. I didn't know that I was expendable, disposable. I didn't know I was evidence that must be disposed. I didn't know that I was the only one who had to die so you could get your thrills. I didn't know my life was so cheap. Why is it that your other children are such a treasure to you, but I can be thrown away without a thought? Why isn't my life, despite the behavior of my parents, precious? Why do you show more emotion about a golf game gone bad than about the murder of your child? Is it asking too much for you to at least shed a tear over my tiny, burnt body? Is it asking too much for you to regret killing your child? Is it too much to ask you, who can be responsible for a corporation, to take responsibility for a tiny little life you took part in creating? Is it too much to ask you to care that I had to die to cover your crime? Is it just too much trouble to ask for MY life?

Your Baby Boy

"I had to wonder how can having a child be so wrong for some people that they will pay me to end its life."

– Dr. McMillan

"To be a man is, precisely, to be responsible."

– Antoine de St Exupery

Dear Daddy,

I know what I want to be when I grow up. I want to be like you. I think you're the strongest, smartest, best daddy in the world. When I'm with you, I feel bigger, braver than I do on my own. I love it when you're near Mommy. She must think like I do, she gets excited and peaceful at the same time. Yeah, that's how I feel too. It's like everything is going to be okay because you're here. Yours is the only voice I love as much as Mommy's. I can't wait to meet you. I'm going to open my eyes so big. I'm going to grip your finger so you know I'm strong like you. I'm going to try to smile for you. I want you to love me like I'm going to love you.

But then Mommy began crying. She cried too much. I didn't understand why. We were so happy. She would rub her tummy, and I'd flip and kick for her, then I could feel her laugh. Her laugh is wonderful. But now she clings to her tummy, to me, and cries.

You're leaving my mommy, leaving me. You just can't do it. You just can't be my daddy. Apparently, loving me is asking too much. You can't have me and mommy depending on you, needing you. I wish I could give you some of my love, and some of Mommy's. I'm sure we have more than enough to share with you. What is it about being my daddy that would be so hard? I'll be good. I won't eat too much. I'll be quiet. I'll go to sleep. I'll say, "Yes sir," and "No sir." I'll be your little helper. I'll pick up my toys. I'll put my arms around your neck and hug you so tight. I'll try to be just like you, my daddy.

Why can't you stay? Is it money? Is it something you want to be or do? Is it really somebody needing you, expecting something from you? Is it having to be responsible? Is it the late nights that you would miss out on? Is it my diapers? Is it all that you can't do because you have to take care of me? Do you really think that what your little boy can give you for a lifetime doesn't compare to those things? Do you really think the love between a father and son is something to shrug your shoulders at and coolly walk out on? Do you really think your child is something to throw away? Do you know what will happen to me because you left? Do you know how you crushed my mommy? Did you realize she is so distraught, so brokenhearted that she's going to the doctor to have them kill me because she can't stand the thought of being left by you and raising your son? She doesn't want to go on living. She wants to kill us both, but the people at that place told her ridding herself of me was the answer to her problems, killing me was the answer to getting her life back.

But what about me? How does that help me get my life back? How does it help me cope with the pain of being left by the daddy I love, the daddy I want to be like? How does it protect me, heal me, love me? How am I to understand why something so violent and horrible should happen to me when all I have done is love those around me and grow bigger and stronger?

I know you'll blame her for that choice and remove yourself from any responsibility. But people don't think straight, they don't think for forever when their hearts and lives have been used, trampled, lied to, and walked out on. All they can think of is the quickest way to stop the pain. Pain you caused, Daddy.

I just can't figure out what's so good out there in the world that's worth abandoning Mommy and me. I can't figure out what you're chasing, or what you're running from. What is it that the world offers that loving a child prevents you from having? Why do I have to die? What have I done, Daddy? What have I done? I don't want to die. All I ever wanted was to be like you! Please, Daddy, do something! Don't walk away. Don't leave us! Don't leave *me*! I love you, Daddy!

Your Little Man

"I can do no other than be reverent before everything that is called life. I can do no other than to have compassion for all that is called life. That is the beginning and foundation for all ethics."

– Albert Schweitzer

"Let me give you a definition of ethics. It is good to maintain and further life, it is bad to damage and destroy life."

– Albert Schweitzer

Dear Mr.,

I can't figure out why I used a formal greeting, maybe because an intimate one is not possible. I realize you couldn't care less. Still, somebody has to say something. Mama won't, she hasn't told a soul. So that just leaves me to tell the world what you did to her, me to tell the world why I was killed, and why she is a shell of the person she once was.

Of course you thought she was hot that night, young and hot in that skirt. "Fresh meat! Easy Access." was what you boasted to your friends with a knowing, prowling confident nod. Then you gave her drinks that took her breath away, with a little something extra in case she could hold her liquor. And it worked. She was drunk within the hour and in your room soon after. She doesn't know when she passed out. She doesn't know if she said no. She doesn't remember that part, only the drink. What echoes in her gut with a sickening, nauseous regret is waking up to you behind her, in a victory cry, hooting with beastly pride, and realizing she had just lost her virginity. Humiliated and used. Once you left, she found her clothes and ran. She never told, fearful of what might be said of her. She didn't go out for a long time after that.

But the nausea wouldn't go away, and she knew there was more to the awful night, I was there. She was overcome with the kind of gut-wrenching fear, shame, and desperation that swallows you whole. She couldn't seem to find an escape, and with frightening speed she killed me. Before she knew it her heart was torn to pieces. On that table where she thought she would find her quiet, quick fix to a haunting, humiliating night, she became more broken than before. A new panic overtook her as the physician did his work, as I began to die, a soul-crushing fear, a fear of realization that she had chosen wrong! She wanted to stop the unstoppable, rescue the doomed, save the little baby that had fretted her so. She kept thinking there had to be another way, but it was all too late. My tiny body was burned inside and out with a lethal poison reserved for babies just my size, and I was trashed. You should be able to understand that, it is the same kind of consideration you had for my mama. The hole you began in her spread with a feverish intensity. It keeps devouring her, even today. The waves of shame you shoved her face in that night have pooled around her, stagnant, drowning her heart. Don't misunderstand me; it's not her regret that makes killing me wrong. It would be wrong whether she felt it or not. After all, you don't regret what you did to her, but it remains wretched and wicked. Me being killed is wrong because it is wrong to kill defenseless people who show up in our lives uninvited. Her regret is still there, though, and still very real.

Of course, I wish I could have told her there was a way out. I wish I could have told her there were people who could help. I wish I could have told her there was something to take away the shame and guilt. I wish I could have told there was a place to go, a place to hide away. I wish I could have told her about medical withdrawals, transfers, pregnancy centers, and the compassionate people who have been where she has been, people who know how to help. I wish I could have told her she could keep me or find someone she felt safe giving me to. I wish she could have stopped panicking long enough to see another way. I wish she could have trusted someone to be her friend, to stand by her, to love her until she could love me. Because these are the things that would have made survival possible in her mind, these are the things and the people that would have given her the courage to do what was right for us both, despite the treacherous way you used her. I wish I could have shown her that even though you don't deserve me, she does. I wish she could have seen how much I deserved to be loved. I wish she could have held me. But you took that from her. You took me from her. She knows I am real, she knows I am her child. It is YOU that doesn't understand my humanity or hers. It is YOU that scrapes the bottom of depravity. It is YOU that doesn't grasp the beauty and dignity of a life, or the purpose of one. It is YOU that needs to be stopped, not *me* that needs to die.

HER *Daughter*

"Bad news never had good timing."
– John Mayer

"It is a great pity that a child must die so that you might live as you wish."
– Mother Theresa

Dear Daddy,

I know you're scared. You don't want to lose her, that beautiful, graceful lady you love, the one you want to spend your life with. She isn't my mommy. I'm not growing inside that great lady. My mommy is that girl from that night where you drank too much and got caught up in the passion of the moment. The night you regretted and put out of your mind, the night that made you distant and moody for weeks to the one you love. Your love thought it was her, thought you didn't love her, thought she'd gotten too close, thought you needed space, thought you were going to break her heart. You saw her hurting and wanted to comfort her and tell her it was you, but you couldn't because then you would lose her, and you couldn't let that happen. It would be better if she just thought it was her problem, then she wouldn't question you too much. Then after a few weeks you could get it out your head and things would be like they were before. You would hold her and love her, and it would be over.

You didn't know, of course, that *I* began that night. When my mommy called and told you, you jumped into damage control at full speed. The objective was the status quo, the secret kept, the night gone. You offered her money you could afford to give her, money that would go unnoticed by your love. It couldn't be too much, that would raise suspicion. It couldn't take too much away from what you had planned to spend on the ring, the one you knew she adored. A few hundred dollars was all that was needed to get rid of this problem, to get rid of me.

But that stupid girl, the one you were beginning to loathe, she wanted to keep me. She wanted help *raising me*, instead of ridding the world of me. All you could think of was how to convince her, how to persuade her, how to make us both go away forever. If you didn't, you would lose everything, the beautiful girl, the happy life. And you would be stuck with a person you didn't want in your life, and me. You've been unable to think of me in all of this, of what I look like, of who

I am, of my tiny precious life. You, and what you want, is all that matters to you, even if it means killing me. Of course, it doesn't help to think of me. It doesn't help to take that risk. Empathy, compassion, responsibility, justice, these are threats to the decisions you have made, threats to your choices, threats to your best-laid plans.

What do I say, Daddy, that my life is more important than your love story? It is, you know. My life, although it will mess up yours, is sacred, NOT worthy of being destroyed for your sake. It is my life, not yours to grant to me, not yours to bestow or withdraw rights upon, not yours to live or yours to kill, MINE! Your love may not be able to get over your betrayal, but worse to her, worse to all that is right and good is what you plan to do to me when I'm too small to defend myself, too small to stop you when you crush me, too small for my cries to be heard. She is the kind of woman who could not tolerate a baby being killed so you could have her as a prize. And my mommy, despite the situation she's gotten herself into, wants to do the right thing. She just needs help. Daddy, don't make me beg for my own life. Don't do that. No one should have to do that, even though it happens too often. Maybe it's time to take a new course, plan a new life, one where you do the right thing and consider others instead of yourself, one where you do not create casualties to cover up your crimes and you take the loss instead of create the loss, one where you see that my life and my story matters as much as yours.

Matthew

"Guilty? Yes. No matter what the motive, love of ease, or a desire to save from suffering the unborn innocent, the woman is awfully guilty who commits the deed. It will burden her conscience in life, it will burden her soul in death; but oh, thrice guilty is he who... drove her to the desperation which impelled her to the crime!"
– Susan B. Anthony, The Revolution, 1869

Dear Grandpa,

You don't know about me, but I am your granddaughter. I was killed before I was born. My mommy, your daughter, killed me because of you. I know, it's hard to hear, but it's true. You have always been so strict, so tyrannical, so terrifying and cruel that she couldn't even imagine the course your anger would run. There would be the screaming, the slapping up side the head over and over again, maybe another eardrum ruptured. That was what happened when she came home an hour late and didn't call. Then there was the name-calling, the really hurtful, degrading names that destroy the heart of a young girl, she knew them well. This would prove the names true. And then there would be the humiliating torture of being shamed in front of her family while they all stood there silent, everyone afraid of you. Of course she would be kicked out with nothing, for dramatic emphasis, and warned never to return—disowned. And then she would be alone, with child, too young to provide for herself or a baby, terrified, ashamed, broken, desperate, without hope.

So you see, I'm dead because of you. The fact that my mommy tried to find love, affection, and home in the arms of a boy she thought loved her is your fault too. She was too hungry, too naïve to know it wasn't real, to desperate to know that she made it more than it was because she so needed to be loved, so needed to know a kind touch. She knows what she did to me was wrong. She really didn't know what else to do. Her reality left her captured by fear, with no safe place. Her guilt has eaten her for a long time. I wonder how many other babies die because of cruel grandpas like you, because you refuse to give love or mercy or grace or compassion or forgiveness or second chances. But a heavy hand, intimidation, condemnation, shame, fury, control, those you shower generously, liberally.

My mommy lives with a broken heart every day because of my not being with her and her not being strong enough to find courage back then. But in truth, she has been broken for a long time. You broke her too. Her one comfort is in knowing another Father, the one who made us both. She reminds her sorrow that He has forgiven her, and tells her grieving, regretful heart that her beautiful baby is in His arms and one day she will hold me. She sings to her scared, lonely spirit of His unfailing love that has known her and loved her all through the ages. He is her comforter, especially when she is reminded of you and all that you took.

It's awful, wretched indeed, that so many young girls live never knowing love and find their fragile hearts trapped between fear and survival, making decisions they regret for a lifetime. Regret is so much worse than fear because well, because it's for forever. With fear you're scared because you don't know what will happen, but with regret you can never change what you did. Not all of these young girls will know or accept the grace of God, the one hope for their weighted, weary hearts. Some cannot for they can't forgive themselves. Some cannot for they can't accept what they did. Some cannot because all they have ever known of a father is the kind of hurt you offered. But maybe if there were more love, more hope, more healing, more open arms and safe places for scared little girls to run to there would be less loss, less hurt, fewer dead babies, replaced with stories of courage, love, and survival.

You have destroyed much, but all is not lost. There is hope for you, that is if you can learn to admit you were wrong, and that you are as needy as any person. I hope you do learn to love. I hope you learn to tell your baby girl you are sorry for everything. And I hope you will do something about it, something to help girls like my mommy. I hope everyone who has had a hand in hurting these girls or abandoning them and the tiny persons growing inside them will put their hands up to help. I pray my baby girl prayers for safe places for young girls to finish growing up far from hate and anger, far from condemnation. I pray my baby girl prayers for people to love these girls and give them a way to save their lives and the lives of babies like me. I pray my baby girl prayers for the money they need, the education they need, the jobs they need, the childcare they need to become the self-sufficient women who can love and provide for the babies they love. I pray for the hurt to go away, not through denial, not through pretending we are not real so they can keep the guilt away, but through the forgiveness of a real Father who will always make a way and a safe place for the meek.

Your Granddaughter

"Think occasionally of the suffering of which you spare yourself the sight."
— Albert Schweitzer

Dear Papa,

I know you don't want to hear this. I know you don't want to hear me. I guess like all of our family's secrets the only way you think we can survive is if we all pretend everything is fine. We have to buck up, smile, but never, ever speak and say the awful, ugly truth. We have to keep up appearances, keep the image intact, patch and paint the cracks, and trash anything that tarnishes the golden image, the perfect family, the proof that supports your proud pose and gives you permission to look down your nose at the messed up, dysfunctional excuses for families. But not you, Papa, not your family. No disgrace will ever befall your family. With the steely defense of a warrior, you destroy anything that threatens that perfect picture. So I guess it seemed logical to you that would include me. I was a threat, and was dealt with as such—killed, *quickly*, before your scared, foolish daughter could find the courage to resist you. Your little girl would have the perfect life, marry the perfect man, have the perfect children. The picture of perfection would not be comprised. I would not stand in her, or really *your* way. You acted like she had done this awful thing to *you*, that it was *you* who had been wronged. The fact that she did not want to kill the baby that grew within her, the baby she knew she could and would love, the way she tried to tell you and beg you, these facts and pleas you discarded with little more than a grimace. You would protect your family from disgrace and shame, from your daughter's stupidity. You knew what was best for her, Papa. And apparently, you knew what was best for me too, butchering and a trashcan.

But tell me, Papa, is your pride so great that you think you somehow have the authority to determine who lives and dies, that you somehow get to choose which child you will proudly claim as your grandchild? Why should one generation be allowed to kill another? Is that what age, wisdom, and experience bestow on you, the right to kill if it suits and protects your interests and your image? Do you actually think because you are older that you are more valuable than me, more worthy of life? That's like saying four-year-olds are less human than five-year-olds. It just doesn't make sense.

Maybe you think you don't know me, that I am a stranger to you and that you do not owe me any consideration as such. But, Papa, I am your flesh and blood! You know me as well as you know any grandchild that is growing inside your child's womb. Besides, not knowing someone gives you even less authority to claim the right to say they live or they die. That right belongs to no one, *no one*, Papa, not even you, "*no one has the right to choose to do a wrong.*"²⁹ And killing family, how can you possibly justify it? Do you really think that the things and the image you have built are worth more and should be protected more than a breathing, bleeding, tiny human being that even carries your blood and your genes? But those are just lies you tell yourself to justify my death by your order. It is really just about you and how you look and what people think of you. So I am dead so other people will think well of this phony image you present. I guess it will work as long as the skeletons keep quiet.

So tell me Papa, when you held the right baby, the one that came after the perfect man and the perfect wedding, did you think of me? Is that baby, my sister, more real, more human than me because everything was as it should be? Is she more real because she is more wanted? Did you give her that right, Papa, the right to exist, to be alive, to stay living, to not be killed because she came with all the trimmings? Silly me, I guess I just thought that being here, living and growing, the offspring of my human parents was all that was required to be a person. I didn't realize I needed someone else's permission to exist. I didn't realize I should be okay with being ripped to pieces because somebody else didn't like the picture the way it would look with me in it. I didn't realize I was property, that I belonged to someone else. I guess I thought I belonged to myself. I guess I thought I was worth being protected and fought for simply because I possessed the same nature as every person ever since the beginning of time, a human nature. I thought that was all I needed.

I know you don't know this because you won't listen to others. But your little girl, with the perfect life and the perfect grandchild, well, she is not so perfect now. You see, when she held my sister, she couldn't think of anyone but me. The truth, the skeleton from the closet haunted her. She couldn't see why this child deserved to be loved and

---

²⁹ Abraham Lincoln in a debate with Douglas in regards to slavery. Douglas proposed that if people want to have slaves, then they should have a right to them.

her other baby, me, didn't. She can't seem to love this new baby; she doesn't think she is worthy of her after what happened to me. She is dying inside, and in a few months it will be too much for her and she will take too many pills to make it all stop. The picture will be broken then for good. But the thing is, it has been broken and a lie for a long time. And telling yourself lies, even for decades, can never make the lies true.

I guess, Papa, I think what should have died was your pride. I think you should have had the courage and the humility to say nobody's perfect, no family is perfect, but we can find enough love for everyone, even the unexpected. I guess I wish you had realized it wasn't about you at all. I guess I wish you had accepted a new picture, even if you didn't know what it would have looked like, one with a stranger who had your smile.

Love,
Your Grandson

Dear Grandma,

What I am going to tell you is going to break your heart. You don't know it, but you have two dead grandchildren... yes, two. I know you think there is no way this is true, that you have raised your son to have respect for life, to be moral, upstanding, good. But he doesn't want you to be disappointed in him, doesn't want to break your heart, doesn't want to bring you shame, doesn't want to live that stereotypical story. He wants to stay the picture of the perfect Christian son. He knows how much you care how everyone thinks of your family and all you stand for. He knows how much you have tried to show others how they should be living. "Live the standard," that's what he always heard you say. So he told his girlfriend he would dump her if she had that baby of theirs. So she got rid of me. I am the first. Then she got pregnant with my little sister. He issued the same threat, so she did the awful deed a second time and now that beautiful little baby girl is dead too.

Our mommy is still waiting for that marriage proposal so she can live that perfect picture with your perfect son and they can live a perfectly pretty life. You have wondered why she has gotten quieter over time. You saw the sadness, and the funny way she acted around babies. I wonder who you would be angry at if you knew the truth about us. Would it be your perfect son, or our stupid mommy who kept getting pregnant? Why is it always the girls who get blamed for being so stupid? Is it *all* their fault? Do you think they really want to do this wretched thing that makes them ache inside forever? What is it that these boys and girls have learned that makes them so afraid of admitting they made a mistake and didn't wait like they were told at least good *girls* did? I think it is shame they are running from. Shame that traps them into an identity for a lifetime, making dignity and respectability impossible, shame that makes them always and forever less than others, labeled, not as a humble soul, but a humiliated, dirty one, incapable of honor. They think the guilt would be easier to carry. I don't know which is easier to live with for a lifetime. I just know that one of them involves dead babies.

So why am I telling you, right? Your breaking heart wants to defend the way you have raised your son. I think what has been missing, what you didn't teach, is grace, grace in the face of failure, grace when goodness is gone, grace because no one can truly and honestly live the picture perfectly, grace because we all screw up, grace because little lives are at stake, grace that gives love and honor instead of shame and loneliness. Grandma, give grace, abundantly, generously, not lowering the standard, but standing on the same level with all who haven't met it, holding little people's hands so they won't be afraid. That is what honors the King, pointing to the One who lived the perfect life, while loving everyone who didn't.

One day, you will meet us. I long for that day.

Love,
Your Grandchildren

"It is not because the truth is too difficult to see that we make mistakes... we make mistakes because the easiest and most comfortable course for us is to seek insight where it accords with our emotions—especially selfish ones."

– Alexander Solzhenitsyn

"A system of morality which is based on relative emotional values is a mere illusion, a thoroughly vulgar conception which has nothing sound in it and nothing true."

– Socrates

Dear Nanna,

That's what my sisters call you. You're my Nanna, too. I know how much you love them, adore them, how they're your pride and joy. But not me. I was just as beautiful, just as precious, just as worthy of your love and pride and bountiful gifts. But you didn't think so simply because of my ill timing. I had the audacity to show up when she was young, not yet married, not yet at the time and circumstances of life when a baby is an appropriately timed joy.

When my mommy told you about me, you took control. You weren't going to let this happen to your daughter. You most definitely weren't going to let it happen to you. You'd raised a good girl, and I was putting both your reputations at risk. You weren't going to let some unplanned pregnancy ruin her life. Besides, you knew a baby would mean you'd have to put aside your plans, your freedom, when you were almost done with mothering. There would be the disdainful pity from friends and of course having to accept failure for the nearly two decades you'd just spent mothering, *failure* because you hadn't raised an upstanding girl. Her mistake was yours, her shame you shared, all of which you found unbearable. The thought of starting over with a baby and helping that much for an *illegitimate* grandchild, well, I guess it was just easier to pay somebody to take care of the problem so that there wasn't one. Love, that was what you called it.

A problem, yes, I guess it's easier to kill me if you remove any thought of referring to me as a child, as a person, as your granddaughter. Yes, I guess calling me "problem" makes doing the unmentionable tolerable. You stood beside your young daughter and held her hand. You stood stoic, strong, unyielding, urging her, coaxing her as she faltered, wavered, attempting to love me, attempting to defend me, attempting to find courage in that wretched, wrong, fateful moment. You shushed her, told her she'd thank you one day, that she'd thank you for all that you were saving her from. Reassuringly, you uttered your consolation for my death: "Of course, you don't wish anyone harm dear, but remember you don't have any obligation to remain tied to this child. Now lie down. It will be over soon." My mommy couldn't control her panicked breathing or her heart. That's why you were there, to make sure she didn't do something stupid, like love me.

Where you went so wrong was in valuing one life more than another because it suits your interests and design. Claiming the authority to have power over life and death, that just doesn't belong to you. Do you really think that a person only has a right to live if someone wants them, if time and circumstance are agreeable, as if those things can determine the worth of a human life? I just can't see why *you* get to say if *I* live or die. When do I get a say? When do I get to appeal? Why are my sisters precious and I'm rubbish?

No obligation? No obligation to me, her child? Well then why is she, why are you, so willingly obligated to my sisters? *Because you want to be? Because there's a ring? Because you don't fear what an obligation to them will cost you as opposed to what I might?* I'm as much her child as my sisters are, and as human too. I'm your GRANDDAUGHTER! What part of that do you not get? What part do you not understand? I don't see how you not wanting her to *have* to be a parent gives you the right to encourage her to kill me, to pay someone in a white coat to poison me like a human pesticide. She doesn't own me and neither do you. I don't see how you or anyone choosing to be responsible suddenly gives another human being their worth. What about being liable to not hurt me, a helpless human being, not to mention not assisting in the destruction of your own grandchild? You treat your precious pedigreed dogs better than you treated me. What about being devoted to helping your scared little girl do right instead of wrong? What about those finer, ethical obligations of motherhood? But I guess that isn't couture these days with the ladies at the country club, is it? Fine, if you don't want your daughter to raise a baby when she's so young, she could have given me to those who would welcome me, but only, ONLY if she wanted to let me go. You should have let her choose, let her control her life, by choosing who raises me, not choosing who dies.

Obligation, obligation, yes, we're all obligated despite our resistance and struggle with circumstance and responsibility. Just think, *think* of all the fathers who don't want to be fathers, don't want to pay child support, don't want to be held responsible, but obligated they are, and rightly so! They see no good from being fathers, no good from the inconvenience of parenthood, but our government ignores their demands to choose or deny the requirements of fatherhood and garnishes their wages accordingly. Many citizens can see no good from the taxes they pay and demand exemption, demand a choice in the taxes they pay, but their taxes are still withheld. Think further of how many young students can see no good in going to school, no use in education, and choose to play hooky. No school board, teacher, truancy officer, or parent would grant them such a choice. They demand attendance and dare to require the child who knows better to go to school. They remain stoic, uncaring, inconsiderate, indifferent to the child's wishes and rights to roam free. As far as obligation, I think we're all obliged to not willfully harm another. It seems so simple. I can't understand how people have twisted it so. If we demand taxes, attendance, child support, and even speed limits and stoplights, surely we can insist parents not kill their children before the rest of the world has seen their precious face and glimpsed their undeniable humanity, sucking their tiny fingers. Surely we can require that people let another life live unharmed, even if they pull out in front of us, right in our lane, and cause us to slam on the brakes.

This is the other thing I can't understand. How do you stand beside your daughter and hold her hand as I am ripped to pieces and then hold her hand another day as she gives birth to my sisters? How can you be so... so... two-faced? Of course I find fault, I'm dead because of you. You could have stood beside my mommy and loved her through this. You could have helped her love me. She wanted to love me; she was just scared—very, very scared. And you, the person who could have been her strength, used it instead to help her do the unthinkable, the unchangeable. How I wish I could have been your love, cuddled in your lap and kissed your cheek. Oh, how I wish you had room in your heart for me, for the unexpected joy you didn't expect I could bring! I wish you'd seen me for what I really am and had courage instead of pride, love instead of an agenda.

The end, the picture that you find so pretty which gives you so much pride, you think it justifies the means because it looks the way you planned it. The means, ME, my body, my life, thrown away like waste, will never be justifiable for the simple reason that you took what was not yours, treated like refuse what was priceless and precious, and destroyed what could never be replaced!

*Your **First** Granddaughter*

"He who oppresses the poor reproaches his Maker, but he who honors Him has mercy on the needy."

– Proverbs 14:31(NKJV)

Dear Grandma,

I need you, I need your help. My mommy needs you too. She's going to tell you I'm growing inside her. She's been trying for weeks. She keeps choking on the words, her throat goes dry and her mind goes blank. And her heart, it races so fast it scares me. But nothing comes out of her mouth. She keeps hoping you'll somehow just know, and you'll ask so all she'll have to mutter is "yes." She's terrified, absolutely paralyzed with fear. She's scared you'll hate her, be ashamed of her, never ever forgive her. She's scared of what will happen to her. She doesn't know what to do. It's so... There just doesn't seem to be a word that covers it all. She needs you, that's all she knows.

Please, Grandma, I know you don't know me yet, but please, please help my mommy. I don't want to die. She can keep going if you don't leave her side. She can hope if you do too. She can believe if you tell you her that a baby is a good thing. She can choose what direction her life will take if she knows that there's help and hope and love.

When she tells you, please don't be angry. I know you didn't think she was doing such things with boys. She thought he loved her. Now she isn't so sure. She feels so alone. When she finally tells you, be kind. Wrap your arms around her and tell her you love her no matter what. When she tells you, help her, please. She isn't strong right now, and she needs you to help her do the right thing. I think people think you should just do the right thing just because it's right, but I think they underestimate the power of fear and loneliness. I wish they understood how much strength and courage and power they could give to those they expect right actions from, strength, courage, and power that could save a little life like mine, and a heart like hers.

I know you weren't expecting to be a grandmother so soon, and you have younger kids, and what kind of a message does this send, and where did you go wrong? But none of that matters when you compare it to a whole little life made by the One who made all of us. None of it, the expectations, the lessons, the failures, what people think, none of it can compare with the beauty and purpose that is found in one little life, designed by Him, for Him.

So please, for my sake, and my mommy's, love her, love me, help her, help me. For your love can do wonders, a mother's love always can. And in acknowledging and loving my unexpected life, you honor the One who made us all.

Love,
Your Grandbaby

"A person's a person no matter how small."

– Dr. Seuss, <u>Horton Hears a Who</u>

...and deserving of the rights God gave to us all.

Dear Stranger,

I am not yours. I do not belong to you any more than you belong to me. I am not waste to do with as you see fit. I am not research material. I am not lifeless tissue, despite how you have treated me. I am not your cure to be sliced and diced, studied and replicated, killed and used for your benefit. You do not own me.

I am not worthless because I am so small. I am not disposable because someone who does not recognize my humanity placed me on a Siberian shelf. How people treat me is not where my value comes from. I am human. I have a human nature. I have the same significance, the same unalienable rights as you because of what I am, a human being, not because of how small I am, the most helpless of all. You do not define me.

From my very beginning I was a boy, some of us are girls. From my very beginning all that is me, my talents, gifts, figure, freckles, and flaws were all here. I don't lose that because you treat me like a thing, like some *thing* that you have a right to take, own, use, and kill for your own purposes. Being sick does not mean you get to kill others because they are small and helpless. Being sick does not mean you get to kill them just so you can use them to get better. That is not noble. That is utterly, inconceivably wrong. You do not own me.

You are not more valuable than me because you can do things I cannot do yet. You are not more valuable than me because you know more people than I do. You are not more valuable than me because of the way I came to be. You are not more valuable because you raise money for research, research that kills babies like me. You are not more valuable than me because you have been on TV. You are not more valuable than me because of who does or does not want me. You don't get to use me and dispose of me because not you or anyone else owns me.

Each person is distinct. Each person is unique. Each person, each human being is a self, completely. People do not own you. People don't get to kill you. People do not get to use you because you are one of those distinct, unique persons, living, human, and precious. Me too.

Tiny living baby Boy waiting for a name

Dear Abba,

You said if we cried out, You would hear us. You said if we cried out, You would answer. You said if we cried out, You would run to our rescue. You said You are our defender, our hope. You said You would listen to us, catch all our tears, plead the plundering of our souls, and deliver our very lives from the strong who seek to destroy us. You said You have heard our sorrows, and seen our blood. You said Your wrath is hot against those who kill and crush us. You said Your heart is with those who have no helper and Your eyes see all, even those as small as we are. You said You knit us, You said You know us, You said You love us. You said we could trust You. You said power belongs to You, our Father. You said You will not fail or be discouraged until You have established justice on the earth. Does that include us; do we get justice too?

You said to those with weak hands, feeble knees, and fearful hearts to be strong and not to fear, for You are coming to save us. You said You, our great God, will hold our tiny hands that You made. You said we would know You are the Lord when You break our yokes and deliver us from those who claim to own us, who say we are nothing. You said You, the judge of all the earth, do *right!* You said You save the needy, You shut the mouth and hand of the mighty, You shut the mouth of injustice. You said You will maintain our right and our cause. You promised You would not forget our cries, You will remember us. You said You are our hope, that we should trust in You. We do.

You said You hate it when the people You have made are crushed and when those with power grind the faces of the helpless. You hate it when women with child are ripped open so people can increase their wealth. You hate the lies told about us. You hate it when people eat, recline, and sing but do not grieve for the weak and the afflicted. You hate the violent perversion of justice. You said You hate it when there is no justice, You hate it. You hate it because You are just. You love justice. The works of Your hands are truth and justice. You said You are on the side of the weak, on the side the helpless. Are there any more helpless than us, too small to speak, to scream, to stop the hand that reaches in to rip us to pieces and crush our tiny bodies when we have done nothing wrong?

You warn those who decree that which is wrong, and those who write misfortune so they can rob the voiceless of justice, take what is right from the needy, and rob the fatherless of that which is theirs. You have told the people You made to execute justice and righteousness. You have told them to rescue the plundered from those who plunder. You have told them to do no wrong, to do no violence to the stranger, to the fatherless, to the widow, to shed NO innocent blood.

You said no one calls for justice, nor does any plead for truth, and that is why righteousness stands far off and equity cannot enter. But we cry, Abba, we cry. Our bodies, our blood, cry out to You. We cry out for you to save our precious lives from the lions. We cry out for you to gather us, guard, and number us among your stars. Oh, that we had wings like a dove and we could fly away from those who seek to destroy us and cast us away like trash. We are poor, we are needy, our bodies are wounded and crushed, our spirit overwhelmed, our hearts distressed. We cry for this to stop, we cry for the laws that allow our bodies to be ripped apart to be no more. We cry for You to establish us, claim us as Your people, protect us as human beings made in Your magnificent image. We cry for You to vindicate us, We cry for Your deliverance, for Your justice, for our lives. Free us from their hands; free us from their unjust laws. Make haste our help, Father of the fatherless, lover of our souls, O LORD, do not delay! Your mercy is good, deliver us.

They say You do not see, that You are not real, that You do not care. They gnash at the upright, at those who plead our cause. They gather together to condemn the guiltless, to condemn innocent blood. They hate us for no reason. Do they not see that the One who made us made them? Do they do not see that the One who made the eye can see all they do? Do they not understand that the One who made the ear can hear the lies they spread? Do they not know that You who gave knowledge and declared right and wrong will execute justice? Show them, Father, let them see Your goodness, Your faithfulness, Your Justice. Let those who despise us see Your love for our lives and Your deliverance and be ashamed. For we believe You. We believe You are good and You will do all that You have promised. We trust in You for our hope. We trust in You to establish us and put us in a safe place. And so all you who love the Lord, praise His name. The needy put their trust in Him and are not ashamed, for He is good and His mercy endures forever!

Love,
Your Children

- Every single sentence in this letter originates from a verse in God's Holy Word, a promise from the One who is truth and cannot tell a lie.

To Those Who Propose an Easy Answer:

Adoption, here's the thing about it. Sometimes it is the answer. Sometimes it rescues mother, child, and barren womb. Sometimes it is the miracle of love that saves lives. Sometimes a young woman rejoices knowing her child is alive and safe somewhere with a family. Sometimes it is a happy ending. Sometimes it is wonderful.

But sometimes it's not. Sometimes it breaks a young girl's heart to give her baby away. Sometimes she is pressured, forced to give her baby up to a stranger and never know her again. Sometimes she spends her whole life missing someone she loved but never got to know. Sometimes she wonders at every face she sees. Sometimes she feels that a part of her was taken and she will never be whole again. Sometimes the happy home that she sent her baby off to wasn't happy at all. Sometimes she realizes too late that she could have done it, she could have kept her baby and her life. Sometimes she aches at what could have been but can't now fix. Sometimes her baby spends a lifetime wondering why her mother gave her away and where she is. Sometimes, that happens.

But sometimes a girl fears the unknown over the known, choosing to know what happened instead of not. That fear sometimes makes her choose to end her child's life rather than give her child a chance simply because she wants it be over, to know the end of the story, to not wonder and long for a lifetime. But really it is a choice that is just the beginning, the beginning of the guilt that won't go away, the hurt behind the horror of knowing, a hurt that doesn't dull in time, a hurt that cannot be comforted with thoughts of a safe, happy child somewhere out there.

If only these girls knew that there were ways to know, other ways to choose. If only they knew, they could choose who would raise their baby. If only they knew, they could catch glimpses of their child's life as they grew. If only they knew the hope and comfort of choosing life. But they don't know now and are afraid they can't live loving, but not knowing.

The thing is, no one knows the end of the story, nor does anyone know how things might have been. As Aslan said, "Child, did I not explain to you once before that no one is ever told what *would have happened?"*[30] We make these decisions and they change our lives because we are dealing with life itself, not a peanut butter and jelly sandwich. Life is no little thing to give away or throw away and simply get over. We struggle and we make mistakes, we love and we lose, and it changes us.

So because it is life, human life, we must be not just willing to do right, but determined to do so. Because it is life, human life, we must take every opportunity to protect, every chance to cherish, every pound to provide, always seeking that which honors life by honoring the one who bears it, always protecting those who can't protect themselves, always showing the smallest lives that they matter simply because they are here, and always giving their mother love and the help and hope that what is today will not be for always.

---

[30] C.S. Lewis, The Voyage of the Dawn Trader

DO YOU KNOW HOW MANY OF US BABIES DIE?

Abortion is one of the most common medical procedures in the United States.[31]

Every year more human beings die from abortion in our country than any other cause, making abortion the number one cause of death in the United States.[32]

At least 1.2 million children, and some years over 1.3 million, are aborted each year in the United States.

Since 1973 there have been over 47 million abortions in the United States, which averages out to:

> 1,300,000 abortions each year, 108,333 every month, 27,083 every week, 3,735 every day, 155 babies every hour, 2.6 babies every minute, 1 baby every 25 seconds.

22.5% of all children conceived in the United States are aborted, this number excludes miscarriages.[33]

But sometimes the numbers are so big you don't see them as what they are: the numbers of babies who were killed instead of born. Sometimes you have to take a closer, smaller look to see the bigger wrong. So look at these numbers and then tell me if you see a great wrong happening in our great country.

FULTON COUNTY, GA 2007 (latest available statistics from the Georgia Division of Public Health – OASIS)

15,372 Babies Aborted

13,802 Babies Born

1,570 More Babies Aborted than Born[34]

I wonder how many of us have to die before people see abortion as the wrong it is...

---

[31] Abortion in the United States: Incidence and Access to Service 2005. Perspectives on Sexual and Reproductive Health, 2008; Jones, Zolna, Henshaw, Finer
[32] Center for Disease Control
[33] Statistics from Alan Guttmacher Institute, Copyright 2005; www.agi-usa.org
[34] Georgia Division of Public Health 2007 OASIS

"I will neither give a deadly drug to anybody who asked for it, nor will I make a suggestion to this effect. Similarly I will not give to a woman an abortive remedy. In purity and holiness I will guard my life and my art."

– Hippocrates (Excerpt from the Hippocratic Oath)35

"10 A.M. on a sunny day in Seattle and 25-year-old Anna* is sitting on the end of a gynecological exam table, naked except for her baggy gray T-shirt and the blue paper blanket draped over her lap. Her body is trembling but not from cold– she's pregnant and she's scared. Deborah Oyer, M.D., the owner and medical director of Aurora Medical Services, where Anna is about to have an abortion, asks Anna to put her feet in stirrups. 'The more you relax, the less pressure and pain you will feel,' she says. Dr. Oyer dilates Anna's cervix and turns on the vacuum aspiration machine. She inserts a tube through Anna's cervix, and a gentle whirring sound fills the room. She barely has to raise her voice to explain, 'The cramping you feel is totally normal.' Anna lets out a few gasps before Dr. Oyer clicks off the machine, signaling the end of the five-minute procedure. 'We're all done,' Dr. Oyer says. The young woman groans and holds her stomach, but still smiles a bit. 'Really?' she says. 'That was not nearly as bad as I thought it was going to be.' Dr. Oyer isn't surprised by Anna's reaction. 'I hear that refrain almost daily when I perform abortions,' she says later. 'It's as if women expect me to come at them with whirling knives.'"36

It's all so pleasant and gentle. Do you think anyone in the room cares that a child was just killed? Do you think this is what Hippocrates had in mind?

---

[35] The classical version of the Hippocratic Oath is from the translation from the Greek by Ludwig Edelstein. From The Hippocratic Oath: Text, Translation, and Interpretation, by Ludwig Edelstein. Baltimore: Johns Hopkins Press, 1943.
[36] Liz Welch; *The Serious Health Decision Women Aren't Talking About. Until Now*; Glamour Magazine: March 2009; p. 248

"The catching business, we beg to remind them, is rising to the dignity of a lawful and patriotic profession... The trader and catcher may yet be among our aristocracy."

– Stowe[37]

"But who, sir, makes the trader? Who is most to blame? The enlightened, cultivated, intelligent man, who supports the system of which the trader is the inevitable result, or the poor trader himself. You make the public statement that calls for his trade, that debauches and depraves him till he feels no shame in it; and in what are you better than he?"

– Stowe[38]

"The gross perversion and destruction of motherhood by the abortionist filled me with indignation, and awakened active antagonism. That the honorable "female physician" should be exclusively applied to those women who carried on this shocking trade seemed to me a horror. It was an utter degradation of what might and should become a noble position for women."
– Dr. Elizabeth Blackwell, the first female physician, in her diary, where she recorded her thoughts regarding Madame Restell, an early New York abortionist, 1845.

Dear Doctors,

What is it you do? Our experience with you has been rather limited. We have only seen you do one thing, catch, evict, and kill us for money. Do you do anything else, or is that your whole job? Do you ever heal? When you were a kid, did you dream of growing up and killing the unwanted and helpless? Was that what you dreamed you could do and be?

Are you licensed to kill? Do other doctors give you a paper and a number after you go to school and learn how miraculous and intricate and complex and phenomenal human beings are from their very first moment, a number that gives you the authority to destroy the miracle you have just spent years studying? Is that how you get the authority to do what the rest of the population goes to jail for doing? Does anyone else have a constitutional right to destroy another life for profit? Isn't it true that no one else gets to kill an innocent, helpless human being under the protection of the law? What was it you learned in school that taught you human life was disposable, negotiable, worth several

---

[37] Harriet Beecher Stowe, Uncle Tom's Cabin; p. 75
[38] Harriet Beecher Stowe, Uncle Tom's Cabin; p. 138

hundred dollars to be rid of? Which course taught you that? When you learned that life can only come from life and a being can only reproduce after its own kind and a separate distinct human being begins at conception how were you able to deny my life and the value and rights that came with my humanity? What was it you learned that justified one person owning and destroying another? Is it because you have a skill in killing that you have this privilege, or do you lack a heart? How do you go from one hospital room and deliver a premature, living, breathing tiny human being and then to another room down the hall and destroy a tiny human the very same age? Do you just fill orders? Save this life, end that one. Does your bank account make it all okay? Are you one of the successful and esteemed, ridding one life of the problem of motherhood and another life of *life*?

What makes you different from the men who in decades past were paid by people owners to hunt down, capture, and kill the people they owned? Did the fact that it was legal for them to capture and kill people who wanted to live, who wanted to own their own life, make it right? Was the reward money not dirty? What makes your profession acceptable, the fact that the people you kill can't run, so the chase happens in a controlled, clean facility under your killing expertise? But to kill and capture wasn't enough, was it? You found another way we could benefit you. So tell me, when you profit off our body parts, how does that make you any different from the poster boys of evil who made lamp shades from babies' skin and mattresses from human hair and accumulated gold from the mouths of their victims? How are you different? How are you a doctor? How is it you heal? Tell me, what is different when you use and destroy our bodies for research from when the sinister Nazi doctors used and destroyed the human beings they thought worthless for medical experiments which would result in saving and improving the lives of Aryans?[39] The end justified their means, their gains justified their carnage, their findings justified any faults. Or did it?

Why does it sound so wrong, so hollow? Is it because they stole someone else's life and used it for themselves? How is this noble? How

---

[39] Robert J. Lifton; The Nazi Doctors: Medical Killing and the Psychology of Genocide (New York, 1986). Hugh C. Gallagher; By Trust Betrayed: Patients, Physicians, and the License to Kill in the Third Reich (New York, 1990). Christian Pross & Gotz Aly; The Value of the Human Being: Medicine in Germany, 1918-1945 (Berlin, 1991).

is this good? How is it a right? What medical discovery can ever be traded for a soul? Shouldn't the study of our natural world, science, be harnessed if it harms, hurts, uses and kills humans? Human beings sacrificed to the pursuit of science, it is all so eerily similar to the child sacrifices performed by the ignorant tribes of old, who killed children for a blessing instead of a curse, who thought a child should welcome their death if it benefited the good of society. How are you and your agents any different in your murderous pursuit of science and wealth from the esteemed doctors of Hitler's regime or the murderous tribal rituals in their pursuit of blessing? Is there nothing precious but the profits you make and the interests of our mothers? And how did it ever become legal to do this to tiny children for the benefit of those all grown? Where are our defenders, our rescuers, our great generation to end our nightmare, our holocaust?

If I could work my whole life and pay you more than what you would make today, would you not destroy my tiny body? I shouldn't have to ask you not to kill babies like me. No one should have to beg for their life. But here I am begging a professional healer to leave our little lives alone, my little life just as it is. I am not even begging you to heal us, there's nothing wrong with our bodies, they are just small and young. I am just begging you not to kill us. Is that asking too much, o' healing one? Or are you too much of a hypocrite to take the Hippocratic oath, too much of a businessman to be honorable, too greedy to do good? Are you too concerned about your wealth to care about my health? And don't throw the blame on my mother, you don't care about her health, she is just your 2:30, your 3:00, your 4:15, your revenue for a day's work. There is nothing you are doing to make her body better. If she chose to keep me, would you help her with the cost of having me, of raising me? Of course not, there's no money in that for you. But my body, well, it does put cash in your pocket, doesn't it?

I wonder if you ever think about us, about me, when you look on the screen and see my heart beating 140 beats a minute and you adjust the monitor to make sure my mommy can't see me moving and being. I wonder if you think of me when you see me sucking my thumb on the screen as you reach in with your tools to rip me apart. I wonder if you wonder how I feel. I wonder if you have a pang of guilt about the murder you are about to commit when you pull most of my body out of my mommy and you hold me firmly as I kick my legs and try to grasp with my hands. I wonder if you care that it hurts more than you could ever imagine. I wonder if, as you ask your nurse if all my appendages and bones are accounted for, I wonder if your stomach hurts. I wonder if you wonder what we, or even just me, would have become if you hadn't put us to death. I wonder if you care how broken those women are who you are helping, how breaking us to pieces breaks them. I wonder if you realize that when they leave, they leave a piece of their hearts they can never get back. I wonder what lie you tell yourself to justify what you do, how you justify doing this to another human being. I wonder how it is that a profession existing exclusively to heal the human body could allow itself to get wrapped up in the killing business. Do you regret? I wonder if anyone who works for you cares about all the wasted humans discarded in the wastebaskets of your business. Does the $372 for my life ease your conscience? Or do you need more to make it worth your while? How much more do you get for selling my body parts, my flesh? Aren't my eyes worth $75, my limbs $150, my spinal cord $325, my torso $500, and my brain $999? Don't you follow instructions for making sure my leg with my entire hip joint is available for sale when I am twenty-two or twenty-three weeks grown? Don't you carefully follow procedures to make certain my fully intact lungs are dissected when I am seventeen to twenty-four weeks old? Aren't you certain to note my sex, my race, my age, and measure my foot? Can't you make $50,000 a week by selling the babies you abort piece by piece?[40] I guess when you see our hearts beating, legs kicking, bodies being, you see a gold mine. That must be why you rip us apart in pieces and pack us so quickly in dry ice because our bodies deteriorate so rapidly without oxygen. What efficient, economical, brilliant advances in research and medicine! That must be why the procurators can offer "Fresh Fetal Tissue harvested and shipped to your specifications... where and when you need it," and how they can boast "the highest quality, most affordable, freshest tissue prepared to your specifications and delivered in the quantities you need when you need it."[41] Wow, Doc, you must good at what you do!

---

[40] 20/20 Investigation, Chief Correspondent Chris Wallace; aired March 8, 2000; The Harvest of Abortion; World Magazine, Lynn Vincent; October 23, 1999, Vol.14 No.41.
[41] Brochure from fetal transplant company, Opening Lines, revealed in 20/20 investigation and confirmed in testimony before House Commerce Subcommittee, March 9, 2000; all quotes from brochure.

I guess what the brochure said is true, you have learned how "you can turn your patients' decision into something wonderful." You have seen how profitable it can be when "Consultative and Diagnostic Pathology will lease space from your facility to perform the harvesting and distribution of tissue. The revenue generated from the lease can be used to offset your clinic's overhead." And what a relief when you realized, "Consultative and Diagnostic Pathology can train your staff to harvest and process fetal tissue. Based on your volume we will reimburse part or all of your employee's salary, thereby reducing your overhead." Should I continue? *Oh, how I profit thee, let me count the ways.* It certainly does make one wonder, how much cash does my death bring you?

Do you know the story of the two arrogant, educated doctors? An old, dirty, sick, smelly man was brought into the hospital desperately needing treatment to survive. The two doctors conversed in front of the man about whether it was worth their time, expense, and trouble to save this wretched, worthless human being. But being discreet, they conversed in Latin. To their surprise, the old worthless man rose up and rebuked them. *"How dare you call him worthless for whom Christ died!"* And the doctors stood there stunned to their very core, for he had accused them in Latin. You see, physician, the human beings you are paid to heal are more than what you see, more than broken, worn-out, flesh, more than the insignificance you place on them because of their size or vulnerability, more than the costs they incur, and more than the money you can make from selling them piece by piece. For it is the life and being inside the body that makes the body so valuable, so worthy of being healed, so worthy of the life that was given to them, to me, not you.

So, Doctor, what is *your* measure of *my* worth, of others made and treasured by their Maker? Is it how much you will make off our lives, the power, the prestige, the success our death bring you? I have yet to figure out how it is that our bodies become your human property to sell, your raw material, your potential revenue. I can't see what we were given in exchange.[42] But what I really want to know is how much longer is this going to continue? How much longer will doctors be licensed to kill instead of heal? How much longer will the value of a human being

---

[42] Professor of Biology & Embryology at Oxford University, Sir Richard Gardner proposed at a conference in March 2009 that aborted fetuses organs be used for transplants in addition to research, reported by UK's Daily Mail, 3/11/2009

be determined by their size, their circumstance, or their place of residence? How long till we are safe inside our mommies and out? How long till we are precious? How long?

Urgently,
The Whole Souls of Those You Sold

Averaging $372 per abortion, with 1,287,000 abortions performed in the U.S. each year the abortion industry generates $400,000,000 annually for destroying innocent human life. Figures from Alan Guttmacher Institute (AGI), Planned Parenthood's special research affiliate monitoring trends in the abortion industry. This figure does not include estimates for grants and donations received or revenue generated from the "site fees" abortion facilities charge wholesalers or "procurement agents" who then harvest the fetal tissue and bill various researchers for "retrieval" costs.

"A trade founded in iniquity, and carried on, as this was, must be abolished, let the policy be what it might—let the consequences be what they would."
– William Wilberforce

What the abortionists say in their own words...

"The most merciful thing a family does to one of its infant members is to kill it."
 - Margaret Sanger, Founder of Planned Parenthood, (editor) *The Woman Rebel*; Volume 1, Number 1, reprinted in Woman and the New Race: New York; Brentanos Publishers, 1922

"...human weeds,' 'reckless breeders,' 'spawning... human beings who never should have been born."
 - Margaret Sanger, Pivot of Civilization, referring to immigrants and poor people

"We should hire three or four colored ministers, preferably with social-service backgrounds, and with engaging personalities. The most successful educational approach to the Negro is through a religious appeal. We don't want the word to go out that we want to exterminate the Negro population. And the minister is the man who can straighten out that idea if it ever occurs to any of their more rebellious members."
 – Margaret Sanger's December 19, 1939 letter to Dr. Clarence Gamble, 255 Adams Street, Milton, Massachusetts. Original source: Sophia Smith Collection, Smith College, North Hampton, Massachusetts. Also described in Linda Gordon's *Woman's Body, Woman's Right: A Social History of Birth Control in America*. New York: Grossman Publishers, 1976.

"Eugenic sterilization is an urgent need... We must prevent multiplication of this bad stock."
 – Margaret Sanger, April 1933 *Birth Control Review*.

"Eugenics is... the most adequate and thorough avenue to the solution of racial, political and social problems."
 – Margaret Sanger. "The Eugenic Value of Birth Control Propaganda." *Birth Control Review*, October 1921, p. 5.

"Since the National Revolution public opinion has become increasingly preoccupied with questions of demographic policy and the continuing decline in the birthrate. However, it is not only the decline in population which is a cause for serious concern but equally the increasingly evident genetic composition of our people. Whereas the hereditarily healthy families have for the most part adopted a policy of having only one or two children, countless numbers of inferiors and those suffering from hereditary conditions are reproducing unrestrainedly while their sick and asocial offspring burden the community."

- "The Law for the Prevention of Progeny with Hereditary Diseases" proclaimed July 4, 1933 by the Third Reich of Nazi Germany forcing sterilization of the unfit, the preceding step in the T4 euthanasia program which killed an estimated 200,000-250,000 and was used to plan the Final Solution.

"Today it is possible for almost any patient to be brought through pregnancy alive, unless she suffers from a fatal illness such as cancer or leukemia, and if so, abortion would be unlikely to prolong, much less save life."
- Alan Guttmacher, M.D. Former president of Planned Parenthood

"We have yet to beat our drums for birth control in the way we beat them for polio vaccine. We are still unable to put babies in the class of dangerous epidemics, even though this is the exact truth."
- Mary Calderone, M.D. Former president of Planned Parenthood

"Women are not stupid... Women have always known there was a life there."
- Faye Wattleton, The then President of Planned Parenthood when she made these quotes on May 15, 1989, *Donahue Show*, Transcript #3288 NBC

"[Pregnancy] may be defined as a disease... [and]... treated by evacuation of the uterine contents."
- Warren Hern, Nations leading abortionist and author of *Abortion Practice*; (J.B. Lippincott Company)

"The first time, I felt like a murderer, but I did it again and again and again, and now, 20 years later, I am facing what happened to me as a doctor and as a human being. Sure, I got hard. Sure, the money was important. And oh, it was an easy thing, once I had taken the step to see the women as animals and the babies as just tissue."
- Abortionist quoted from a radio talk show by John Rice in "Abortion" Litt D. Murfreesboro, TN

"The procedure changes significantly at 21 weeks because the fetal tissues become more cohesive and difficult to dismember. The calvaria [upper skull] is no longer the problem; it can be collapsed. Other structures, such as the pelvis, present more difficulty... A long curved Mayo scissors may be necessary to decapitate and dismember the fetus..."
- Warren Hern, *Abortion Practice*, p. 134

"'After an abortion, the doctor must inspect these remains to make sure that all the fetal parts and placenta have been removed. Any tissue left inside the uterus can start an infection.' Dr. Bours squeezed the contents of the sock into a shallow dish and poked around with his finger. 'You can see a teeny tiny hand,' he said."

- Abortion clinic worker quoted in *Is the Fetus Human?* "The Abortion Conflict: What it Does to One Doctor," by Dudley Clendinen, *New York Times Magazine* August 11, 1985, p. 26

"I was trained by a professional marketing director in how to sell abortions over the telephone. He took every one of our receptionists, nurses, and anyone else who would deal with people over the phone through an extensive training period. The object was, when the girl called, to hook the sale so that she wouldn't get an abortion somewhere else, or adopt out her baby, or change her mind. We were doing it for the money."

- Nina Whitten, chief secretary at a Dallas abortion clinic under Dr. Curtis Boyd

"Every woman has the same two questions: First, 'Is it a baby?' 'No' the counselor assures her. 'It is a product of conception (or a blood clot, or a piece of tissue)' Even though these counselors see six week babies daily, with arms, legs, and eyes that are closed like newborn puppies, they lie to the women. How many women would have an abortion, if they told them the truth?"

- Carol Everett, former owner of two clinics and director of four. "A Walk Through an Abortion Clinic" by Carol Everett ALL About Issues magazine Aug-Sept 1991, p. 117

"'Let's just say for instance we took a different view, a different tact and we left the leg in the uterus just to dismember it. Well, we'd probably have to dismember it at several different levels because we don't have firm control over it, so we would attack the lower part of the lower extremity first, remover, you know possibly a foot, then the lower leg at the knee and then finally we get to the hip.'

Describing an abortion that did not prevent a child from being born alive, Dr. Haskell said this, 'It came out very quickly after I put the scissors up in the cervical canal and pierced the skull and spread the scissors apart... in the previous two, I had used the suction to collapse the skull.'" (Dayton Daily News; Dec 10, 1989)

- Dr. Martin Haskell, Abortionist who developed the variation of the abortion procedure Dilation and Extraction (D&X, and named it "partial birth abortion" describing in detail the procedure in a 1992 paper entitled *"Dilation and Extraction for Late Second Trimester Abortions"*) in 1992 and has performed more than 700 D&X procedures in his office) as reported in an interview with *AMA News* 1993, where he reported that 80% of these abortions were "purely elective, and that doctors in the clinic where he began working typically spend ten minutes with patients but three hours in the clinic, an efficiency problem that he proudly remedied."

"I walked in the laboratory every day. I saw dead babies every day for three years. If I could see fifty, I was so happy. Because, you know what? That meant I was really gonna' have a good bonus in my paycheck."
    - Clinic Worker Hellen Pendley, quoted by Mary Meeham in "The Ex-Abortionists: Why They Quit" in The Human Life Review

"We really need to get over this love affair with the fetus..."
    - Joceyln Elders, former U.S. Surgeon General (Clinton Administration)

"Nobody wants to perform an abortion after 10 weeks, because by then you see the features of the baby, hands, feet. It's really barbaric."
    - Abortionist quoted in M.D. Doctors Talk About Themselves; John Pekkanen, p. 93

"I have been there, and I have seen these totally formed babies as early as ten weeks... with the leg missing, or with their head off. I have seen the little rib cages..."

"The counselor at our clinic would cry with the girls at the drop of a hat. She would find their weakness and work on it. The women were never given any alternatives. They were told how much trouble it is to have a baby."

"Saline abortions have to be done in the hospital because of the complications that can arise. Not that they can't arise during other times, but more so now. The saline, a salt solution, is injected into the woman's sac, and the baby starts dying a slow, violent death. The mother feels everything, and many times it is at this point when she realizes that she really has a live baby inside her, because the baby starts fighting violently, for his or her life. He's just fighting inside because he's burning."
    - Debra Harry, former abortion worker quoted in the 1989 film Meet the Abortion Providers

"In testimony Wednesday in St. Louis Circuit Court, [abortionist] Crist said that it is not uncommon for second-trimester fetuses to leave the womb feet-first, intact and with their hearts still beating. He sometimes crushes their skulls to get the fetuses out. Other times, he dismembers them."
    - Jo Mannies, "Abortion Doctor Gives Graphic Testimony Describing Abortion Procedure," St. Louis Post-Dispatch, May 25, 2000

"Abortion is killing the fetus... Human life, in and of itself, is not sacred. Human life, per se, is not inviolate."
    - Abortionist Dr. Smith, as quoted in "The Abortionist," by Leo Wang, Berkeley Medical Journal, Spring 1995 Edition

"I look inside the bucket in front of me. There is a small naked person in there, floating in a bloody liquid–plainly the tragic victim of a drowning accident. But *then perhaps this was no accident, because the body is purple with bruises and the face has the agonized tautness of one forced to die too soon. I have seen this face before on a Russian soldier lying on a frozen snow-covered hill, still with death, and cold."*

    - Dr. Magda Denes, PhD; "Performing Abortions" Oct. 26, 1976; pp. 35-37

"The doctor pulls out something, which he slaps on the instrument table. 'There,' he says, 'A leg.' ... I turn to Mr. Smith... he points to the instrument table, where there is a perfectly formed, slightly bent leg, about three inches long... 'There, I've got the head out now.' ...There lies a head. It is the smallest human head I have ever seen, but it is unmistakably part of a person."

    - Dr. Magda Denes; <u>In Necessity and Sorrow: Life and Death Inside an Abortion Clinic</u>. (Basic Books, Inc. New York, 1976)

"Even now I feel a little peculiar about it, because as a physician I was trained to conserve life, and here I am destroying it."

    - Abortionist Dr. Benjamin Kalish, quoted in Dr. Magda Denes, <u>In Necessity and Sorrow:</u> p. 140

"My country again! You have a country; but what country have I, or any one like me? What laws are there for us? We don't make them—we don't consent to them—we have nothing to do with them; all they do for us is to crush us."

– Stowe [43]

"...perhaps among us may be found generous spirits, who do not estimate honor and justice by dollars and cents."

– Stowe [44]

Perhaps.

Dear Legislators,

What is it you do? Our experience with you has been rather limited. From our perspective it appears you are chosen to represent those citizens who live where you do, and they expect you to make laws that protect them and help them. Is that true? Well, my parents are both citizens, which makes me a citizen too, you know. I am a citizen of this country because my parents are, not because of where I live or how old I am. And, being a citizen, I am under your care, under your representation. But I have to ask, how are you protecting me, how are you helping me? In your district, those like me, those who are helpless and need laws and people bigger than us to protect us, are being killed every day. And isn't it you who should be making those laws? So where are you, where are the laws for us? How is it that our representative votes against laws that protect us and for laws that deny us help? How is it that our representative votes to fund our death? How can that be? Where is the equality, the protection, the help, the due process in that?

There are some laws that protect us if our mothers want us, and other laws that protect mothers and allow them to kill us if they don't. Sorry, it just seems so duplicitous, so confusing. I can't figure out why one baby matters and another baby doesn't. How is that equal? How is that fair treatment? Isn't that what they call a double standard, where different people have different sets of rules for themselves and other rules for everyone else? Does that mean that our mothers determine which laws apply to us, which law reigns? Do other citizens get to choose which laws apply to them? Do we? Certainly you must know that *the law*

---

[43] Harriet Beecher Stowe, <u>Uncle Tom's Cabin</u>; p. 115
[44] Harriet Beecher Stowe, <u>Uncle Tom's Cabin</u>; p. 324

is very much a teacher. So what does the law teach? If I die, does it really matter who kills me? Is it somehow not killing depending on who does the killing, or where the killing is done, or how old I am when I am killed? Really, it is quite perplexing. One day I matter, one day I don't, one baby's precious, another a predator. If people don't want to care for you, you can be killed, but if they do, then every effort of man must be tried. And so I wonder. Who? Who is the law for? Who gets to choose who is protected? And which laws do they get?

I can't see the help, the protection, the consistency of the laws you have made, or even any basic equality in the laws. If one baby should be protected, if one baby deserves justice, then all babies do. We are supposed to be a government of the people, by the people, for the people. Doesn't that mean all people should be represented equally, that all people have the same rights? Doesn't that mean some people should not be valued more than other people, and one group of people does not get to own or dominate or oppress another? Doesn't it mean because we are all people that we are all equal? And doesn't equal mean having the same worth, the same value, no matter where you are living or who you are growing in? Tell me, sir, what lesson is in your laws?

I thought this country declared its independence from those who were supposed to govern instead of oppress, represent instead of silence, protect instead of crush, help instead of hoard. I thought our people decided that such actions against them justified their seeking to govern themselves. I thought their struggle was the shot the whole world heard, the beginning of a country determined in the cause that all men are of equal worth. So what happened? Where is our equality, and why won't you seek it for us? How is it that our country, our representatives, deny us not only our citizenship, but our very lives? We are not old enough to vote for you, we are not old enough to make our own laws or struggle for our own independence, we are not old enough to defend ourselves or even object to being killed or appeal our death sentence or seek justice against those who seek to abandon us or crush us or sell us. We have no choice, no choice but to depend on those who have a voice, who have power. And that, sir, is you. So where are you? And what have you done with justice?

Does bipartisanship matter more than the lives of babies? Is getting the budget passed more important than fighting for what's right? Are the only interests you need to consider the interests of those who can vote and contribute? What is it about your position that makes you think you can abandon good and right for money, power, and influence? You know, as bad and as wrong as it is when you do, I think it really is all too common among your kind. You would think that those who have been chosen to hold power would be the most courageous of us all. But too often they are not, and for the most part haven't been even in our own history. Those who crafted our country despite their wonderful true words, withheld from some the equity and justice that would have made the words reality simply because of their own self-interests and fears. They lacked the courage to do the right thing at all costs, even if it actually cost them all they had fought for. They chose compromise instead of courage, power instead of protection, government instead of virtue. Those who lost were those not acknowledged as persons despite the humanity they shared with those in power. But the same story keeps being played out large and small, over and over, throughout our history. And it is a strange thing indeed, what power itself becomes to the powerful. For the power that should bolster and activate the courage needed to do good, actually becomes the thing to protect, the thing to hold dear, the thing that restrains them using their power to fight for what is right, equitable, and just. Oh, the things that power, goodness, and courage could provide, if only there were any who had them all. So maybe, sir, maybe I should ask you, where is your courage, and what have you received in exchange?

It makes me wonder, when you were little did you dream that one day you would grow up and take money from Political Action Committees and do whatever they said so you could keep your comfy, prestigious spot on high? Did you dream you would be the kind of man that would help scared women kill their children? Did you dream of abandoning the helpless and fighting to insure there were less of them to educate and provide basic services for? Is this what you dreamed you could do and be?

I realize we have not yet earned any wages and cannot contribute to your reelection bid, but does our inability to speak and donate take away our right to be protected, our right to be valuable? Do other citizens lose their value because they lose an ability? Do they lose their rights, as well? Do they lose their humanity? Tell me, Congressman, which ability is so primary, so necessary, so preemptive to one's claim of rights and humanity? I was human when I began, and I am still the same human now—not more human, not less human, the same human, just bigger. You might say we are not viable, not wanted, not planned, but you can't say we are not human; science would never agree. To put it bluntly, being human is all we *can* be when we are alive and our parents are humans. I don't see how something that is tied to my existence as a human being can be acknowledged or denied based on someone else's wishes or fears.

Some people say another person, our mothers, our legislators, some strangers in robes must give us our value or affirm us as a person with rights. But that's not what the people who made this country said, nor all the people who died trying to make it so. They said I have the same rights as anyone, and that I matter as much as you do because of what I am, a person, and because of who made me, the same Creator who made you. You, however, in an effort to weasel out of helping and protecting me (although that *is* your job), might claim I am not a person yet, that being a human being is not the same as being a person. But seriously, "*what is a person being other than a human being?*"[45] And a human being I am, that cannot be denied.

I really think it is just a game of words you all play with the added bonus of attracting the lobbying dollars of certain groups that benefit from our death—how convenient. Instead of devising ways to help scared, vulnerable young women find the best way for their child to be raised given their situation, instead of confronting poverty, confronting abuse, confronting a lack of opportunity and discrimination, you collect the donations from those who profit off our death and actually declare that you are a friend to women, and a defender of choice and freedom, all while raising money to keep yourself in power! However do you do it? And might I ask... whose choice, whose freedom, whose life, and for what cost? This, sir, is not equality. This is not justice.

I wonder, sir, when will men who make laws realize that you fight hunger with food, poverty with good jobs, discrimination with fair and equal treatment, ignorance with knowledge, decay with restoration, despair with opportunity, hate with love, and abuse with safety and justice? Killing babies like me does nothing to right these wrongs, it just creates new ones. And nothing in your great debate can change the simple fact that killing the innocent will never be right, no matter how

---

[45] Gregory Koukl, Precious Unborn Human Persons

much they cost to raise, how much time, effort, and energy they consume, or how much they require of us all. Nor will it ever change the fact that no matter how eloquently you speak, your years in public service, or the monies you collect, a *senator is only a man*[46], as human as we.

Waiting for Justice,
Your unborn human constituents,
Affectionately and otherwise known as "our Posterity"

> *"Your feelings are all quite right, dear and interesting, and I love you for them; but, then, dear, we mustn't suffer our feelings to run away with our judgment; you must consider it's a matter of private feeling- there are great public interests involved- there is such a state of public agitation rising, that we must put aside our private feelings."*
>
> *"Now, John, I don't know anything about politics, but I can read my Bible; and there I see that I must feed the hungry, clothe the naked, and comfort the desolate; and that Bible I mean to follow."*
>
> *"But in cases where your doing so would involve a great public evil-"*
>
> *"Obeying God never brings on public evils, I know it can't. It's always safest, all round to do as He bids us."*
>
> *"My dear, let me reason with you."*
>
> *"I hate reasoning, John—especially reasoning on such subjects. There's a way you political folks have of coming round and round a plain right thing; and you don't believe in it yourselves, when it comes to practice."*
>
> – Stowe[47]

---

[46] Harriet Beecher Stowe, Uncle Tom's Cabin; adapted from chapter title; p. 82
[47] Harriet Beecher Stowe, Uncle Tom's Cabin; pp. 84-85

> *"If the law says that, sir, then the law is an ass."*
>
> – Charles Dickens; <u>Oliver Twist</u>

Dear Court,

What is it you do? Our experience with you has been rather limited. But it appears that you determine what the laws of the land say, whether they support "unalienable" and "enumerated" rights or deny them, and whether or not these laws adhere to our Constitution, on which our government is established. Is that so? Who gave you that power? Did our Constitution? Did you get that power from us, did you get the consent of the governed, from the place where the power originates? No? Well, then who gave it to you? You? Oh.[48]

So you gave yourself the power and authority to declare laws right and wrong, valid and invalid. You gave yourself the power to determine who is included in the jurisdiction of the Court Supreme, and who is eligible to receive their rights *unalienable*, rights guaranteed and protected by the Constitution, even though given to *all* by their Creator. How is it you have also claimed the power to say who is and who isn't real, who can and can't be killed, who can and can't kill? Where did you find that power in our Constitution? What qualifies you to determine the value of a life, of my life, and who owns me? Were you elected by the people you claim jurisdiction over? No? Wow, that's a lot of power to claim from and over someone and never to know the fear of a ballot box. Power AND exemption, pretty incredible.

---

[48] The Constitution of the United States establishes our positive grant system of government, meaning that because our government gets its power from the consent of the governed it can only exercise those powers which are expressly granted to the government by the people. The Tenth Amendment states: "The powers not delegated to the United States by the Constitution, nor prohibited by it to the States, are reserved to the States respectively, or to the people." In Marbury v. Madison Chief Justice John Marshall declared the Judicial Act of 1789 to be "unconstitutional" claiming the Supreme Court did not have jurisdiction and Congress did not have the power to alter or increase the jurisdiction of the courts, determining the law to be in conflict with the Constitution, and establishing the power of the court to make this determination and interpret Acts of Congress. This means the Supreme Court gave itself the power and authority to nullify Acts of Congress, a power never granted to them in the Constitution, even though the Constitution specifically reserves all powers not expressly given. While judicial review has case history and 200 years of precedent and has played a significant role in our nation, the case which originally served to recognize and enforce the limitations of power and jurisdiction of the courts has been used to grant an ever-expanding, unlimited, unchecked power to not only review law, but create and establish law. If we, the people, have not expressly given the courts this power and authority, it is being exercised unconstitutionally and should either be expressly granted to them with the limitations other branches must adhere to or denied, remembering that it is a government of the we, the people, not they, the courts.

I mean, it's not as if you have been consistent over the years. Some people get rights, some don't. Some people get nothing, some get it all. According to your long, gloriously inconsistent tradition some people don't even have to be people to qualify for the protection intended for citizens while you simultaneously deny the humanity of *actual* people. How, I will never be able to figure out, were corporations people, but black people, women, and babies not? How, I will never be able to figure out, were you able to declare that states had no right to protect their citizens from those corporations who tried to exploit their labor, their humanity?

There must be some measure to recall you if you abuse these powers, some way to hold you accountable if you misuse these powers you hijacked, broaden them, or claim new ones. No? Hmm... Well, why is the federal government only allowed to exercise powers specifically given to it by the Constitution, but you, although part of the government and established by the Constitution, get to exercise any powers you give yourself with any method, any standard you decide upon? Why and how is it *you* who holds this power over who I am, over what I am? Why and how is it *you*, the unelected, unaccountable, self-proclaimed interpreter, who holds this power over whether I have any right to be here and any right I have to claim the protection and guarantees of my government, established for me, *Posterity*? Please, tell me!

Didn't our declaration and our beginning announce to the world what was already true and evident, that everyone is equal, everyone has the same value, that everyone has rights which belong to them, to protect them, recognize their worth, keep them from being owned or crushed or used, and to free them to pursue their own happiness? Didn't our Constitution recognize and include those not yet born, "*Posterity*", as bearers of those rights, and establish the Constitution with the purpose of securing the "*Blessings of Liberty to ourselves and Our Posterity*"? Those who went before us rightly realized you have to acknowledge a person's right to exist, to be alive, and the value of their life before you could recognize the liberty that belonged to that life, and their pursuit of it. They claimed these rights were "unalienable," much more so than the right to speak freely or bear arms because these things could not possibly be as important as a person's right to be alive, to not be killed when they had done no wrong, their right to be recognized as what they are, a human being, equal to all. Besides if a person is not allowed to exist, how can they freely do all these other things? Dead people, we all know, are the least likely to use their right to speak freely, the least likely to speak the unspeakable... well, at least until now, for the crimes done to us, the extermination of our lives and our liberties force us to cry out against you who have made it a right for others to destroy us. So, I have to ask, Your Honor, of all the rights out there, large and small, which one matters most of all?

Since you have had such a delightfully diverse opinion through the years on the people who get to be people in this country, it makes me wonder, is the value of a human being absolute or relative? If it is relative, how can it be unalienable as well? If we are not valuable, not equal, who else isn't? What makes a human qualify for their unalienable rights? Can we separate rights from those to whom they belong, for whom the rights exist? Does someone else have the right or authority to affirm or deny my nature? Do you? Why? Is my life, my value, really yours to vote up or down, 7-2, 5-4? Why would you say, *"Pregnancy often comes more than once to the same woman, and in the general population, if* **man is to survive it will always be with us**"[49], and then turn right around and say you don't know if I am human or not? Did you really have some other purpose, some other reason to avoid truth and reason? How did you find the authority to make my life negotiable? Does it go something like this? So and So with such and such degree says I'm nothing because I can't do some particular thing, because I make my mommy's life much, much harder, because *where* I am determines *who* I belong to and *what* I am. But another So and So with same said degree says I am a living, growing, heart-beating human being, that I have all the right stuff, and that is all I need to qualify for my human rights, all I need to demand to not be killed, to stay alive because I am already here, already a human. Is my humanity, my personhood determined by law, by the degrees, interests, and persuasion of the smart, rich, powerful people, by economic, personal, or political interests, by culture, by how much of a burden I am, undue or otherwise? Or is it possible that who I am and what I am are not under your jurisdiction to determine, that if you must decide, opine, or even err that the better decision is the one which recognizes, safeguards, and protects the

---

[49] Justice Blackmum, Roe v Wade

HUMAN LIVES of the smallest of citizens, the smallest of persons, instead of willingly killing the innocent, willingly making a human life negotiable? Is this liberty, equity, justice for all?

Of course, you don't have much of a track record for impartiality or even righting your own wrongs. Over and over again you have denied access to the blessings of liberty you are supposed to be the guardians of. Over and over again you have sided with the powerful over the weak and denied the equal protection for all guaranteed under the law. Over and over you have subverted and contrived reasons to exclude certain groups of people from the protections that were theirs. The people had to struggle and wrestle and amend the rules by which you interpret to make adamant what was inherent. The 14th Amendment did not suddenly make slaves persons, nor did the 20th spark the humanity of women. All these amendments did was acknowledge what was already there and guarantee them the rights their nature demanded as human beings. These great acts ended *your* great wrongs! And the doors of life and liberty opened wider.

So what did these amendments say? What great wrong did they stop? What great injustice can they prevent? The 20th Amendment gave women full citizenship and rights they had always been denied. The 14th Amendment overturned an excellent example of your skewed vision of equality and liberty, where before people had been things to buy and sell. It acknowledged and protected life, liberty, and property, with the guards of due process. And people, people could no longer be property. People could no longer be things. People had rights to be protected. But what were those rights unspoken?

Certainly all of the rights free people inherently need to pursue their liberty are not listed in our Constitution. Certainly all of the rights not given to the government are reserved for the states, and most importantly for the people. How ironic though that the amendment overturning the previous precedent which had allowed one group of people to be the property of another would be used to justify babies being things, would permit women to own them, and would even grant women the right to kill their unborn, private property so they could be free from having to be a mommy. How could that be? How could this amendment, abolishing slavery and proclaiming life as something to be protected, be used to create and assume such a broad, expansive right of feminine liberty that denied and superseded a child's right to live? How could an amendment intended to protect life and liberty be used to abolish the rights of some and widen the rights others? How far do these liberties, these rights that free us to determine and define our own concept of happiness, how far do they reach?

Privacy, one of those rights not mentioned, is thrown about as if it is the most primary of all rights, as if anything done in private is acceptable and above the law. But we don't adhere to that logic. Some things we know are wrong no matter *where* they are done, and the people make laws that say so. So please tell me how, explain to me now, because the thing done privately that you protect with this assumed right is the thing that breaks my body into pieces to be trashed or sold in pieces. This right you found makes me a thing, a nothing, instead of what I am, a human being. It makes the *interests* of one more important than the *life* of another. I will never be able to understand your twisted logic, for how if you treat an animal cruelly in private you are breaking the law, but if you kill your unborn baby in private, it is somehow a protected liberty. It just doesn't make sense. Liberty can't possibly mean no responsibility. Liberty can't possibly mean someone else has a right to destroy me. Liberty, however broad, can't possibly make me a *thing*. It isn't right, it isn't fair, it isn't equal, it isn't just.

Just think, if we allow people the right to kill their unborn child because of privacy, then we must allow people to steal because of poverty. If we allow people the right to kill because they want the freedom to choose their destiny, then we must allow them the freedom to lie, cheat, and ruin whoever crosses their path. If we decide pursuing happiness can rightly include killing the person that would make them a mother, then we should grant this right to men and more. What if the thing that would make a person happy is to take someone else's child, a wretched wrong that destroys like no other; should *that* be permitted? Wouldn't this be the logical progression, intention, and interpretation of *equal protection under the law* and of the unenumerated rights of the people? After all, we should all be able to do anything we want to get what we want, anything necessary to define our own existence exactly as we wish. Isn't this the great promise of liberty?

Or maybe not. Rights exist to protect, and are claims for such protection. But a person's rights stop when they infringe on someone else's. Our Declaration even stated that the authority of governments stop when they become destructive and infringe on the rights of the people, for "whenever any Form of Government becomes destructive of these ends, it is the Right of the People to alter or to abolish it." You see, a woman should be able to choose if she wants to be a mother, she should be able to choose whether to "bear and beget a child," but not kill one that is already here. She should be able to decide if she wants all the responsibility, but not whether her child should live, for the simple reason that the life does not belong to her. It is her child's. And one of those lives belongs to me. It is mine! Not yours, not hers, MINE!

But what can you do when the child is too small to defend its rights and claims and everyone says my mother's interests are greater than any who would try to speak for me, even if they are trying to represent me? Aren't we a representative government? Don't we pride ourselves on legal representation? How is it that in this case, anyone who speaks for me is considered an intruder, but anyone who speaks for my mother a hero of liberty? Your Honor, I want my rights that are endowed to me and guaranteed for me. I want my right to life and liberty! What will you do? Do you ignore me, deny me, violate my rights; do you protect those who kill me? Or can the defenseless have someone speak on their behalf when they can't speak for themselves? Yes! An advocate, a defender, a guardian, *that*, that is what we need! Is there any such thing? I think you, the Court, call them guardian ad litems. They represent us and help us; they *are* the voice of the helpless. They intercede for us on our behalf and on behalf of the state who guards our rights. But what business is it of theirs you ask? What right has the state, their ad litem or their attorney, to meddle in and violate the intimate associations a woman chooses not to have? Well, quite simply it is this... The law states clearly that the interest of the state begins when the safety of the child is threatened. Certainly it doesn't take a genius to recognize that if my mother seeks to kill me, take my life, that qualifies as my safety being threatened. How much greater threat needs to be shown? How much more than the life of one of its smallest citizens endangered, does the state need to prove to show an interest?

You said the state did not have enough historical, traditional interest in protecting the life of the unborn, that they had not acknowledged the unborn before and therefore didn't need to now. Well, if that is true, then the state, which had no traditional or historical interest in acknowledging or protecting the rights or humanity of slaves, should have never had to do so. But just because it was that way, that didn't mean it should stay that way. All of it, the injustice of it, the inhumanity of it, the callousness of it demanded to be changed because it was **wrong!** Because it went against all that we said we were, all that our history said we believed, all that we were supposed to be! The state might not have acknowledged me before, except for the obvious fact that it did try to protect me with laws. Isn't trying to keep someone alive, defending their life, protecting their right to grow and live, doesn't that show an intent, doesn't that show acknowledgment? And what about when our Constitution acknowledged us, those not yet born, *"Posterity"*, as those for whom the Constitution was being established? Really, it is you who isn't willing to acknowledge me. And because you have claimed the right and power to bestow human rights on whom you see fit, I find myself pleading my case to you. All that needs to be done now is for you, Your Honor, to acknowledge what is already here, me and my humanity. That is unless the people limit or reclaim that power from you, or declare my rights so you can't deny them anymore. The people have that right you know, they have both the right and duty to alter the Constitution and limit your power since you have used it against those it was intended to protect.

As usual, I expect you will perform legal gymnastics to avoid the obvious, the right, the just. You will say the fetus might be human but isn't a person. Do you hear yourself? It defies logic and reason. Tell me, Your Honor, *What is a person being other than a human being?*[50] You can't answer, can you? That's because you don't mean 'being', do you? You mean 'doing'. You interpret a difference in the value of a person based on their abilities or how strong or viable they are, or if they drain or contribute. But show me, Your Honor, *show me* where in the Constitution where rights are granted by ability, by what a person is able to do! Such a test defies the foundation of equality! Such a test creates caste! Such a test screams that each man has a different value and will be granted particular rights based on the interests and desires of those who hold the power! Such a test denies liberty and readies itself to support a government bent on tyranny over the weak and power to the strong! Is this not what we ran from, all we stand against?

---

[50] Gregory Koukl; <u>Precious Unborn Human Persons</u>

Sadly, there are many who think the weak man, the man of manual labor, the poor man, the common man and his descendants are a great tragedy, not worthy of equality or the rights of liberty—better off dead. There are many who say your value is based on what you do rather than what you are. But this thinking is the inherent belief behind oppression and abuse. This is how the elite think. This is the thinking that empowers the arrogant to put more value on themselves and grant themselves permission to exploit, crush, and deny those they view as less than them. When slave supporters suggested that owning people who do their manual labor freed them to the greater pursuits of art, literature, and inventions not possible if they did not have slaves to do necessary labor, this was the lie they believed, the lie that humans are not equal but some *occupy lower rungs on the human ladder.*[51] So, Your Honor, does the law, does the Constitution say that? Does the Constitution say that women have a right to claim ownership of their child and kill their child because their child will burden them and prevent them from pursuing greater things? Killing is punishment, the taking of one's life. How can another person, even a child's mother, be given a right that takes that child's life without due process and destroys it? How can another person, even a child's mother, defy equality and claim a supremacy and a liberty so strong that no matter how alive I am, how separate and distinct a human being I am, I can be destroyed if she so wishes? Is this the freedom the 14th Amendment was all about? Is this equality?

But you have determined the health of a woman is more important than anything else that needs to be considered. You have declared there is nothing wrong with her putting her needs first. Even if she has to kill, her rights protect her violence against her child. Her desire to not want the burden of motherhood, her desire to flee shame, her desire to get rid of anything that gets in her way, her emotional and mental health, you have determined that how she feels is more important than me. Can you possibly mean that? Is an emotion or a fear greater than a life? Is doing wrong acceptable if it makes you feel better? Is doing wrong okay if it is legal? Is this what the law says? When Adolph Eichman defended himself by claiming the law required him to starve, torture, and kill Jews, was this a justifiable defense? Why not?

---

[51] Dr. Raymond Dennehy, <u>Anti-Abortionist At Large</u>; p. 145

Could it be that *legal* wasn't then and isn't now the same as *right*? Could it be there is a greater good than the wrong which one justifies for one's own good? Could it be that the Israeli High Tribunal in 1961 was right when they told Eichman that although the laws of Germany required the killing of Jews, he should have known that what he had done, that killing innocent human beings was unquestionably **wrong**.[52]

Your Honor, no person has a constitutional right to kill the innocent, no matter how burdensome a child might be. No person has a right to deny another person their life, their personhood. No person has the authority to claim a power to give or withhold life, especially for their own self interests. The law doesn't say what you have claimed, which makes you, not the law, an ass. Trust me on this; I won't stop fighting till I have back what was always mine, my life, my right to be.

Respectfully,
Posterity
(A Friend of the Court)

---

[52] Dr. Raymond Dennehy, <u>Anti-Abortionist At Large</u>; p. 89

CASE: ROE V. WADE
TRANSCRIPT : ORAL REARGUMENT 1972

JUSTICE BYRON R. WHITE: Regardless of the purpose for which the statute was originally enacted, or the purpose which keeps it on the books in Texas today, you would agree, I suppose, that one of the important factors that has to be considered in this case is what rights, if any, does the unborn fetus have?

MRS. WEDDINGTON: That's correct...

WHITE: Well, is it critical to your case that the fetus not be a person under the due process clause?

MRS. WEDDINGTON: It seems to me that it is critical, first, that we prove this is a fundamental interest on behalf of the woman, that it is a constitutional right. And, second—

JUSTICE WHITE: Well, yes. But about the fetus?

MRS. WEDDINGTON: Okay. And, second, that the State has no compelling State interest.

And the State is alleging a compelling State interest in

JUSTICE WHITE: Yes. But I'm just asking you, under the Federal Constitution, is the fetus a person, for the protection of the due process clause?

MRS. WEDDINGTON: All of the cases—the prior history of this statute—the common law history would indicate that it is not. The State has shown no

JUSTICE WHITE: Well, what about-would you lose your case if the fetus was a person?

MRS. WEDDINGTON: Then you would have a balancing of interest.

JUSTICE WHITE: Well, you say you have anyway, don't you?

MRS. WEDDINGTON: Excuse me?

JUSTICE WHITE: You have anyway, don't you? You're going to be balancing the rights of the mother against the rights of the fetus.

MRS. WEDDINGTON: It seems to me that you do not balance constitutional rights of one person against mere statutory rights of another.

JUSTICE WHITE: You think a State interest, if it's only a statutory interest, or a constitutional interest under the State law, can never outweigh a constitutional right?

MRS. WEDDINGTON: I think-it would seem to me that—

JUSTICE WHITE: So all talk of compelling State interest is beside the point. It can never be compelling enough.

MRS. WEDDINGTON: If the State could show that the fetus was a person under the Fourteenth Amendment, or under some other Amendment, or part of the Constitution, then you would have the situation of trying-you would have a State compelling interest which, in some instances, can outweigh a fundamental right. This is not the case in this particular situation.

JUSTICE BLACKMUN: Tell me why you didn't discuss the Hippocratic oath.

MRS. WEDDINGTON: Okay. I guess it was- okay- in part, because the Hippocratic oath—we discussed basically the constitutional protection we felt the woman to have.

The Hippocratic oath does not pertain to that. Second, we discuss the fact that the State has not established a compelling State interest. The Hippocratic oath would not really pertain to that.

And then we discuss the vagueness jurisdiction. It seemed to us that the fact that the medical profession at one time had adopted the Hippocratic oath does not weigh upon the fundamental constitutional rights involved. It is a guide for physicians, but the outstanding organizations of the medical profession have, in fact, adopted a position that says the doctor and the patient should be able to make the decision for themselves in this kind of situation.

JUSTICE BLACKMUN: Of course, it's the only definitive statement of ethics of the medical profession. I take it from what you said that your... you didn't even footnote it, because it's old? That's about, really, what you're saying?

MRS. WEDDINGTON: Well, I guess it is old. And not that it's out of date, but that it seemed to us that it was not pertinent to the argument we were making.

JUSTICE STEWART: Well, if-if it were established that an unborn fetus is a person, with the protection of the Fourteenth Amendment, you would have almost an impossible case here, would you not?

MRS. WEDDINGTON: I would have a very difficult case.

JUSTICE BLACKMUN: Well, do I get from this, then, that your case depends primarily on the proposition that the fetus has no constitutional rights?

MRS. WEDDINGTON: It depends on saying that the woman has a fundamental constitutional right; and that the State has not proved any compelling interest for regulation in the area.

Even if the Court, at some point, determined the fetus to be entitled to constitutional protection, you would still get back into the weighing of one life against another.

JUSTICE STEWART: That's what's involved in this case? Weighing one life against another?

MRS. WEDDINGTON: No, Your Honor. I say that would be what would be involved, if the facts were different and the State could prove that there was a "person" for the constitutional right.

JUSTICE STEWART: Well, if-if it were established that an unborn fetus is a person, with the protection of the Fourteenth Amendment, you would have almost an impossible case here, would you not?

MRS. WEDDINGTON: I would have a very difficult case.

JUSTICE STEWART: I'm sure you would. So, if you had the same kind of thing, you'd have to say that this would be the equivalent—after the child was born, if the mother thought it bothered her health any having the child around, she could have it killed. Isn't that correct?

MRS. WEDDINGTON: That's correct. That—

CHIEF JUSTICE BURGER: Could Texas, constitutionally- did you want to respond further to Justice Stewart? Did you want to respond further to him?

MRS. WEDDINGTON: No, Your Honor.

The OYEZ Project. U.S. Supreme Court Media

I've got soul, but I'm not a soldier...[53]

Dear Mr. Senator,

You said you would do what you had to do to make sure there weren't so many black babies. *Did I hear you right? Who do you think you are?* Did your racism and arrogance come with your office, or did you bring it with you to justify the things you vote against? You know we've got words for that. But tell me somethin', Mr. Senator, who made you and all those treasures you see yourself as guardian over? Which do you think He expects you to protect, money or people? Which does *He* love? Which did *He* send *His* son to die for? Do you think He who made the eye does not see what you do? Do you think He who made the ear does not hear what you say? Do you think one day He'll say to you, "Well done, good and faithful servant, you saved money?" Call me crazy, I thought He was in the people savin' business. I'll tell you this, Mr. Senator, there are people out there who think we matter no matter what color we are, people who are willin' to look like fools to save us. They don't know yet what you said, but just you wait, we'll tell 'em.

    You know, you sure think a lot of yourself. What I can't figure out is how you got such a big head with such puny little thoughts. Who are you to say one color of baby is more valuable or has more potential than a baby of another color? After all, He made us all, and He makes no lesser, lower, discount version of Himself! He loves every color baby He makes. We are all beautiful. We are all made for Him. So, who are you to help us die? Do you think you're doin' us a favor! Or maybe, you're really just tryin' to make sure there's nobody left to need help. It makes me so mad when I think how hard you work to make sure we don't ever see sunlight. I wonder how He must feel when He sees the children He knit so carefully and tenderly *destroyed* because people don't wanna' be bothered with raisin' a kid. Do you not know He is our father, our defender?

    Maybe you don't know. In fact, when I think about it, I don't even think you really know what this country is supposed to be all about. You think it's about bein' free and gettin' rich. But it's not. Don't get me wrong, that stuff can be a part of it. But that's like startin' in the middle

---

[53] The Killers, *All These Things That I've Done*

of a story and just tellin' *how* somethin' *did* happen. What you're leavin' out is the *who*. That's what makes the story so great, the people. This country is great because of its people. And the way we love and help the people is by makin' sure they're free, and they have a chance to use that freedom. You see, freedom is for people, not just some of 'em, but all of 'em. Gettin' rich is what can happen when people are free, when they aren't crushed, when they aren't devalued and dehumanized. It's what happens when people have a chance, an opportunity. That's what this country is about, makin' sure **all** its people have an opportunity to fully realize all the great stuff God put inside 'em, 'cause all those people are who freedom is for; He made us all. I bet the thing you have never truly believed is just that, you and me, that we're equal. You and me, though you've got lots and I've got nothin', even though we look real different, and don't think much alike either, our value is the same. It always has been and always will be, despite you tryin' to make some people more important than other people.

I know you see us babies born to poor, young girls, and it sickens you instead of movin' your heart. Well, did it ever occur to you, things are the way they are for a reason? You throw scraps at us and tell us we're nothin'. You take all the jobs and wonder why we're poor. And then you mock us because some of us take our empty bowls and dare to ask, *"Please, sir, may we have some more?"* Did it ever occur to you that instead of killin' us you could help make things better? Is that really too much to ask?

Maybe you think it's just fine to create a problem, sustain a problem, or ignore a problem and then condemn all those mired in the mess that is so beneath you. Maybe you're foolish enough to think all we can do is jump and run and entertain you. But you don't know what lies unearthed in that great sea of human potential. There is more, so much more. Right now we know and do only what we have had a chance to learn. But once we can take a step beyond just survivin' you'll see. Our country will be proud of us. You see, when we are given the tools we can learn, we can teach, we can build, discover, govern, we can love, we can give, we can think as well as anyone.

We do want more, more chance to thrive, more opportunity to learn, more of the things all human beings need to grow to become all they can be. We want more of us gettin' to stay alive than gettin' to die. Man, it's just bad, real bad. We need ya'll's help. Cuz right now in that same county where you do all your important work, every year 'bout 13,000 babies are born and somewhere 15,000 to 19,000 are killed... Yeah, you read that right. More dead than alive, a lot more. That's just wrong. Anybody can see that. And we never did no wrong. It might cost more money to invest in more children, but doin' the right thing is always better than havin' more things. Sir, what we want, what we need, are the very things you would give your own child. A fightin' chance to be alive and free.

Michael

> *"Better is a little with righteousness, than vast revenues without justice."*
> *Proverbs 16:8 (NKJV)*
>
> *"The generous soul shall be made rich, and he who waters will also be watered himself."*
> *Proverbs 11:24 (NKJV)*
>
> *"No one has ever become poor by giving."*
> – Anne Frank

"When you're only informational you can bend it all you want."
– John Mayer

"Journalists won't give you receipts."[54]

Dear Press,

What is it you do? Our experience with you has been rather limited. But it appears you tell all the different things that are happening in our country and in our world. Is that so? Do you get to say anything you want? Does everything you say have to be true? Do you get to not tell the things you don't want to be heard? Do you tell all the sides of a story, or just the sides you agree with? Do you get to control the story? Do you get to control what the public sees and hears? Do you get to bend the truth?

    Pardon me for stating the obvious, but the stories you tell about us, those who are too small to be cuddled, don't ever include the ugly, awful, bloody truth about how and why we die. Why not? Isn't that part of the story? Why isn't the direct killing of over 3,000 tiny humans **each day** in this country news? You hide what happens to us and protect our murder with claims of legitimacy, feminine liberties, and constitutional rights. Does anyone else have such a right that you protect so fiercely? Do you tell stories to make it seem virtuous for anyone else to kill the innocent so they can pursue being happy? Why not? Why do only women have that right? Why is it only the smallest of human beings whose story, whose death, isn't important enough to be heard? Why is our, why is *my* death, a right instead of a wrong? Please, tell me... Oh, I see, **only YOU get to report what YOU want to, and I don't get to decide** whether or not I should be alive.

    I wonder if you realize how much sense you don't make, how hypocritical you are, and how unjust. I wonder if you realize the word games you play with the most helpless of human lives. Surely you must know, surely you must see the inconsistency in the stories you choose to tell. Don't you remember these stories? One story where a man callously kills his pregnant wife and throws her and her baby away in the San Francisco Bay is covered with a voracious demand of justice. Two bodies were found on two different days. One a woman, another a baby boy,

---

[54] Ludwig von Stueb quoted in King Leopold's Ghost

both bodies apparently demanded the justice you, the press, *rightly* intended to cover until it was accomplished. Another story was about another woman who, though likely raped, carried her baby conceived in the most hateful of ways and waited painfully, patiently for her day of truth and justice. When the same man who raped her later killed and burned her body *privately* in his backyard to destroy both crimes, you, the press, were there, furiously telling the story, telling the great wrong, demanding the evil done to this woman be met with justice. You, the press, stood horrified at the story that made a hardened investigator fight back tears as he told the country about the remains of both the mother and child, whose tiny hand was still clenched in the tiniest of fists, still inside his mother. You, the press, demanded the man's capture. You demanded justice for both mother and unborn child.

What about the stories where young girls kill their newborns in bathrooms and bedrooms and go about their proms and practices as if they were just taking the garbage out? What about the boys who beat the bellies of their girlfriends? Is their motive or the outcome so very different? Why does this make you, the press, so irate, so vigilant, so adamant that these wrongs be righted? Why are entire episodes devoted to these babies, and yet the other babies who are killed are completely ignored as if they are nothing? We are all babies. We are all helpless. We all need to be protected. Please, explain it to me. I just don't understand why I don't matter too. Where is my great story, my righteous coverage?

Why if the same thing happens to the same helpless person, why is it okay one day and evil the next? Why do you consider the babies in one trashcan "crimes against the innocent," but the babies in a different dumpster or sold piece-by-piece "nothing to be concerned about," or even "a right to protect"? Does it matter *who* the trashcan belongs to or *where* the waste container is or *who* put these tiny, human beings inside them? It is a trashcan! Human beings don't belong in them, EVER! Why does one story, one baby's death, unleash your fury, and the thousands like those babies whose grave is a dumpster a "constitutional right" you use your power and influence to protect? Why? Do you see what I mean? It doesn't make the least bit of sense when you open your eyes to the whole story, to the story of every life wrongly taken.

There is another story too, a story about a little two-year-old girl in Florida whose mother killed her so she wouldn't have to be a mommy anymore, so she could be free. Do you know the story? The press, and everyone else, thought this a great wrong. But I find it strange. If this same little girl had been killed when she was inside her mommy for the exact same reason, you, the press, would have seen it as reasonable, understandable, constitutional, even wise. But tell me, tell me how if this same little girl is killed by the same person for the same reason, does it really matter where or when it happens?

Unborn or unwanted didn't change the greatness of the wrong done to these children. How they were conceived, where they were when they were killed, or who did or didn't want them, none of it mattered when confronted with their helpless, lifeless bodies. No right or choice or privacy or liberty could be heard over the cries of justice their bodies demanded. And you, the press, have answered the call. You, the press, have been their voice.

But why not me? Why does my body, broken in pieces for the profit of a stranger, for the happiness of my mother, why does that not appeal to your sense of justice? Why do you have two different standards? Why do you treat some children one way and other children another? Why are some children trash, and others precious, deserving of your passion, your concern, your <u>coverage</u>? Tell me, why do I deserve your disdain, your repulsion, your disregard? Tell me, please, what are your criteria? If I never get a chance to live my life, how can I achieve what you consider to be the greatest of all achievements? If you don't consider my *life* worthy, how will I ever become *newsworthy*?

Maybe if you stopped at just ignoring me, your hypocrisy wouldn't be so evident. But you don't. Relentlessly you attack anyone who attempts to tell the truth of our death. You accuse them of illegitimately and crudely using graphic portrayals to appeal to emotionalism and sensationalism. You accuse them of propaganda, of attacking the constitutional rights of women. But why is it okay when you tell the emotional appeals of women who justify killing us? Why is it okay when you show victims of epidemics, catastrophes, starvation, or wars? Why are these images acceptable, even necessary, to show the truth, but the pictures of our bodies not? Why can't our truth be shown? Could it be that the public doesn't want to see what it willingly allows to be done to children of this country? Could it be you don't want to tell the whole ugly truth because of just how ugly and wrong it really is?

Please don't misunderstand me; I don't place the value or significance of my life or babies like me on what the press thinks of us. We don't need your permission to be important. We don't need your permission to tell the truth. Our value, worth, and rights all lie wrapped up in our human nature, something you have no control over. But since you ignore our nature, distort, crush, and disregard who and what we are, I am forced to address it, forced because it is *you* who is responsible for telling the whole story—including ours. And as of yet, *you* have left it untold. You don't even have the courtesy to acknowledge us, much less care about what happens to us, even though enough us of die *every day* to fill a high school. We are human and you close your eyes. We are human and you shut your ears. We are human and you call us anything else to silence our story, anything else to distort the truth. Is this really that much different than when the Nazi propaganda machine depicted the unwanted as deserving of any label, any fate the state wished to confer upon them? Do you really think we are only what you declare us to be? Does what we are change depending on the story you are telling? Wow, stop the press! What an evolutionary feat!

We all know what you do. It is the same thing that is always done when those with the power want to withhold the rights of some particular unwanted group of humans. With remarkable effectiveness they spin a tale, they pretend these humans just aren't human at all, and they name-call. And that is exactly what you do. You know how important language is and the power your words have over how people think. Even though you have been trained to call a particular people group by the name they choose to call themselves, even though you have been trained to always use a common, everyday term whenever possible, even though you have been trained to be fair, oh, what does all that matter? You don't have to if you don't want to! You can tell the story any way that suits your interests and attack anyone who questions you. When you have to mention us, you use words to separate us from our humanity. You call us, you call *me*, a *thing*.

"Fetus," your favorite word choice, is used by you with condescension and indifference to make our death sterile, impersonal. You act as if when I have grown enough to be called a "fetus," I have somehow not grown enough to be a human. But adult, adolescent, child, infant, embryo, fetus, even zygote just tell how long I have lived, how much I have grown and developed. They have nothing to do with whether or not I am human.

"Fetus" is just Latin for "young child" or "young one". Didn't you go to school? Don't you know every creature has these different stages of life, but it is always the same life it started out as? No matter how much they change no one can ever become a different being. And if my parents are human, that is all I can be. Good grief! It is just so plain to see, why do you keep denying me? Of course you know all this, but you have a goal, an intent to deny my humanity so the only relevant human interest is that of my mommy. To you women are more important than babies. But you don't call our mommies the strange Latin term for a pregnant woman, do you? I bet most people don't even know there is one because you don't use it. I haven't heard any pregnant women called "gravidas". Why not? Does it distract from their humanity? Does it make them nothing? You probably don't insist "gravidas" be denied equal protection under the law. You probably don't justify their murder for hire. They are women, no matter their size or status, women with child. But me, you manipulate and deny, so you can help cover up how I die. You know if you use the word "baby," all of a sudden I matter, all of a sudden I am someone to protect instead of a something to get rid of.

With all your word games and spin stories, the truth is hard to find. But know this, what you call me doesn't change who I am. When men try to destroy the heart and spirit of women by calling them hateful, spiteful, cruel demeaning names, it hurts, but it doesn't make them true. When bullies use slurs and name-calling, when racists hurl their hateful rhetoric, it is still just words. All of it is just words, that is until people start to believe them. The danger lies when we believe words that make others less than us because they are different to us. The danger lies when we forget equality in favor of practicality, or value prosperity over life. The danger lies when we believe the words that justify us destroying someone else for our own interests. And these are the words you, the press, are responsible for spreading, words of half-truths and half stories, words that deny who I really am and how much I really matter.

Do you remember another story? It was a story of one of us, a story where a mother found out something was wrong with her baby, and instead of killing her helpless baby growing inside her, she sought out someone who could help. And a doctor, a doctor who actually believed health meant healing instead of killing, operated on this tiny baby while still inside his mother's womb, while he was still inside his home. The world could not have known what was going to happen; the doctor most certainly did not. But as the doctor operated on this precious human life, the little life, the little unborn boy reached his hand out of the opening in his mother's womb, the doctor put his finger near the petite fist and the child clenched hold of the doctor's finger with a tiny, firm grasp of humanity. He in that one moment spoke for us all. He said what all of us want to say but aren't given the chance to say, "*I am here. I am a separate human being. I am real. I am alive. I live. I matter...*" "Fetus" just isn't the best word to describe the miracle of life inside a womb, is it?

So to you who have been wise enough to realize that "suicide" bombers are more accurately termed "homicide" bombers, maybe you could be honest enough to call me "tiny unborn baby," waiting to reach out and touch the world. To you who tell the count of our soldiers who die, soldiers who can defend themselves, maybe you could tell the count of how many helpless babies die every day on our soil. To you who show the emaciated bodies of those far away with no food, maybe you could show what happens to our bodies legally right here. To you who are infuriated over the dead children of another country, maybe you could be infuriated over the dead children of this country. But I guess it is a lot easier to point a finger across the world, and much, much harder to point one at yourselves.

You know, you could help us. You could fight to make it safe for our mommies to have us instead of making it safe for our mommies to kill us. You could help make a better world instead of a world with fewer babies. Maybe that could be your philosophy. We all know you have one, we just don't like it. We don't like it because in your worldview we have to die because our mommy is scared, alone, poor, or doesn't care. Certainly, there must be a better way, maybe it is harder, but it has got to be better. What a story that would be...

Hoping for Better,
The Babies

P.S. It is said "when you search for truth, you search for God, whether you mean to or not." Maybe that's what is keeping you from telling the truth about us; you don't want to find Him.

"Who does not know how our great men are outdoing themselves in declaiming against the <u>foreign</u> slave-trade. There are a perfect host of Clarksons and Wilberforces risen up among us on that subject, most edifying to hear and behold. Trading negroes (or allowing babies to die) from Africa, dear reader is so horrid! It is not to be thought of! But trading them (or allowing babies to be killed) from Kentucky-that's quite another thing!"

– Stowe[55]

"But do not do according to their works; for they say, and do not do. For they bind heavy burdens, hard to bear, and lay them on men's shoulders; but they themselves will not move them with one of their fingers...Woe to you, scribes and Pharisees, hypocrites! For you pay tithe of mint and anise and cummin, and have neglected the weightier matters of the law: justice and mercy and faith. These you ought to have done, without leaving the others undone. Blind guides, who strain out a gnat and swallow a camel! ... For you cleanse the outside of the cup and dish, but inside they are full of extortion and self-indulgence."

Matthew 23:3-4, 23-25

Dear Church,

I know what it is you're supposed to do. You're supposed to do justice, love mercy, and walk humbly with God. You're supposed to speak His truth in love. You're supposed to seek His Kingdom come, His will be done first, then all the other things will be added unto you. So why don't you?

What's funny is the world thinks you, the church, meddles in this messy business. The world thinks the church judges and condemns. They assume it's the church who fights for us, the voiceless, the unwanted, the babies. They think the church tries to help us. They believe the church is active in advocating for us. They think the church cares about us. But they're wrong...

What the world doesn't realize is how silent the church is. They don't know how annoyed, even angry the church is when people in the church plead for us. They don't know how those people get treated by the church. The world doesn't see the rolled eyes; they don't hear the constant, unapologetic "No." They don't hear how *everything* else is more important. The world doesn't hear how pregnant women and

---

[55] Harriet Beecher Stowe, <u>Uncle Tom's Cabin</u>; p. 138

babies aren't in the budget. They don't know the church doesn't care about the voiceless because the unborn have no voice, no vote, no power, no money, so they feel no guilt in ignoring them, no urgency to defend them. They don't know how the church would rather close their eyes and pretend it doesn't happen. They don't hear you say, "God willed it so," or see you shrug your shoulders indifferently and walk away. The world is unaware that the church rarely weeps over us. They don't know that the church would rather offer a woman God's forgiveness after it's too late to save me than tell her the truth, that it's wrong to kill her child, and lovingly **help** her do the hard, right thing. They don't know how much more the church cares about how they look to the world than how they look to God, or that the church is desperately trying to woo and please the world by enthusiastically embracing the suffering and causes the world cares about while brushing the abuse of our mothers and the killing of us under the ever-bulging rug. It's as if they forgot that He says, "Do you not know that friendship with the world is enmity with God? Whoever therefore wants to be a friend of the world makes himself an enemy of God"[56] They don't know how cheap the church makes grace appear, as if you can do what you have to and just say you're sorry later and that makes it all okay. They don't know how much more the church cares about how many members they have rather than how many babies are saved. The world doesn't know the only stones the church throws are at its own members, or how popular the church wants to be. They don't know the church wants to be loved by the world. Somehow the world is unaware that the church, His hands in His world, doesn't care about us. They don't know the church doesn't *do* justice unless it's cool and chic and will make the church look good. They don't know you have better, more important things to do.

Of course, there are some churches who do care. But not many. There are some churches that back up their belief that each human being is made in the image of God and seek to protect such innocent and vulnerable life by helping these young mothers through the pain and fear, by offering them help, hope, acceptance, and kindness. There are some churches that actually live out truth and grace by giving these young girls all that they need to do the right thing, a home filled with

---

[56] James 4:4

people to help them. There are some churches that are not afraid to speak the truth in love on our behalf, even if it scares some people away. There are some churches that see us babies as real, even though we haven't met, and believe we are precious and deserve to be protected as much as our mothers. There are churches that believe God's gospel of truth, seeking His Kingdom come, His will be done, includes us, because they believe that the human life that doesn't know it is about to be thrown away is equal in importance to the life that we can see anxiously fearing and living with poverty, disease, and abuse. There are some churches, some believers who think these issues are not in competition with saving babies, that it is not an issue of either/or, but rather both/and, churches that believe the truth lies in seeking Him and what He loves, and believe *He wants* these babies and that's why He made them, so it is the church's job to love and defend them. But not many *believe* this enough to *do* something about it.

Most of our defenders are people seeking to do the right thing for nothing but Him, and are willing to be hated while trying to love us and our mommies. They are not the brutish, self-righteous people the media likes to display. Certainly those people exist and their words thunder in the vast emptiness of their love, for the law that they know, knows no love. There are those that condemn our death, but viciously condemn our mothers as well. They rally and rant, but don't lift a finger to show their faith with love that pours out of a living gospel. Those people have much to say but *do* very little. Those people are not our defenders. It is the others, the ones that know saving us means loving our mommies in every real way they can. They are living out the hard, hard truth in love by loving what He loves even when it's not popular to do so. They are the unfashionable ones, the ones who didn't get the memo that it's not cool, not trendy, not vogue to speak for babies, not wise to speak for us, not prudent to help the shamed, the stupid, the unabstinent. They don't care that the world thinks their concern is passé and tacky. They act simply on the truth that God is not trendy, and He has always hated it when babies He made were treated like trash, and when scared young girls were cast out and forgotten. They see no glory for Him, no good in not caring that I die. I like people like that, people who think I should live and do everything they can to make it happen. I wish there were a whole nation of people like that to fight for us, people with courage and love, who helped others do the right thing because it was right. But right now there aren't. People are too busy thinking about themselves to bother thinking about us.

It does make me wonder though, if you, the church, don't care about us, what is it you do care about? What are the more important things you're doing? You say it is His Kingdom, His Gospel. You say it is bringing more people into His Kingdom *with* His Gospel. Why doesn't that include us? Do we not need the gospel? Do we not need to live? You make it so hard for us to show just how valuable we are. I can't figure it out. Why can't you see? Why are you so blind to us? It's hard to be part of a kingdom when we are denied a birth certificate. It is hard to explain to you why we're important to God when we're never given a chance to see His world. It is hard to compare our value to big multimillion-dollar budgets. Our worth is much, much bigger than that. Our worth was displayed on that cross, by what was spent to redeem us. Remember?

So tell me why. Why are million-dollar buildings on your agenda, in your budget, and millions of helpless babies not? Why do you preach and plead that pledging more bricks builds His Kingdom? Why do you teach **BIG GRACE** and little truth? Why do you preach mercy and not justice, or justice for some, but not all? Why do you please the strong and ignore the weak? Why? Why do you never preach and plead or even mention that children He made, children who bear His image are torn to pieces for profit here where you live by people you know? Why do you not act as if this is so very wrong? Why do you never mention what happens to us as little more than a footnote? Do you not know that your silence is deadly, that your inoffensive neutrality actually puts power in the hands of those who crush? Do you not know that by doing nothing you are doing the very something that ensures we die? Do you not know when human beings are being killed you HAVE to pick sides? Church, it is you, your wanting to make sure you are well liked, that justifies and condones our death.

But tell me, why aren't you just as neutral, just as inoffensive, just as "good-news-only" oriented when it comes to the children in foreign places? Why are you more concerned, more passionate, more giving to children on another continent than you are to the ones right here where you live? Do you think it's more noble when doing so only brings you praise and honor? How hard is that? That's not courage. Do you think doing something generous over there excuses you to do nothing over here? I see no bravery in your overseas compassion. Have you ever spoken truth to the guilty and stood with the broken when it would cost you everything to do so? Have you ever wept for the disposable humans? It's a lot easier to condemn a disease or a system than the actions of people you know and <u>*need*</u>. I guess it's easy to be passionate when you don't have to worry about pissing anyone off. You don't have to temper your message or tiptoe around truth. You don't have to worry that some of the people who hear you will feel guilty, convicted, condemned and attack you. You don't have to worry that some of the people will be angry and leave because they have taken a life, abused a woman, killed without caring, done wrong out of fear. You don't have to worry they will say bad things about the church for fighting such faraway wrongs. There just isn't a downside to advocating for AIDS victims in Africa, or victims of slavery in Asia. The world's on your side. It's vogue. And you're a hero.

But speaking up for me is dangerous. And you are... silent. So either you're ruled by a cowardly, self-interested fear, which you have thoughtfully named neutrality, bipartisanship or "*moderation*"[57], or you just don't give a damn because it's just not your thing. Which is it? Do you even know? What is it you're so scared of? A decrease in membership or tithes? *God is your provider, or have you forgotten?* Are you scared of scaring off the world? Are you scared of the world's rebuke or rejection? Who is it you seek to please? *Shouldn't it be Him?* Are you scared of hurting those who have hurt us, or reminding someone of a pain and guilt they have buried so deeply? Maybe you want to be seen by the world as all loving, all forgiving, and somehow you think that requires not mentioning the very worst things people are guilty of. Maybe you are scared of being branded a fool or worse, or do you tell yourself God is more concerned about saving souls than bodies?

Perhaps, though, you think He really does care, but you don't, at least not too much. You have other things to consider besides babies nobody wants. Maybe you don't want to be bothered. After all, you're "not rabid about abortion," so God must certainly be following your lead. Certainly God must be most passionate about what you're passionate about. One must prioritize. Right? I wonder in all your studying and thinking if you ever realized that this is following backwards.

---

[57] Thomas Paine, <u>Common Sense</u>

But what about me! Don't I matter! If I matter to Him, and I must, then shouldn't I matter to you, too? I know you know our mommies and you care about them, you love them, or maybe you just need them to <u>not</u> be offended, so you judiciously choose not to burden them with such a monstrous weight of truth. And, of course, the most important thing is for them to know His love. I know you would rather just say we're all guilty and in need of a Savior and avoid pointing out such a particularly painful wrong. **They** are loved and forgiven and I am... *gone*. What do I say? *Do I not get to be angry? Do I not get to cry foul?* Am I not supposed to care that everyone ignores what is happening to so many, what happened to me? Do I have no need to know Him and His love? It's me who died violently, my body that was broken, my life that was taken, my story not written. If you knew me, would you be so casual, so reluctant to speak the truth, so eager and quick to pardon and forget I was ever here? Ignoring me or forgetting me can't take away my humanity, my existence, or my worth. He doesn't place more value on a life in there or out here, or determine value per pound. So why do you? Do you not realize I am both body and soul? Nor does God lie to Himself about the children He has made to satisfy your desire to be uninvolved. So why do you? If you don't, then how do you justify doing so little, or more accurately, nothing at all?

You probably think I sound too angry, too full of condemnation, too hostile to be a child, too... brutally honest. It's just that I want this to stop. And it won't stop until people make it stop. And people won't make it stop until they see and admit it for the wrong it has always been. Besides, it was Him who said that the truth so often comes out of the mouth of babes. And nowhere does He say you should not say the truth if it makes people uncomfortable. That is in fact the nature of truth. And truthfully, if you were me, if what was done to me was done to you, *you* would cry just as loudly. You would weep, you would wail. You would want what I want, to live and not die.

The truth is, it's wrong to treat human beings as if we are nothing. It's wrong, deeply, terrifyingly wrong to crush us because we can't protect and defend ourselves, wrong to just let it happen because we don't have any power, wrong to think it's not important enough to throw everything, your whole weight against it until the wrong has been righted and we're safe. It's as wrong today, as wrong as when babies were thrown into pits of fire in that dark, despairing "Kingdom of Night"[58] just a few decades ago in a civilized country where civilized people did nothing. I don't want my mommy or any mommy to shrug us off as if we are nothing, I don't want them to believe a lie, and I don't want them to be swallowed up in guilt, or justify killing us because they have a nice life now because we aren't here. I want mommies to know the truth, the truth about us and the truth about Him. You see, His grace is not made better by making yourselves seem better, more deserving of His grace. His grace is not more powerful because we pretend the wrong isn't as bad as it is. That makes grace cheap. His grace is shown to be the deep, wide covering it is through truth. More truth, more grace. He doesn't run out on those who call on Him because the truth is too much to handle, too ugly to bear. He just spreads His arms wider till it's all covered—all of it. I want my mommy to know just how big His grace really is, just how huge a debt it covers. I don't want her to feel condemned, I want her to know more than most ever will how amazing, full, and wide His grace actually is. That can only happen when she hears the truth of her own heart and the love in His.

As for you, the church, you should love all that He loves, all that He made, all that is right and good and just. The very fact that I exist is proof that He cares, proof that I matter. How I came into being might be an act, or a sin, a mystery unapproved, but I carry His image, and that is in itself proof there are no accidental people. You know the nature of our Maker, and you know better than to think He makes bodies without souls. You also know better than any that *"it is the spirit who gives life; the flesh profits nothing."*[59] So really this is about you, the church, and what you will do to protect and defend us. My death and the death of over 3,000 innocent children each day requires I ask, when will you care more about saving a tiny life than you do about not offending people who have taken one? When will you love them both? When will you decide to be bothered with the wreck of a life on the side of road, delay your important business, and willingly get dirty in God's messy business of saving both bodies and souls, both mother and child? When you will see the church as the body of Christ, not a corporation and realize that in the great division of labor you were not exempt from doing to others what you would have them do unto you? When will you act as if following the

---

[58] Elie Wiesel, Night.
[59] John 6:63 (NKJV)

Giver of Life **requires** defending life and recognize that what you don't do for us, you don't do for Him. Remember?

Maybe you think saving us, protecting us, acknowledging us, changing the status quo is impossible, so no need to waste precious resources and energy. Maybe you lack faith or courage. Maybe you feel you have too much to lose. Maybe you don't realize with Him all things **are** possible. Maybe you don't want to give up too much to help our mommies, to help us. Maybe you don't realize that change becomes possible when humble people speak both truth and grace, stand for justice and equity, live with less to accomplish a greater good, and love both lovely and unlovely. Maybe you can't begin to imagine the stories our lives would have told for Him.

But you can. You can believe the truth, that we matter to Him, and let us matter to you. You can give because He says your well won't run dry. You can love because He first loved you when you weren't lovely at all. You can fight for a world where every child gets the chance they deserve, the chance to live the life God gave them, the chance to know His grace and love Him deeply in return. You can do all these things because these are the things of His Kingdom come, His will be done, these are the acts of truth and love that show the truth and power of the gospel and bring Him the glory He deserves.

His Babies, Your Brothers and Sisters

"If I profess with the loudest voice and clearest exposition every portion of the truth of God except precisely that little point which the world and the devil are at that moment attacking, I am not confessing Christ, however boldly I may be professing Christ. Where the battle rages, there the loyalty of the soldier is proved; and to be steady on all the battlefield besides, is mere flight and disgrace if he flinches at that point."

– Martin Luther

"Truth has no special time. It's time is now- always, and indeed then most truly when it seems unsuitable to actual circumstances."

– Albert Schweitzer

"God didn't ask us to be successful, just faithful."

– Mother Theresa

"Who will go for Us?" Then I said, *"Here am I! Send me."*

Isaiah 6:8(NKJV)

> "When we consider that women are treated as property, it is degrading to women that we should treat our children as property to be disposed of as we see fit."
> – Elizabeth Cady Stanton, in a letter to Julia Ward Howe, October 16, 1873.

Dear Betty (Betty Friedan, author of <u>The Feminine Mystique</u> and founder of NOW),

You talked about so many things. You made so many women not want to be mommies. You made being a mommy seem really small and pointless, even bad. You made it sound so awful to take care of us children. I know it's not easy to give up so much for such a long time. But giving your child love and life is...well, it's the greatest gift you can ever give anyone. I know people didn't make it easy for mommies to keep growing and to be mommies. And I don't think it's bad for mommies to want to do more than just be a mommy. I don't think it makes them a bad mommy any more than it makes daddies bad because they seek to be more than just a daddy. But I still don't see why we little girls and boys so tiny and precious need to die for the sake of our mommies. I don't see why one life matters more than another. I don't see in so many of the things you said were true, I don't see **_anything_** that makes us nothing.

"Anatomy is destiny," those were the words, the conclusions, the teachings you hated, the ones that shackled and haunted women even after their hard-fought battle for suffrage and recognition of their human worth and dignity. They were the fury behind your hunt, the lie to be exposed, the bonds to break. How awful and wretched that a pompous, arrogant, self-serving man could influence the psyche of a nation and tell women they can only be and become what their biological function is: that they are only capable of being a womb, that their only value or contribution lies there. How awful and ludicrous that society bought the lie that took them backwards and told women they *could* only be, in fact, what they *should* only be is *what society says they are, what they are permitted to be.* How awful that woman were treated as property, that they could only be affirmed by those around them, that they were kept from their autonomy, kept from living their own life, and from fully realizing all that was in them.

Betty, you rightly thought women were people, and because they were people they should be free to seek their full potential. You rightly thought their humanity, "no more no less," was all they needed to expect society to give them a voice and an opportunity to determine their own destiny. You rightly thought women should not feel guilty because they wanted motherhood and *more*.

But, Betty, haven't you done to us babies not yet born exactly what was done to women? Haven't you said we are only what our bodies are today, instead of all that we can be because of our humanity? Haven't you denied us the life and freedom to pursue all the potential within us? Haven't you said we are only what society says we are and permits us to be, all so that women can be free to pursue their destiny? Isn't that what men have done to women throughout history? Haven't you said we are the property of our mothers and can be disposed of and treated any way they wish? Didn't men say that of women? Haven't you declared that our value is determined by somebody else choosing to give us value? Isn't that what society did to women? Haven't you made it acceptable for one person to take or let us retain what was already ours to begin with, our life, our *self?* How can that be?

How is it, Betty, that you, who have known what it is to not be allowed to live and pursue all that is wonderful in life, could declare a right for women *alone* to withhold life from those with a whole life to live? You said women are merely human. Then how can one group of humans have rights other humans don't, especially a right to destroy and deny the humanity of others? How can unalienable human rights exist only for certain humans and not all? Why is it only women who get to declare they don't want to be parents and kill their children? How can this possibly be part of dignity, life, and equality? Isn't being limited because of what I can do, because of my age and size, as bad as being limited because of what a woman can do because of her sex?

You exposed to the world what the social scientists and anthropologists already knew, that determining the potential of a human being based on what they could do presently was a "myth... an impediment rather than a prop to scientific progress... that it imposed a static society that could not handle social change... that functionalism was rather 'embarrassing' because it really said nothing at all." You showed everyone that functionalism "closed the door of the future on women." But it is functionalism that has been used to slam the door shut on the future and the very lives of children. Many have said because unborn babies don't presently do certain functions that they are nothing to be valued or protected. They insist that the value of a person and the rights they deserve can only be determined by what they are presently capable of doing or the function they can perform, instead of what their nature says they are capable of. You thought it was wrong to insist that women "adjust to a state inferior to their full capabilities" before they had reached them, and yet that is exactly what you have done to babies because we get in the way of our mommies. It's as if everyone has believed the lie, "I think therefore I am, not realizing the opposite is true, "I am, therefore I think, breathe, love, build, create, wonder, run, rest, fight, dream, fulfill." Being always comes before doing, that's why it is the most cherished, the right that comes before all others.

Betty, isn't there potential in both lives, in mother, in child, that has yet to be reached? Don't both lives deserve the opportunity to pursue their full capability? When you say, "ME ONLY!" isn't this selfish? Isn't this hypocritical? Isn't this *wrong*?

Years later, with your *own* well-defined feminine mystique securely in your grasp, you found yourself conjuring and dwelling on an unborn child, your grandchild, and so many thoughts crossed your mind. You had a reputation, a policy, an agenda, a PAC, a lifetime of work to uphold, a lifetime of defending the legitimacy of shedding our innocent blood. But you couldn't help yourself. Without meaning or wanting to, you couldn't help but love this unplanned, uninvited, inconvenient grandchild, who had the nerve to live, grow, and exist without invitation or consideration of his daddy's or mommy's life plan. He was, like all of us, just... here, just... human. And you struggled to intertwine the matchless love that enveloped your heart for this little baby that was connected to you, and the holocaust you had justified and declared as essential to femininity. You sought to defend both. But your heart betrayed you. We could hear it, truth... life; it beat so clearly despite the latter arguments you crafted to justify our death. They were simply puny when set next to life itself. And we knew life would someday win. But today, let it be known, let it be heard just how much you thought of yourself and your own, and how little you thought of everyone else.

Tell us, those killed, how is it that you can quote Rilke, as you yearn and wonder over your own grandchild almost born...

We are nearing the land that is life.

You will recognize it by its seriousness.

...and yet talk about the need for other little unborn babies to be executed, evicted for the sake of women, as if their life lacks the significance and seriousness that your own grandchild's does? How is it that you can take such sweet delight in your children, the "gifts" of your life, and "wonder what you did to deserve them" but define the "gifts" of others as pests? How is it that you marvel at how "they were so much *themselves*," not yours, not you, but *themselves* "from the very beginning" and yet deny other unique, individual valuable children *their* lives when they are at *their* beginning? How is it you can acknowledge their own individuality and yet claim that their humanity and even their dignity lies in the actions and affirmations of someone else? How is it you can melt at the "enchanting smile" of your grandson, this "priceless new being" but flippantly discuss disposing of other countless living treasures? How is it you can do all these things and wonder at the mystery and beauty of human life renewing itself and yet claim these wonders and priceless, unique gifts of humanity only for yourself and your offspring? Why aren't others just as deserving of the wonder and mystery of life? How is it that you can say your grandchild, as unplanned as the rest of us, as interfering with female career plans as any of us, is priceless and the rest of us tiny people of equal value are nothing but something to get rid of?

You say that a woman's choice is what gives a child their value. How can that be? I don't change or lose my human nature or my individuality based on the thoughts, fears, plans, or aspirations of my mommy. No one does because no one can. I can't become nothing after I am already something. It is literally not possible. Besides, it's so two faced. What you claim for yourself you won't give to others. Just think, if man cannot determine the value of a woman, if it is beyond his reach, how can a woman determine the value of a child? Aren't we all human? Don't we all have the same nature, a human one? Don't we all belong to ourselves and not another? Don't we all exist to coexist, to love, to help one another? What if a woman changes her mind and doesn't want to be a mommy anymore? Does the child suddenly become non-human, non-living, not priceless?

Why won't you admit we are real and you are wrong? Will it really cost you so much? Are you really so selfish, so proud, so determined to destroy the lives of others for your own interests that you will continue to fight for the right to kill us, to own us, to lie about us, to never say you are sorry even when faced with the evidence of our mounting holocaust? It sounds so much like what has happened before. Some people said they mattered more and kept killing with increased speed and efficiency despite the cries of humanity. How many is too many? Six million? Fifty million? When will our cries of "We don't want to die!" be heard over your demand that "You should not be allowed to live?" **WHEN?** What I want to ask is this, shouldn't we get what our mommies get, "no more, no less," the same opportunity to be all that we can be because of our humanity?

Priceless Human Babies

"You see," said Aslan. "They will not let us help them. They have chosen cunning instead of belief. Their prison is only in their own minds, yet they are in that prison; and so afraid of being taken in that they cannot be taken out."
— C.S. Lewis

"They do not change because they do not fear God."
Psalm 55:19 (NKJV)

Dear Abortion Advocates,

I wonder sometimes what you mean. You say things like "freedom" and "choice," "reproductive health," "reproductive justice," and "reproductive rights…" and it makes me pause and puzzle. I might be young and all, but I'm not stupid. The words you use, they are good words, but when you use them you mean death. When you say "freedom," you mean your freedom is the only one that matters even if it robs me of mine; you mean free to kill your baby so you don't have to be a mommy. When you say "choice," you mean free to choose whether your child lives or dies. When you say "health," you mean not having to have a baby because it is not the best decision to keep your life intact, your *well-being* as you define it. When you say "justice," well, I don't think you actually know what that word is all about. You can't possibly mean justice, because justice is when you act on behalf of those who have been crushed, those who are weak and vulnerable. And the weak one, well that's me. You have taken my freedom, my choice, my life, and claimed it as your right. But no one has a right to do wrong to someone else. You see, a lot of people just don't realize that justice is either distributive or retributive. One refers to equity, equal value, treatment, and opportunity, and the other to punishing those who have crushed and taken from others. I have not harmed anyone, crushed anyone, or hurt anyone. I'm just here, that's all, doing what babies do. In fact, real justice would acknowledge me, protect me, give me equal protection under the law. Real justice never abandons the helpless to the interests of the strong. It is the first hand extended to those who need one.

If you mean justice as equity and insist women should not have constraints on them that men don't have, or that the poor or less advantaged should not have constraints on them that the better advantaged don't have, then I would argue equity too. It's true that "children do indeed tie a mother's shoes" and keep them from the work that will make them the economic and social equals of men, keep them from becoming vulnerable to so many destructive things. It's true that children cost money and time and energy to raise. It's true that it is so very hard for women to do both on their own and thrive. But isn't it possible to untangle those knots so women can reach down and hold the hand of their child and keep moving forward with both their lives, and not cut those living, breathing heartstrings? I just don't see how the path to justice and equity for women of all circumstances should include or require the death of their children. We don't fight cancer by killing the patient. We don't fight poverty by killing the poor. We don't fight ignorance by killing the uninformed. If justice for all is opportunity for all, then isn't that the thing that is missing, real opportunity for women who have a baby and not much else? Wouldn't reproductive justice actually be achieved for women if those women who have reproduced, who have a child, have the opportunity to not be discriminated against because they need to care for that little life? Wouldn't reproductive justice be achieved by childcare assistance, affordable food, energy, and housing, flexible education and working environments, adequate, accessible healthcare, and good pay? Wouldn't reproductive justice be achieved by promoting the well-being of both women and children instead of shaming them and giving them little chance of survival? Wouldn't justice be better served by not pitting women against their own children? Wouldn't justice be promoted by acknowledging the equality of all people no matter their size or ability and protecting the most helpless by condemning death and violence, and offering hope and help?

As for responsibility, yes, I think men should take some, a lot actually, more than they have ever known. I think they need to pay for the children they have a part in making. I think families should take some. I think business should take some, I think the church should take some, and I think government should take some. Yes, I think we all should take some part, even some pride in caring for our smallest citizens. It's like anything really, when you invest in something you begin to nurture it, help it, protect it, love it. Would that really be so bad if we all took part in the greatest resource and opportunity for potential and growth we have, our children? Doesn't the Creator of us all, who knows and understands equity, who is all that is right and just, doesn't He say it best when He tells us, *"For where your treasure is, there will your heart be also"*? Can you imagine what it would be like if all children, not just the wanted children, not just the planned children, not just the children of the rich, not just the perfect children, but **all** children were regarded as the treasure they have always been? Can you imagine if all children were not just created equally, but were treated equally? Can you imagine the hope for good if every child was a reason to rejoice? Well, they are, you just haven't done so. And it really does take a village. But that isn't a bad thing. Investing in people and giving them the tools they need to become independent is not detrimental to all that we value. Helping mommies does not hurt children, it makes the burdens lighter, it makes hope burn brighter. It is simply what any good parent would give their own child. In fact, it is good, very good. Instead of burdens, children, no matter how we are conceived, should be called what we are—gifts, the future. The future is always a good investment. The wise know this. The foolish can't see past the end of their nose, and it is sadly, the only nose they care about.

For too many the answer to problems is to kill anything that costs them something. But we are talking about human beings, human beings with the same value as anyone who does or does not pay taxes. When you kill people, no matter their age or present skill level, you kill the things people will one day do. When you kill human beings, you kill science, business, technology, medicine, law, philosophy, literature, theatre, comedy, engineering, agriculture, manufacturing, architecture, journalism, business, banking, teaching, football, baseball, basketball, swimming, tennis, soccer, music, art, dance, poetry, fashion, photography, cooking, charity, love... We can never even begin to know what unique, great gifts were hidden in the humans we allowed to be treated as trash. Who can tell how much music has been lost, how many dances have gone undanced, how many jokes have gone untold, how many discoveries still lay hidden, or how many books have gone unwritten? How will we ever know how many battles have been lost, how many structures have not been built, or how many trees have gone unplanted? How many races and records have gone unrun, unbroken, how much progress has been stalled, how much love has been lost in the heap of humanity not allowed to live and give of the gifts within them. What should we do? Keep adding to the pile? Or maybe, we should treasure every life, no matter the price tag.

Mommies too need to be valued. The unending, demanding, selfless work they do has no match. But they need the same hope, the same chance as everybody else to know the full the potential that lies inside them. Mommies shouldn't have to lose their own lives because they have a little one to love. Being able to feel life grow inside you, well, that's a gift only given to women, an opportunity to give the world something only you can. Between the hearts of mother and child there is something so special, a bond which knows there is only one *me*, and I can only come from *you*. Mommies shouldn't be punished for bringing a life into the world any more than a child should be punished for existing. It is the world that should accommodate mommies. Sometimes a baby might feel more like a burden than a gift, but that's because of how women are treated, not because you carry a life inside you. I know women haven't been treated right, but little babies don't have to die to right that wrong. There are much better answers to those problems, answers that give mommies and babies a chance to pursue all the things that make life so wonderful. And life really is wonderful, when all people get a real chance at it.

I guess what I mean is this, you want women to thrive and that's good, but the words you use are misleading, untrue, and wrong. Justice, rights, equality, health, freedom, these are good things meant for all people, even children. You have refused to admit you have been wrong. But it doesn't change the truth. You have hijacked the language to make it for women alone. But we are taking it back. From now on those good words belong to women *and* babies, to anyone who finds themselves helpless and vulnerable. The justice you desire is in our shared equality, not the destruction of children, in our lives, not in our deaths, in the opportunity for us both, not in denying humanity of those too small to defend themselves. Justice *is* equity, both lives matter, not one group over another, not one life over another, but *liberty and justice for all.*

Babies for Justice

"*How can there be too many children? That is like saying there are too many flowers.*"

– Mother Theresa

"You don't have a soul. You are a soul. You have a body."

– *C.S. Lewis*

Dear America,

This is my country.
I want to ask you a few things...
If I don't understand life, can my life be taken?
If no one knows me, does that mean I am not alive?
If I do not know I am going to die, is it okay to kill me?
If my death is covered up, does that mean I never existed?
If I am asleep or unconscious and you kill me painlessly, is that acceptable?
If no one wants me or cares to take care of me, does that make it okay to kill me?
If I won't or can't remember what happened to me, can someone take my life from me?
If I am too small to defend myself or to survive on my own, is it okay to destroy me?
If I don't look like you, or do the things you do, is it okay to destroy my body and use parts of me for other people?
If it costs a bunch of money to take care of me, it is reasonable to kill me before the bills add up?
If more of us are killed than get to live, is it still a right?
How many have to die before it's a wrong?
If I don't contribute anything, can others take my life?
If I don't make any noise, do I belong in the trash?
If there are too many people alive, can some be killed?
If I am the smallest of small, do I have no worth at all?
When do I deserve to be protected?
When is my life my own?

The things you say scare me because you treat life so callously. They say if it happened before, it can happen again. And don't we all remember when...

"THEY CAME FIRST for the Communists,
  And I didn't speak up because I wasn't a Communist.
THEN THEY CAME for the Jews

And I didn't speak up because I wasn't a Jew,
THEN THEY CAME for the trade unionists
And I didn't speak up because I wasn't a trade unionist.
THEN THEY CAME for the Catholics,
And I didn't speak up because I was a Protestant.
THEN THEY CAME for me,
And by that time there was no one left to speak up."
- Martin Niemoller

Every human life, in its entirety, no matter how big, no matter how small, no matter what it can or can't do, no matter how feeble or silent or expensive, no matter how many cells that make up a human body, every human life deserves our protection at every stage because the life inside the body is a human one.

A small American citizen, small but equal to all

Dear Sojourner Truth,

I am afraid of what you would see today. I wonder what your words of truth would do. Would they work? Would they possess women and move women and overwhelm women as they did before? Would women see no other way but the right way? Would women seek good for all human beings, needy and not, instead of just good for them and them alone. I wonder...

The women you helped free are now demanding a right to kill me. Is this what you meant when you demanded, *"Ain't I a Woman?"*

When you said, "Look at me! Look at my arm!" and bared your powerful muscles that plowed and planted so all could see just how strong a woman can be, did you mean for women to use their strength to crush the weak and kill their children and defend it because, *"Ain't I a Woman?"*

When you said you could work as much and eat as much and be beaten as much as any man, did you mean to show that strong women should be free to do anything they wish to whomever they wish to get what they wish and no one should be allowed to stop them because, *"Ain't I a Woman?"*

When you cried a mother's grief over your children that you bore, when no one but Jesus heard your tears as they were taken from you and sold into slavery, did you mean that women should execute their own children so they wouldn't have to bother messing up their lives with loving a child? Is that what you meant by a woman's, by a mother's, grief? Is that what you meant when the rafters roared with the cheers of women as you shouted, *"Ain't I a woman?"*

When you asked what intellect had to do with women's rights or black folks' rights, did you mean it is understandable and acceptable to withhold what belonged to a person because of something they can or can't do? Did being a woman mean mothers should be able to own and destroy their children like they are property because they have not gotten as big and as strong and as smart and as able as a woman?

When you insisted on a cup full of rights, no matter the size of the cup, and it was wrong and mean for men to withhold what belonged to someone else, did you mean it was okay, acceptable, even good for women to withhold the same, small cup full of rights from their children because, "Ain't I a Woman?"

When you dared to declare the audacity of men thinking they have more rights than a woman, did you mean, however, that it is acceptable for women to take away the rights, even the lives of their children because "Ain't I a Woman?"

Well, ain't I a person? Ain't I the same value as a woman? Ain't I just as important as any person no matter my size or my smarts? Ain't I got the same rights and need the same protection as anybody else for this simple reason, *Ain't I human?*

Inspired by Sojourner Truth's speech, "Ain't I a Woman" at the 1851 Women's Rights Convention in Akron, Ohio

The Classic Report as recorded by Frances Gage in 1863, President of the Convention

Several ministers attended the second day of the Woman's Rights Convention, and were not shy in voicing their opinion of man's superiority over women. One claimed "superior intellect," one spoke of the "manhood of Christ," and still another referred to the "sin of our first mother."

Suddenly, Sojourner Truth rose from her seat in the corner of the church.

"For God's sake, Mrs. Gage, *don't* let her speak!" half a dozen women whispered loudly, fearing that their cause would be mixed up with Abolition.

Sojourner walked to the podium and slowly took off her sunbonnet. Her six-foot frame towered over the audience. She began to speak in her deep, resonant voice: "Well, children, where there is so much racket, there must be something out of kilter, I think between the Negroes of the South and the women of the North—all talking about rights—the white men will be in a fix pretty soon. But what's all this talking about?"

Sojourner pointed to one of the ministers. "That man over there says that women need to be helped into carriages, and lifted over ditches, and to have the best place everywhere. Nobody helps *me* any best place. *And ain't I a woman?*"

Sojourner raised herself to her full height. "Look at me! Look at my arm." She bared her right arm and flexed her powerful muscles. "I have plowed, I have planted and I have gathered into barns. And no man could head me. *And ain't I a woman?*"

"I could work as much, and eat as much as man—when I could get it—and bear the lash as well! *And ain't I a woman?* I have borne children and seen most of them sold into slavery, and when I cried out with a mother's grief, none but Jesus heard me. *And ain't I a woman?*"

The women in the audience began to cheer wildly.

She pointed to another minister. "He talks about this thing in the head. What's that they call it?"

"Intellect," whispered a woman nearby.

"That's it, honey. What's intellect got to do with women's rights or black folks' rights? If my cup won't hold but a pint and yours holds a quart, wouldn't you be mean not to let me have my little half-measure full?"

"That little man in black there! He says women can't have as much rights as men. 'Cause Christ wasn't a woman." She stood with outstretched arms and eyes of fire. "Where did your Christ come from?"

"*Where did your Christ come from?*" she thundered again. "From God and a Woman! Man had nothing to do with him!"

The entire church now roared with deafening applause.

"If the first woman God ever made was strong enough to turn the world upside down all alone, these women together ought to be able to turn it back and get it right-side up again. And now that they are asking to do it the men better let them."

"How wonderful it is that nobody need wait a single moment before starting to improve the world."

– Anne Frank

Dear Everyone,

So what can people do? Sometimes when you're stuck in a problem, all you want is out. And whichever solution offers the shortest, easiest, cheapest road, that is the road people want to take. Even more often people want to do the thing that is in their own best interests instead of the interests of everyone. It's very human and very common to think that way, but it doesn't make it right. What we all know is that the difficult choice, with its roadblocks, limited resources, and torturously long journey to an unidentified destination is the one that should be taken, however *less traveled*[60]. Despite selfish, fearful hearts, the hard road and the right road remain the same road.

But that doesn't mean our mommies should have to travel that road all by themselves. Everyone should help because we all need others at some time in our lives; and no one is as self-sufficient as they think they are. If everyone would just step back and take a larger, longer look they would see how much all our lives are intertwined and the small things that could make a big difference. Like a cup of cold water[61] when someone is dying of thirst, the help you offer can save our lives and our mommies—literally. That is just what the world needs, people who will give to make the world better for others, and make the journey down that right road not quite so hard and lonely.

For some reason, this is a hard idea to embrace: *needing, helping, saving* all sound like something reserved for losers, something most are too proud to accept. I guess I can see how it happened, how children became expendable in the drive for all that's achievable. Since everyone was young, all of you have been taught that one's character, who you are and how others perceive and judge you, is based on your ability to not need others, to be completely self-sufficient and independent. With this as not just the ideal, but the standard, it became easier for everyone to overlook selfishness, pride, ruthlessness, greed, and even corruption, as

---

[60] Robert Frost, <u>The Road Less Traveled</u>
[61] Matthew 10:42, "And if anyone gives even a cup of cold water to one of these little ones because he is My disciple, I tell you the truth, he will certainly not lose his reward." NIV

long as the process and the end result created the **self**-determined and the **self**-sufficient who had only them**selves** to thank. And yet we, the unplanned people, make all that you value nearly impossible for our mommies to achieve. When little people begin inside young women who, like everyone else, have been taught to value things, status, pride, and appearance by the work of their own hands, they quickly recognize that being a mommy makes them more needy and, therefore, more condemned than they are willing to be. Too often they believe there is no way to choose the right way. And seeing others value all the wrong things and get rewarded makes them think they were right about the wrong they did.

The truth is the problem of unexpected pregnancies, unexpected people, unexpected lives will always be with us until a way can be found to prevent boys from being boys, and girls from being girls. And I dare to say condemning our mommies hasn't worked. Yet even though we are an expensive annoyance to all the people with better things to do, new human beings with infinite worth, well... we are NOT a bad thing. What we are is wonderful beings. Despite how we came to be we have always been in the mind of our Maker, made for a purpose, with a reason and right to be alive, just like every other life. That's just like God, using all your mishaps and mistakes to make something miraculous. And here we are, your neighbors, your fellow citizens, as deserving as the blessings and opportunities of liberty as any of you. We and our mommies are both precious and full of potential and need your help to get through this hard time so we can live the lives we were meant to live.

Even though your culture tells you to think badly of people who need help, to hate people who cost money, and to determine the value of someone's life based on how much they acquire or the glory they gain for themselves, our Maker tells you to go out of your way to love people left for dead on the other side of the road. He tells you to *spend yourselves on behalf of the helpless, consider others more important than yourself, love others like you would want to be loved, to count everything that you earn, value, and determine your worth as LOSS, as NOTHING compared to knowing and loving the Son of God, and to treat those in desperate need as if they were HIM–CHRIST.*[62] He tells you to "Love without hypocrisy, abhor what is

---

[62] Isaiah 58:10, Philippians 2:3-4, Matthew 7:12, Matthew 22:39, Luke 6:31, Philippians 3:4-9, Matthew 25: 34-45

evil, cling to what is good."⁶³ So what has happened? Is our violent death so that our mommies aren't needy and consequently judged unworthy by the world... *good*? Is needing help now *evil*? If I HAVE nothing, does that mean I AM nothing? If you can be labeled a degenerate because of how much you have or earn, then can the same be said for the Son of Man who had no place to lay His head? Why do so many, even people who claim to know and love the Savior of mankind, do nothing to help us and our mommies and feel just fine about it? It's as if the world has so distorted the creed of Christ people behave as if they believe that He measures people by the things the world values. Yet if that were so, if He thought the way the world thought, why didn't He say...

"*Be successful. Win. Dominate. Go, and acquire great wealth for it will be with you always. Put your trust in money and be proud of all you have accomplished. For it was all because of you. **You** are all **you** need. Blessed are the rich. Blessed are those who are proud, and refuse to suffer for what is right and good. Be arrogant, for you have much to be proud of. Go, and judge those who don't have as much as you because they obviously don't work as hard and aren't as smart as you. It is permissible to kill the innocent or do nothing to help them if protecting and providing for them will cost you something or prevent you from achieving your goals and desires. Appearance is everything. Don't help those who are experiencing the consequences of their promiscuity. Make certain they are shamed and shunned and poor for their entire lives. Remind them of their failures, and brag about how good you are and how grateful that you aren't like them. Don't help. Don't give. Close your eyes and walk away from those who are suffering. HOARD, because you will be able to keep your money forever and after all, this is the chief end of man. Let the giving you do only be done for purposes of tax credits, your interests, and for boasting. The tiny gifts the poor give are truly pathetic and do not deserve to be compared to the great sums, percentages, and generosity of the wealthy.*"

But He didn't say that because that's not Him. He said LOVE ... *love like I have loved you*. And when you look at how much He loved us, how much He gave us, and how much none of us deserve Him, any can see this is a good goal, worthy of our time, energy, heart, and even money. Because the simple truth is that God loves people, not money, and it is people that He wants to save, not 401K's. Too many have

---

⁶³ Romans 12:9 (NKJV)

forgotten that He calls the poor, the humble, those who suffer fighting for what is right, *Blessed*. Too many have forgotten what He loves and where His heart is and put their trust in things which can never last. But God is good and full of mercy. He reminds people not to trust the deceitfulness of wealth, [64] which has a tendency to sprout wings and fly away,[65] but instead pursue Him, His Kingdom and all that it stands for, then He will provide all the other things you need.[66]

"But I do think hardly of you," I said; "and I'll tell you why- not so much because you refused to give me shelter or regarded me as an impostor, as because you just now made it a series of reproach that I had no 'brass' (money) and no house. Some of the best people that ever lived have been as destitute as I am; and if you are a Christian, you ought not to consider poverty a crime."
– from Jane Eyre, Charlotte Brontë

So could you please help us? Could you join the human race instead of the rat race? Could you chase Him and help us instead of keeping up with the Joneses? Would you put your treasures in heaven instead of here on earth, and love us, the helpless, more than yourself?

You see, we babies feel like we are either despised, forgotten, or ignored. Some people want to solve this problem of women and children by getting rid of us, by freeing women from motherhood, so women *appear* demure, responsible, chaste, successful, in control of their lives, all that is supposedly comprised in being good, but in reality it just looks good. You know I do wish there were more goodness, not the kind that says "Look how I follow the rules, what's *your* problem?" but the kind that is busy treating others well, binding up broken hearts, and loving the unlovely, the kind of goodness that gives, not expecting anything in return... But anyway, other people want to solve the problem of us by quoting statistics of how many of our mothers have children out of wedlock, the slur, the label, not so subtly simmering under their numbers. *Everyone* knows what they mean. The ugly statistic brands the mothers who are unwillingly counted and grouped according to their ring finger and their womb. They are told what they are because of what they have borne, and shame is bestowed and expected of them. If they attempt to reject shame, they are labeled rebellious or worse.

---

[64] Matthew 13:22
[65] Proverbs 23:5
[66] Matthew 6:33

Yet no one ever tells us how many men are with girls they aren't married to, how many lies they tell, how they manipulate, how they use women, how many they impregnate, and the obvious disgraceful state of their character for such activity. It's as if our foolish mommies get pregnant all by themselves, carelessly wrecking civilized society in the process. If that is the great wrong, if it is just sex outside of marriage that is so unacceptable, then certainly both our mommies AND our daddies would be chastised and labeled. But they're not. Why? For what reason are only the girls who have sex, get pregnant, and **don't** kill their child the ones who get stuck with the scarlet letter and carry the blame of ruin? How many grown-ups have been with someone before they were married, or worse, to another person when they were married to someone else? How many have had *many, many* partners and where is the outcry against them? How many men have used women like they are things? Why is it only unwed mothers that are shoved to the bottom of the pile so everyone can stomp on them? Why is pregnancy the crime to be punished? Does this somehow make society better? Does this help these women, these children, or those of us just growing and not big enough to be born? There is so much hypocrisy and cruelty and no one seems to see, no one seems to care.

The way people crush and blame, I wish you could understand what it does to the heart of a girl and see how tiny babies are treated; I wish you could see the heaviness carried in so many hearts. But all I can do is point out the truth and hope people big enough and brave enough will do something to change it. Some people tell women to "not get pregnant," and if they do, "suck it up and take responsibility, while you listen to us to tell you what a whore and a loser you are because you are not self-sufficient, not married, because people who are successful and who have achieved are having their money taken from them to help stupid, irresponsible, lazy girls like *you*." Still others tell our mommies we don't matter, we are nothing, that we need their permission to keep living because we are their property. And then, of course, is all the talk about the "wrongs brought on by liberalism, by the sexual revolution, and the deploring state of present affairs because so few practice morality and virtue." Maybe that's true. But I think there is much more to the mess. Besides, I don't think the self-righteousness that passes for virtue is really all that wonderful. It tends to leave a great many girls vulnerable to a great many wrongs and allows a cruel, condemning pride to grow in the hearts of others where it shouldn't. Greater than promiscuities is something else which compels. I think quite simply everyone wants to be happy. Some people think pleasure will make them so. Far more, especially girls, think it will come from being wanted, being desired, being held intimately by the boy they adore. That is what their hearts tell them. *"Cause when you're fifteen and someone tells you they love you, you're gonna believe them."*[67] Others discover a child is inside them through no will of their own and find themselves raped of the happiness they were pursuing. The little human lives that begin inside *all* these different young women are not evidence of feminine "virtuelessness," but rather of the restless, yearning hearts inside them, running from pain, or desperately seeking and believing they will be happy in all the wrong places. How shallow do your theories, mandates, and statistics sound when weighed against the yearnings of a human heart. How much sweeter are the words, "How may I help you?"

I would be remiss if I didn't mention that this is about more than just how to help us and our mommies. The other truth just as powerful at maintaining the destruction of innocent children is that no one wants to be judged. No woman joyfully embraces the reality that she has killed her baby. It is a truth that crushes, which is why it is so furiously denied. The lie is a lot easier to live with. It is true that some brutes enjoy pointing a self-righteous finger at these conflicted, denying hearts. Still others clumsily try to speak truth in love. A hurting, hostile front awaits their attempt, justified by the callousness of those before them who have not known this particular hurt and fear. What makes it so hard for you and others to take a stand against our death is that so often the women who have willfully ended their child's life are women you love, women who are lovely, kind, generous, feminine, women who have gone on to become good mothers. How can you oppose them? You love them... But it's not okay to ignore the reality of all that happens to us and accept apathy just because you love the people who believed the lie that they had no choice. Kind people can do cruel things, good people can walk by on the other side of the road, generous people can steal, honest people can tell lies. And a lie is a lie no matter who tells it. What many don't realize is that this is the same battle waged so long ago in our country, the one that kept so many mouths shut, and so many

---

[67] Taylor Swift *Fifteen*

from fighting for what is right and good and just. People were afraid to fight against slavery, against the idea that any person could own another and do whatever they wished for any reason they wished, because they personally knew so many people who were guilty of it. They didn't want to say the truth they knew would convict. But this is never a reason to NOT do right. Truth requires courage as much as it requires love.

And the wonderful truth is... God is merciful, and there is hope and redemption in Him. He wants us to recognize the wrong we all do and weep over it, casting it on the cross, not hiding it in our hearts. He wants us to say, "I was wrong," instead of insisting a wrong is a right. For the fearful and convicted, I guess I would tell you to remember that the man whom God chose to lead His people out of an oppressed land to a promised one was a murderer, the boy whom God helped kill a giant and rule a nation was one too, and the man whom God's Son chose to build His church denied Him at His darkest hour. *BUT* with God's grace and God's goodness they were able to speak truth and do right, not because they denied what they had done, but because they accepted the mercy, power, and love of God, whose forgiveness is limitless to those who put their trust in Him.

Since no one is perfect, and some have faults and flaws and failures that aren't worn around one's belly for the world to see, maybe instead of pointing fingers you could offer that kind, helping hand without prejudice, just love. Maybe you and others could all work together to save lives instead of letting them get crushed. Maybe you could work for the good of all, instead of just good for yourself. But how can that be done, how does it translate from words to works?

When you are talking about living and dreaming, one thing must come before all else, surviving. Our mommies need a way to carry us, keep us, and survive before they are able to thrive. And that means all the things that are required to live a life need to be within their means. It's true some girls have families who support the daughters they love in all these ways. But too many don't. These girls are on their own attempting to do right, but without the means to do so. It is not a lack of work ethic. Anyone who has been a mommy knows how difficult it is and how much it takes from you. "*As hard as you think it is, you'll end up wishing it was that easy.*"[68] It is a lack of worth being placed on the work

---

[68] *Terms of Endearment*

they are limited to. It is a lack of jobs that will pay enough for all their expenses and us. It is a lack of time they can give because their time is demanded by these little ones they love. The fears are real and as unwavering as an eviction, an empty refrigerator or gas tank, a hungry child, and no power. They don't see how they will be able to work enough and earn enough money to live and raise their child. They don't see how they could ever give their child away, never see them again, and not live every day with a broken heart. What will you do for them? What can be done to make loving us little ones and living reachable, possible, and dare I say affordable, so people don't die or wish they had?

So you see, *many* things need to change to begin things again. But first people will need to change. You will need to value different things. You will need to treat others like you would want to be treated if you found yourself in the shoes our mommies don't want to be in either. You will need to do what is best for all, not just some, not just yourselves. You will need to stop deciding right and wrong based on how much it will cost. You will need to measure responsibility with opportunity, compassion with discipline, and frugality with comfort and love. I'm certain these are words that run the risk of infuriating a great many, but that's okay, as long as enough people step up to love, we'll be fine. After all, the wisest of old fools recognized that the evil attack virtue far more often than the righteous defend it, and if you are going to fight, you have to make do with what's at hand.[69] So I guess we are just waiting for the fools from La Mancha, who will rush in with courage and love, to rescue and defend no matter the cost, image or otherwise, because *who* they save is greater than *what* they give up.

From,
All of us

For it is He who died for her and it is His image she bears. "*She is the human and sacred image; all around her the social fabric shall sway and split and fall; the pillars of society by shaken, and the roofs of ages come rushing down; and not one hair of her head shall be harmed.*"
– G.K. Chesterton

---

[69] Dr. Raymond Dennehy, <u>Anti-Abortionist At Large</u>; prologue.

"Something is out of whack in our society. For people ought to be able to provide their own needs. When will and effort are organized and still fall short, this means only that the resources needed are locked up somewhere. And no amount of talk about 'private property' or 'free enterprise' will ever touch the real moral issue of our responsibility to others."

– John Perkins

Dear Big People,

Money. Is it so strange that a child would bring it up? Maybe. But I have to talk about it because it is very much a reason why our mommies pay someone to kill us, and why the poor, those with barely anything, barely surviving, are by and large mommies and their babies. Everyone knows that everyone needs money to buy the things needed to keep living, but too many have forgotten that money isn't worthy to be compared to the nature and value of life itself. When I think about living and dreaming and the life I would live if I get the chance, it's not money that I dream about. Maybe that is the dream for some, but for us little ones that don't know that everything has a price, we dream differently. To call making money **"The"** American Dream falls so short and demands that a country of free people all seek the same dream. It's silly and small-minded.

You see, some of us dream we will fly, some of us dream of exploring a big world, or growing, building, creating, and some of us dream of loving, teaching, and sharing the good news of a *God who so loved the world*. Those are all good dreams, and they are American dreams because little Americans dream them. Maybe all of you big people wouldn't be in such a fret over trying to figure out right and wrong based on how much things cost if you realized that making lots of money shouldn't be a dream we are all forced to seek just to survive and justify being alive. If you are right and money is what matters, then when should children realize they are supposed to dream and live to seek money? How old should a child be so that, *"When gazing at a graph that shows the profits up, their little cup of joy should overflow"*? Should all the moneymakers nod and rejoice saying, *"Yes, Quite right. Exactly"*[70]? What a sad thought. How are so many oblivious to what really matters, to the

---

[70] *Mary Poppins*

dreams and hearts of children who know so much better what true joy is and where it might be found, or how money, despite its uses, doesn't last? The truth is more dreams need to come true for more people, and everyone needs that opportunity despite the things that happen that no one ever plans. Even I, as young and as poor as I am, have a dream, and it is just as valid as any even though my dream is not about taking more, demanding more or having more.

My dream is that every life would be seen as precious and valuable, not because of its net worth, but because of its human dignity. I believe valuing and protecting people just because they are people honors us all, and makes Him smile.

Love,
Little People

> She told him she'd rather fix her makeup than try to fix what's going on...
> We're so confident in our accomplishments, look at our decadence...
> Life is more than money, time was never money.
> Time was never cash, life is still more than girls.
> Life is more than hundred dollar bills and rotor-tom fills.
> Life is more than fame and rock and roll and thrills,
> All the riches of the kings end up in wills
> We've got information in the information age
> But do we know what life is outside of our convenient Lexus cages?
> She said, he said live like no tomorrow
> Every moment that we borrow brings us closer
> to the God who's not short of cash
> Hey Bono, I'm glad you asked.
> Life is still worth living, Life is still worth living.
> Life is more than you are.
>
> Gone – Switchfoot

What are we striving for anyway? Why are we here? What is it that makes life worth living? As C.S. Lewis pointed out, the problem with our desires is they are "not too strong, but too weak. We are half-hearted creatures fooling about with drink and sex and ambition when infinite joy is offered us... We are far too easily pleased."[71] It is easier to make love and sex, money and possessions, titles and praise be the end-all purpose of life. Much harder is the commitment to seeking truth, righting wrongs, speaking truth, stopping injustice, loving the unlovely, doing the right things for the right reasons, seeking to glorify Truth Himself with every thought, word, and deed, and forgetting ourselves in the process. But it is this walk that offers such joy and demands such courage that it somehow makes the journey and the destination offer more than the original tiny distractions could ever pretend to hold. I said many things need to change, but people will need to change. They will have to want what is truly worthwhile and good—life, liberty, and true joy for all.

For it is not only the pretty pictures, the pretty lives that are worth saving, and it is wrong to allow this thinking in any measure. The struggle, the ugly, painful, dirty, hard stuff is what should make us strive for something better and grow into something beautiful, full of strength, grace, and love. I'd hate to believe that humanity was only willing to grow to the point of being cute and self-serving, as if the

---

[71] C.S. Lewis, The Weight of Glory, originally published in Theology, 1941.

maturity and selfish whims of toddlers was our highest ideal, complete with tantrums when things don't go our way. Certainly we can see and even seek the goodness that comes when people push through the pain to become the best kind of humans, the kind that care about everybody else.

These children and their mothers need our help to stay alive. It is our job to care. It is our job to make life possible. We don't have a colored ribbon, a multimillion-dollar campaign, and the support of the media, the government, the courts, or the culture. All we have is our time, our gifts, our money, our love, and the truth which belongs to a God who cares and answers us when we pray. We think that is all we need as long as we determine to speak truth and love through everything we say and most importantly everything we do. We seek the will and the help of the one who made both mother and child for *Himself*, and do what pleases Him, love them.

> Give me Your eyes for just one second; Give me Your eyes so I can see
> Everything that I keep missing, Give me Your love for Humanity
> Give me Your arms for the broken hearted the ones that are far beyond my reach
> Give me Your Heart for the ones forgotten, Give me Your eyes so I can see
> – *Brandon Heath*

Dear Young Mother,

I know you are so scared. So was I. I know you are poor, hungry, far from home. So was I. I know the man with you is not the father of your child. Neither was mine. I know you feel shame, and being accused of something you're not is a very real fear. I know you are scared of what people are saying and how they will treat you. Me too. I know you don't know how you are going to make it. I didn't either. I know you didn't plan this. Neither did I. I know you feel like a castaway, a stranger. So did I. I know you are terrified of what your life will be like now. Yes, I know that fear well. I know how hard it is to sleep with the weight of the world on you.

But I was blessed. And so are you. I had hope. And one day, so will you. I had hope because of what I knew about Him. Promises I knew to be true. I knew that He promised to scatter the proud and put down the mighty. I knew He promised to exalt the lowly and fill the hungry with good things. I knew He promised mercy to those who fear Him from generation to generation. I knew He kept His promises. I knew Him to be true.

It's your turn now, your turn to see His mercy and goodness and love. It's your turn to find out the blessing that you carry inside you. Peace, peace... that is my prayer for you until the day you know joy like you have never known before. And love, yes that too.

Love,
Mary

> *Silent night, holy night*
> *All is calm, all is bright*
> *Round yon virgin, mother and child*
> *Holy infant, so tender and mild*
> *Sleep in heavenly peace,*
> *Sleep in heavenly peace*

Do not be afraid, Mary, for you have found favor with God. And behold, you will conceive in your womb and bring forth a Son, and shall call his name JESUS... For with God nothing will be impossible... And it happened, when Elizabeth heard the greeting of Mary, that the babe leaped in her womb; and

Elizabeth was filled with the Holy Spirit. Then she spoke out with a loud voice and said, "Blessed are you among women, and blessed is the fruit of your womb! But why is this granted to me, that the mother of my Lord should come to me? For indeed, as soon as the voice of your greeting sounded in my ears, the babe leaped in my womb for joy."

Luke 1:30, 37, 41-44 (NKJV)

– The Beginning–

In the last public speech of William Wilberforce's life on January 1, 1833 he said this, "I say, and say honestly and fearlessly, that the same Being who commands us to love mercy, says also, 'Do justice.'" Suddenly, a ray of sunshine shone through the hall; seizing the moment the old warrior of reform said, "The object is bright before us, the light of heaven beams on it, and is an earnest of success." July 26, 1833 the House of Commons voted to spend a sum equal to 2 billion dollars today to purchase the freedom of all enslaved in the British colonies and abolish slavery throughout. His thoughts were of extreme gratitude to God to have witnessed the day when his country would spend such money to abolish slavery. He died three days later on July 29, 1833 having spent his life fighting fearlessly for the abolition of the slave trade, slavery, and 70 other reforms.[72]

APPENDIX

Ideas For Promoting A More Just Society

To some the words "just society" sound like socialism, progressivism, liberalism, or some other -ism. To me they sound like what my Savior told me to pursue, a kingdom on earth that seeks the things that honor the King of Heaven, "His Kingdom come, His will be done, on earth as it is in Heaven." Hopefully, you will see ideas in this appendix that could do exactly that. The following pages contain some suggestions that could be implemented to promote an atmosphere where the lives, work, and dreams of all people are valued. However, I humbly recognize others may have plans better than my own, and I encourage them to pursue them. My reason for including these thoughts and ideas is that I did not want to leave this subject without suggesting some solutions and course of action. Harriet Beecher Stowe concluded *Uncle Tom's Cabin* with an array of thoughts and ideas, William Wilberforce addressed social problems with pragmatic solutions and the volunteer efforts of societies promoting good across the British Empire, and William Booth published *The Darkest England and the Way Out*, which exposed the ills facing the impoverished and his solutions for these problems, which included the need for employment offices, missing persons services, and other agencies which are an integral part of our

---

[72] Kevin Belmonte, <u>A Journey Through the Life of William Wilberforce</u>

society, but which were revolutionary at the time.[73] Never did any of these heroes of justice and seekers of truth promote that killing the helpless or unwanted, or ignoring, trivializing, or condemning the suffering of fellow citizens was the path or solution needed to promote "liberty and justice for all." Still today, good people pursuing what is good for all is the best answer to our worst problems. So please permit me a few pages to share a few ideas and let yourself imagine where such changes could take us.

⋯

---

[73] Jesus Freaks Vol. 2; dc Talk; p. 166

ECONOMIC POLICY – PRO GROWTH/ PRO BUSINESS/ PRO LABOR

"It is the interest of the commercial world that wealth be found everywhere."[74]

In the great span of American history we have been blessed with many heroes for many purposes. Wisdom requires we learn from them and emulate them to promote the general welfare of the American people. Like many, I love President Ronald Reagan. To me he was all a president should be, heroic, stalwart, idealistic, efficient, with a great love for the people. While not every policy was perfect, there were general principles that guided him that can guide us as well. Everyone knows he hated taxes and constantly sought to stimulate the economy by lowering them. Yet that wasn't all, besides communism, despotism, and taxes there was something else he hated—inflation. He viewed inflation as much an enemy of the people as high taxes. Wisely he recognized inflation ate the wages of Americans like nothing else, and that is why he promoted true competition in the marketplace and the decrease of burdens on business so they could lower prices.

Others as well used their wisdom and work to grow this nation. Henry Ford has always been a favorite of mine. The great genius of Henry Ford was not the Model T, his efficiency and economy, the freedom that the automobile provided, or even the assembly line. Quite simply, his genius was in realizing that if he wanted to mass-produce a product to generate great wealth, he needed a mass population to be able to afford to purchase his product. He paid his employees wages that allowed them the ability to purchase the product they built and to participate in the rewards of their labor. In doing so he fueled the economy, built a middle class, and rescued many from poverty.

Today a similar wisdom is necessary in this difficult and changing economy. The reality is wages and the supply of jobs have not kept pace with food, gas, housing, and the rising cost of living. Economic theories teach us that by lowering taxes companies should have more money to invest, hire new workers, and raise wages with the increase in revenue,

---

[74] Edmund Burke, English Statesman

which is the logic behind the trickle down theory. But real life tells a different story, a reality in which profit does not trickle down, but over, over to investors and stockholders whose wealth, barring corruption and a complete collapse of the stock market, continues to increase or at the very least be a priority over maintaining or improving the wages of employees the wages of employees. When there is an economic downturn or reduction in profit, wages and employees are viewed as a cost only, something to cut, something to discard, after all, those who invest have a right to expect a return on their investment. Those who control the capital do not let it trickle down. They determine the labor done by the least is of little value and pay accordingly. (Although, serving on boards, lavish executive perks and parties, and running companies into the ground is apparently work worth millions per executive per annum!) Many hard working employees have seen their hours cut down to nearly nothing while prices are raised and companies show profits to reward investors and attract new investors. In several industries they are able to continue to raise prices by producing a limited supply, therefore creating demand and competing companies charge equivalent, as opposed to competitive prices. Efforts to protect workers by raising wages and raising taxes have most often resulted in job loss, reduced growth and profit, and inflation, making the increase in wages ineffective, and keeping all people from spending money, resulting in more profit and job loss.

However, with all the talk about the stock market most Americans are just trying to pay all their bills and have enough left over to take the family out once in a while to actually attempt to enjoy life. Dreams are a luxury they cannot afford. There is not even enough extra left over to do something as wise and luxurious as saving or investing. If that is not enough, every day those with very little get to hear themselves reproved and rebuked for what they lack by those who have "worked hard, who have achieved, who are successful." Apparently the measure of hard work, achievement, and success is how much you have accumulated. Having a dream that does not produce wealth or a life circumstance that prevents you from creating such wealth becomes evidence of your work ethic and character. And yet telling people they are losers and they don't deserve homes doesn't help them find sufficient employment to help them lose the label. What I am trying to say is this: Americans do not want handouts, Americans want good jobs. They want their effort, their labor, to be enough to actually pay for their and their families' needs and dreams and to experience the dignity and fulfillment that follows.

So where and how can we apply the wisdom of Ford and Reagan? How can we offer opportunity and prosperity to a greater number of Americans and to a greater degree? How do we protect against policies that destroy growth? How do we facilitate self-sufficiency among the citizenry despite the many different skills and circumstances of individuals, knowing that in doing so we liberate ourselves from depending on the government, as well as liberate government to focus on its most pressing responsibilities. How do we create good jobs so people of all stages can support themselves and their families and contribute to the economy and the country?

There is a solution that can provide for workers while promoting an environment for growth and profit for investors. The idea is that companies could have the option of paying the standard tax rate or qualify for a tax rate as low as 10%. The lower tax rate would be a direct result of how much they pay employees who fall into the lower income brackets. For whatever % wages and hours are increased, a corresponding reduced tax rate would be applied.

The benefits would include the increased spending power of laborers without raising inflation, which would stimulate the economy, increase profit, provide more opportunities for investors, boost the investment capital of companies, and reduce the amount of welfare needed by the most poor, thereby decreasing the offensive "nanny" role of government. Companies would not lose money from the increase in wages because this expense would be offset by lower taxes, and because they could still choose the wages and tax rate which best fits their circumstances. Additionally, if it is in a company's interest to pay their employees better wages, then the relationship between labor and management could improve, resulting in less need for and power of unions. The opportunity for a low tax rate would encourage foreign companies to trade with America, create an atmosphere where entrepreneurs could begin new enterprises, which would provide more jobs at every level, and an alternative to outsourcing for American companies. All of these activities would stimulate the economy, thereby increasing the tax revenue of the American government, which could be used to pay off the national debt and strengthen the dollar.

So that's one idea. I do not think it is the only one. But I think it is a good one that could help owner, worker, investor, and state. I think it could help single mothers and children by providing more money for the jobs they find themselves confined to when they are young and have not yet gained the experience and education that would provide better employment, or when they have the constraints of motherhood and are limited by what hours they can work. I think it could save lives because it could sustain life. Earning more money makes surviving more possible, more realistic, with the added benefit of something invisible. When money is earned by the work of one's own hand and meets a person's needs, it provides something else just as essential to self-sufficiency, the confidence, the hope, and the dignity to strive further, dream bigger, to endure through the hard times.

Here is another idea. Repeatedly we hear about relief organizations going out into impoverished countries and empowering women to feed and provide for their own children by helping them set up small businesses with micro-loans, the small percentage interest charged being used to continue the program to help more single mothers, each loan not only a stepping-stone to their own independence and self-sufficiency, but a small part of a big plan to help countless others. All that has been required to qualify is to be in need. The assistance, ethical conduct of the agencies loaning and distributing the money, and the ultimate goal of independence have made a remarkable difference in lives and communities all over the world. Why can't we do that here? Is it because of the bad credit of those single mothers, the lack of related experience, the lack of capital or assets, the smallness of their small business venture that makes single mothers here are not worth the risk? Don't people see that the poor here are the same as the poor anywhere? We are not called to pity the poor in foreign countries and despise the poor in our own. It is the same problem, women with children, alone and struggling to survive. I just don't see why a solution that can work all over the world couldn't work here. Sadly, I think it is because doing good doesn't produce a profit. But if people had vision, if they could see what these young women could become if given the opportunity, maybe then they would see the dreams of these women are worth the investment.

These two ideas alone will not create an environment where those in the most desperate of circumstances can choose right, choose life and not starve. The cost of living must come down, especially the cost of housing, but food, energy, clothing, and transportation, as well. How do we do that? Competition. Something has happened to competition in this country. It used to be that a business would offer a better deal, better product, better price. But the oddest thing has happened in the marketplace. Businesses are offering goods that are of lesser quality for higher prices. One company raises prices, and the rest follow instead of compete, or even dare to do the wise, compassionate thing and lead the way to a truly free and competitive market. Profit, not people, are all that matters.

...

"He says their faults are owing to us, and that it would be cruel to make their faults and punish it too. He says we shouldn't do any better, in their place."
— Stowe 180

OBJECTIONS IN PURSUING A POLICY THAT VALUES THE WORK OF THE LEAST

"If he needs a million acres to make him feel rich, seems to me it 'cause he feels awful poor inside hisself, and if he's poor in hisself, there ain't no million acres gonna make him feel rich, an' maybe he's disappointed that nothin' he can do'll make him feel rich."[75]

Of course there will always be greedy voices that will viciously seek to crush the poor and keep them that way because they have not been in such shoes. But I believed all I was taught. I believed people cared and they were just standing on sound conservative economic principle and theory. But I was wrong. Like a good little girl who was taught how a government operates, that is by the people, that her representative was her voice, I took my ideas to people bigger than myself. My congressman after listening and liking this new idea asked me to contact several different conservative lobby organizations and send them the proposal to see if they could help me with the numbers and with promoting the idea. Apparently, a lobby is how to get things done in government, so I contacted them. One foundation never responded to my inquiries. Another said it sounded too hard and *had I not heard of the Fair Tax?* Still another nearly snarled with hateful rhetoric and barely let me speak. Just the idea of paying the poor more for their labor offended him.

---

[75] John Steinbeck, <u>Grapes of Wrath</u>.

"There are people doing work out there that's not even worth the minimum wage!"... (To which I tried to explain that the minimum wage was needed because of the cost of living, the costs of goods.)... The insults kept flying until the final declaration: "The only reason those people are stuck in those bad, low-paying jobs is because of the bad life choices they've made!" ... I knew the rich hated the poor, but I was stunned by these words. I gulped in my own condemnation by someone I had never met. As I pondered his words I realized the bad life decision I had made, the only decision I had made that kept me needing these "bad jobs" was choosing to have my children. It is and was the one and **only** thing that has kept me from seeking financial freedom. There was nothing else that prevented me from the only American dream apparently **worth** seeking. The same is true for every single mother like me, who by and large make up the detestable poor. I guess the wise, prudent, financially responsible choice would have been to abort our children so we could be free to make money. Far worse is my and others' foolish expectation that our labor should be able to pay our most basic needs! God forbid I let my child stand in the way of being ambitious, successful, or rich! (Since the only crime I and my leechlike counterparts have actually committed to obtain this vulnerable, detestable predicament is that of having sex, I of course, am certain those promoting this rhetoric are not hypocrites. I'm sure they would never utter such words unless they were as chaste as nuns. But somehow I think this unlikely.)

...

COST OF LIVING: PRICES & COMPETITION

As the destitute and impoverished family prepares to leave for California in Steinbeck's Grapes of Wrath *they discover some merchants are cheating them even in their needy state. The grandfather observes, "Fella in business got to lie and cheat, but he calls it somepin else... You steal that tire an' you're a thief, but he tried to steal your four dollars for a busted tire. They call that sound business."*[76]

Why is everything so expensive anyway? When I first began to write this portion of the appendix, I felt very small. I imagined all the

---

[76] John Steinbeck, Grapes of Wrath.

pundits and people who want to make lots of money saying how naïve and foolish my comments are. But then I realized that my thoughts and perceptions DO matter, for the simple reason that I am a consumer. And while important people might want to make this about indexes, rates, fluctuations, quarter profit margins, and confidence in the market, it's really very simply about how much consumers make each month, what they need and want, how much of it there is, where it comes from, and how much it all costs. These concepts are not only completely within my ability to understand, they are intertwined in most every decision I make. Additionally, I have the ability to see how the greed of others is passed down to the consumers, what effect it has on prices, how supply and demand are manipulated and controlled, and the truth about wages. It really is all simple common sense. So I will not only comment, I will criticize and critique, and I even dare to do the audacious act of recommending appropriate and fair action. Yes, I might just be an ordinary citizen, but that is precisely the reason why my thoughts matter, because it is in my vested interest to make living for the common man more affordable.

I was discussing inflation with an official of Bank of America. I used the example of retail and discussed how the price of a T-shirt five years ago in almost any clothing retailer was $10-$20, a top $25-$35, a dress $40-$70, jeans $30-$50 and how today the same T-shirt is $30-$60 (a T-SHIRT!! Are you kidding me?), the same top is $80, the same dress $150, same jeans $120, often of less quality. Even discount sellers have raised prices significantly. They will often raise prices for a short time and then advertise new low prices that are actually more than the original price. Yet no cotton crop has failed, there has been no **drastic** increase in the cost of production or generous trickle to labor. In fact, most of the production has been sent to countries where laborers are paid one/tenth of wages in the U.S., so the costs to actually make the products are extremely low. Wages here increase in fifty-cent increments biannually if, and only if, it's in the budget, although workers receive fewer and fewer hours. That means they make *less* money now than they did years earlier when goods were at lower prices. What has risen is the profit and earnings of top executives and investors. Consumers have a choice in style, but little in the way of price. It is as if there is an unspoken monopoly or cooperative price fixing that eliminates competition. The Bank of America official nodded as I explained and said, "Yes, we see the same thing in banking. We raise our fees from $20 to $25 to $35 and everyone is in an uproar, but as soon as it quiets down all the other banks raise their fees equal to ours." When speculators forced gas prices to jump to $4 and $5 a gallon, we were forced to pay that price if we needed to go anywhere or buy anything that had to be shipped; and today when a barrel of oil is approximately $50, the gas companies have not lowered the prices back down to the prices they were when oil was that price. They are still overcharging. All of them. Where, might I ask, is the competition?

Companies depend on the consumer to survive, but collectively demand more and more for what they offer. They have collected power by fleecing the American public together, *collectively*, despite all the talk about free enterprise. They are as much about co-ops and consolidating power for their own purposes as the most ardent community organizer. They just have the ability to conceal their prosperous alliances. It's as if everyone forgot why monopolies, price fixing, price gouging, and a lack of choice are bad. It's because "power tends to corrupt; absolute power corrupts absolutely." Faceless robber barons feast on a public that does not have the means, the land, the tools, the horse to grow their own food, make their own clothes, and transport themselves. We are at the mercy of their greed. We have no choice but to pay whatever they charge. Some might say because I point out unfairness in the marketplace that my words incite class warfare. But instead I remember, and I quote an old book that speaks truth and justice by the One who is both, "The LORD abhors dishonest scales, but a just weight is His delight... A kindhearted woman gains respect, but ruthless men gain only wealth... The wicked man earns deceptive wages... *Though they* join forces, the wicked will not go unpunished, but the posterity of the righteous will be delivered... 'So I will come near you for judgment; I will be quick to testify against sorcerers, adulterers, and perjurers, against those who defraud laborers of their wages, who oppress the widows and the fatherless, and deprive aliens of justice, but do not fear Me,' says the LORD Almighty." Proverbs 11:1, 16, 18a (NIV), 21 (NKJV) & Malachi 3:5 (NIV).

...

"But the age of chivalry is gone. That of sophisters[77], economists, and calculators has succeeded; and the glory of Europe [and America] is extinguished forever."[78]

---

[77] Those who practice sophistry, which is a method of argumentation that seems clever but is actually flawed, dishonest, or intended to deceive (American Heritage Dictionary).

HOUSING AND THE GREAT DEMAND... for more

"The grabbing hands grab all they can, all for themselves, after all – It's a competitive world. Everything counts in large amounts."[79]

Housing, well so much has been said, I prefer to discuss apartments to make my point, which is where most of those lazy, degenerate, single mothers reside with their children, myself included. But general opinion is this; many have blamed the housing problem on the poor or stupid who bought homes they couldn't afford. However, what can the poor afford? Where are the houses that are clean, safe, and in a decent school district that are in their price range? Why were homeowners charging more and more than their homes were legitimately worth? Because they could? Why were most builders raising the prices of the homes they built for $100,000 in each phase they began instead of building homes that matched the wages of workers without the need for creative lending? Because they could? Why are there so many people who can only afford to live in apartments and how much do they pay to live there? Is it reasonable? Typically, there are corporations which run several large properties in various regions. What has happened across the country is they have also raised prices as builders and homeowners raised prices on homes. Then, wanting to continue to make more money, rent was radically raised on their units across the board every year. The result is those who do not have much, who "don't deserve a home", are forced to pay much because they have no other option, which means they can't wisely save as a good girl should for the home that could protect them from landlords. Each year the landlord raises their rent, often $100 more a month as a *thank you* for their continued patronage. Other complexes, instead of offering a dramatically competitive price, instead of saying, "What that community is charging is ridiculous and is robbing the poor, the ones who need money the most to just survive. You can live here for so much less!" They charge $50 less and call that competition. Businesses think, well, they got away with it, why shouldn't we? We want more. Eureka! We will CHARGE MORE TOO!" Wow. What a radically innovative idea to make money. However did they come up with it?

---

[78] Edmund Burke, English Statesman
[79] Depeche Mode, *Everything Counts*

There is a true story from the American frontier that can teach us all a great deal about prices, supply and demand, the cost of living, and right and wrong. Many of you will recognize it. There was a time in our history when people built homes from the trees that grew on their land, a time when people would gather together to build a home or a barn, a time when people usually worked together for the good of all instead of demanding the right to exploit each other or judge each other by how much each possessed. Greed and selfishness when it did emerge rose in shocking contrast to what was right and how neighbors and citizens **should** treat each other. In Laura Ingalls Wilder's book, <u>The Long Winter</u>, an entire town is cut off from all resources and food and is on the verge of starving to death. The young, heroic Cap and Almanzo ventured off into a frozen prairie to find a rumored storehouse of wheat and return, nearly freezing in the process, but delivering the wheat to the local merchant. The next day the local merchant priced the wheat at a price so high that the pioneers would have to give him everything they had just to keep their families alive. Certainly, economic theory was on his side. He controlled all of the limited supply and there was a great demand. He should be able to charge what the market could bear, which in reality is what the people will pay. The people would pay anything, in fact, everything to keep their families fed. *"The wheat's mine, and I've got a right to charge any price I want to for it."* Mr. Loftus said. *"That's so, Loftus, you have,"* Mr. Ingalls agreed with him. *"This is a free country and every man's got a right to do as he pleases with his own property... If you've got a right to do as you please, we've got a right to do as we please. It works both ways. You've got us down now. That's your business, as you say. But your business depends on our good will."* After more argument Mr. Loftus says, *"What do you call a fair profit? I buy as low as I can and sell as high as I can; that's good business."* But the hungry crowd of men in front of him, stood there unflinching for what was right, insisting on fair treatment and fair prices, insisting that people mattered more than profit. Finally, the merchant relented.[80] What that merchant realized is the same thing more American corporations need to realize, and that is just because you **can** charge too much does not mean that you **should** charge too much. That sometimes the best business decisions are the worst human ones, for there is no industry, no quarter profits that can ever justify

---

[80] Laura Ingalls Wilder, <u>The Long Winter</u>, chapter title "Free and Independent"; pp. 301-306

mistreating people, taking advantage of people, or using people to take more money than you should, more money than something is worth. It is always wrong, *always*. "*Therefore to him who knows to do good and does not do it, to him it is sin.*"[81]

Taking more than you should, more than what you are selling is worth – you see this mindset with gas prices, food monopolies, subsidies, housing, and more. It is not every industry or every business, but it is too many of them that people need to survive. Because we are no longer an agricultural society, with each family raising their own food and being as self-sufficient as one can be living off the land, individuals are now dependent on what others tell them their labor is worth and what others demand for the goods they provide. Additionally, the one thing that does seem to trickle down is greed. When one industry raises prices, other industries dependent on that industry have to raise prices to cover their costs, and the greed keeps going until those at the end of the chain pay. Eventually the consumer/worker, the one who earns her money by giving her labor in exchange for money, can't pay more because she doesn't have more and drowns in a sea of bills. So they make choices, desperate ones. Often these single mothers move in with friends or boyfriends just so they can split the rent, which, I might add, is not exactly the best environment to raise their child. They don't necessarily want to; they need to, just to survive. When the relationship gets ugly, they stay because they can't afford to leave. Bad things happen often and they are trapped. But that's okay because we can just tell these women what greedy leeches they are, remind them of their "bad life choices," how little they contribute, and pat ourselves on the back for standing up for what's right.

No one wants people to expect entitlements from the government. But where is the famed private sector? Where are the competitive and affordable products and services? Where is the apartment even a single mom could afford and still be safe? If business wants government to butt out, they need to make the necessities of life they want to profit off of affordable. If the private sector refuses to supply the needs and demands at a cost the poor can afford, and refuses to pay wages people can live on, then somebody has to step up and fill the gap some way. I would prefer that it was the private sector for more reasons than this paragraph can hold, but the truth is business has operated in a way that

---

[81] James 4:17

has hoarded wealth and resources for a few and not answered the need in the marketplace. Additionally, the private sector has abandoned a crucial component of its capitalist doctrine: Competition. There has been an appearance of the great equalizer, the great innovator, but it is about as real as the Great and Powerful OZ. Prices tell the truth. And the truth is competition has been absent for quite some time.

The answer is for businesses to honestly and independently compete for the business of the American consumer, all of them. If you think greed is good, fine, be greedy for their patronage by offering the best for the best price. CHARGE LESS/SELL MORE. Lead the way to a *free* market. For a market with no competition is not free at all. What we need all over the country are prices for goods that are in some relation to their actual cost to produce. That may mean new entrepreneurs who are committed to fair prices and fair wages. It might mean builders who change their focus to build affordable homes for the poor and lower middle class. It might mean more support for organizations like Habitat for Humanity, which provide affordable homes for the poor. It might mean reform among larger corporations, or even TRUE competition. This should create more business, more profit for those who respect the earnings of Americans, which they can use to expand their business and sell in more places to more people for more money. Maybe even celebrities, television networks, talk show hosts, political pundits and commentators could charge less for their craft, their great opinions and shows so the advertising during their popular programs would cost less and allow businesses to charge less for their products and services.

Seeking great riches, while I personally don't see why one would want to make this their life's work when it is the most uneternal dream out there, it doesn't bother me that some people have that dream. What bothers me is the greed, corruption, and unfairness that keeps markets from being free and robs people of their labor and worth. I don't see why top executives could not still make a handsome salary and profit, since they deem their labor so much more valuable than most of us, and pay wages people can live on. If they would only put themselves in their worker's shoes, how much would they deem the labor worth while done in those shoes? Isn't it possible, reasonable for them to consider valuing the labor of the least more, and maybe not having such an inflated view of their own self-worth? Who knows how many employees could live off the money reallocated from the top to the bottom. The tiniest reduction in salaries and bonuses at the top would be plenty to pay workers for labor well done, provide another consumer with the means to consume and be self-sufficient and not need a handout. And the more people who have more money to spend every month, the more our economy will be stimulated.

In addition, if politicians and committees did not solicit companies for contributions, or companies solicit favors and fund PAC's, during the 2008 election cycle businesses like Goldman Sachs would have $6,920,215, Lehman Brothers $2,533,504, Bank of America $3,401,745, AT&T $5,606,074, Time Warner (CNN) $3,048,444, General Electric (NBC, CNBC, MSNBC) $3,900,673, UPS $3,133,801, Blue Cross/Blue Shield $2,502,806, Aflac $2,302,880, and countless other PAC's, companies, and firms would have had more money to pay employees who doubtlessly have continued to work hard for very little, not to mention unions who use the money of workers to give to politicians, of which there are many. (I randomly chose companies from the list posted on **Center for Responsive Politics** under **Top Overall Donors** for 2008. The number of companies as well as the amounts are frightening. In an effort to be fair and thorough, News Corp, although not listed as a heavy hitter, gave substantial amounts to a diverse group of candidates, in addition to lobbying. However, most of the contributions are given from the entertainment as opposed to the news/journalism division.) But I guess it's more important that politicians solicit and receive money from companies than companies say: no, we are going to keep costs low and reward the labor of our workers with the profit we have made as a result of their labor. Maybe politicians could get votes some other way, like I don't know, pound pavement and represent the interests of the voters, no matter how little they grossed last year. Silly me, I thought that is what a republic is. Maybe paying workers a decent wage they can actually live on is redistribution of wealth. I don't think so. I think many of these problems would be solved if those on top placed more value on the hard work of those on the bottom. It is not taking from those who have achieved and giving it to those who haven't. In reality, both labor and owner, both elite and commoner have achieved, however, they have achieved different things. It is instead not exploiting labor for your own profit, it is valuing the hard work and time of others, it is acknowledging that they matter too, and they need to make enough to pay for their most basic needs and enjoy the blessings of liberty as opposed to the despair of poverty. It doesn't have to debilitate a company or an executive. Money is going plenty of places it needn't. I realize a few million is loose change to these corporations. But a few million here, a few million there, a $10 million office remodel or tropical business retreat, and the **$3.24 BILLION** spent lobbying Congress by corporations and unions in 2008,[82] and hey, you've got enough money to lower prices significantly or even, God forbid, raise wages and create jobs. *"For you have eaten up the vineyard; the plunder of the poor is in your houses."*[83] *"Come now, you rich, weep and howl for your miseries that are coming upon you! Your riches are corrupted, and your gold and silver are corroded, and their corrosion will be a witness against you... indeed the wages you have kept back by fraud, cry out, and the cries of the reapers have reached the ears of the Lord Sab'aoth."*[84] It is the people who need to be paid for their labor, not companies for their power and influence, not politicians for their favors. Nor is it even executives and boards who need retention bonuses or pampered retreats for their strenuous strategy sessions as they fret and calculate over just how fat to make the cats at investors' expense. (I personally believe any company trading publicly should have all salaries, bonuses, and retreats approved by the stockholders, since it is their money, and all employees should have an input as well. This one measure of accountability could prevent countless acts of corruption, excess, and waste. Mind you, I didn't say cap salaries; I said owners should pay executives based on their productivity and performance, which discourages waste and excess, while simultaneously keeping executives focused on their job and doing it well. Executives are, after all, employees.) Additionally, I would like to point out the obvious, that our free press is paying the politicians, which does not encourage impartiality or honesty. The bonus is that they receive money from companies advertising on their networks who are also paying so many of these politicians. Now where do they get that money? From the products and services they sell, right? So in reality, we, the people, as we buy goods and services are unknowingly funding the

---

[82] All lobbying amounts and campaign donations were compiled from the information on Center for Responsive Politics/ OpenSecrets.org in March 2009 for the 2008 campaign cycle.
[83] Isaiah 3:14b (NKJV)
[84] James 4:2, 3a, 4 (NKJV)

favors and interests of the powerful. How much **less** would the public have to pay for products if we were not also paying politicians and the excesses and interests of executives? This country is *we the people*, not we the corporation, not we the politicians, not we the wealthy and well connected. It is we, the people, who will have to remove ourselves from our dependence on corporate America if we ever hope to recover a truly free market and country.

...

CHILD SUPPORT

There is so much that could be said about how much women need the fathers of their children to not be stingy with the resources needed to raise children. Some men need to not use money as a means to crush and control their families. Some men need to not vanish without a trace and abandon a mother and her children to poverty. Some men need to not be allowed to use their children as pawns in an effort to manipulate and destroy the mother of their children. Every day in every county in this country there are untold stories of some woman fighting for her children from a father who is more interested in NOT paying child support than he is in being a father. Yet these men pay attorneys outrageous sums while simultaneously refusing to provide the support these women and children need to survive. Women are left bankrupt, broken, and utterly devastated because they dare to fight for their children. The courts allow far too much cruelty and never enough just treatment. The damage done to both these women and children can hardly begin to be calculated. Laws that protect women from men who seek to use the courts to destroy them are desperately needed, as well as laws that hold attorneys and judges responsible for either using the court process to charge never-ending fees while little children go without or for prejudicial judgments from those who abuse their positions and forego justice in favor of favoring men. Judges who can identify, understand, and stop abusive men before years of damage are inflicted are critically needed. But in the end, this all needs to translate into women, the ones who gave up their lives to give these children one, having access to the funds needed to raise their children.

There is much more that can be done regarding the resources needed to raise a child, more that men can do. Sometimes the men who once encouraged a girl to abort their child now recognize and mourn over the little one they will never know. These men could take this opportunity to save another child's life. They could make those child support payments to pregnancy centers and other organizations helping these women. While it won't bring back their child, it will help other children experience the joy, delight, and wonder of life, and calm a fearful mother's heart.

...

CHILDCARE

"Well, what are you doing to correct these bad things with your 'good' theology?"
– John Perkins

Childcare. Someone's got to watch the kids. If you want single women to not abort their children and you want them to be self-sufficient, responsible, and provide for themselves and their child, then while they work or continue their education, someone is going to have to watch their child, or children if we are also going to insist that domestic abuse is bad and women and children should not stay in homes where they are controlled and crushed. It is just common sense. They can't be in two places doing two things at once, and most employers frown on bringing one's infant or toddler to work. Saving their lives means facing their needs squarely with support and solutions that will help them stand on their own. This is love in action. Love, the thing we are supposed to do to our neighbors.

Of course, the next accusing question on every pragmatist's tongue is, "Who's going to pay for daycare?" with mutterings and grumblings of, "I shouldn't have to pay for somebody else's kid." To which I would remind that daycare is much less than welfare, and children should not have to die because they are expensive. This problem has a host of workable solutions, the least of which is telling these young mothers to miraculously come up with the money, which is nowhere near affordable, especially when you are, again, alone and at the bottom of the labor chain, also needing food and a roof. But I have an idea. I do not by any means think this is the only answer, but I do believe it is an efficient and practical idea that addresses a serious need and offers an opportunity to love our neighbors in a very real way. Maybe it will spark an even better solution in a greater mind than mine. But first, permit me an aside.

Church, *Body of Christ*, when I said everyone needs to take some responsibility in helping these young mothers and their children, I was thinking of you. You are the Body of Christ, and Christ said, "Let the little children come to me, and do not hinder them for the Kingdom of God belongs to such as these... And He took the children in His arms, put His hands on them and blessed them."[85] So why doesn't the church take the children into their arms and bless them with a safe place and love while their mommies go to work? You complain about how government is trying to do the church's job. But you don't DO this implied duty of the church, you just complain about government! Of course, people are inclined to think government is the answer when their life is falling apart; they are the only ones offering one! If you don't like how they do it, don't wait for a mandate, meet the need! And that is not throwing a few dollars at it, wringing your hands and saying you tried. MEET IT IN FULL! (One church in one county demonstrated how this could be done. It determined that every child in need of a foster home would have one. At this date there are more foster parents than foster children in this county. This is leadership. This is Christ. This is how to solve the problem of suffering.) Some of you preach against the awful social wrongs of single motherhood, working mothers, abortion, and welfare. I always wondered when I heard these teachings, so often grouped together, if these pastors and teachers realized they made supporting oneself impossible if you were unwed and pregnant and obeyed this teaching. It's not even hard to see, but you hear it all the time. When I would question people I can't even remember how many would say, "Well, those girls need to get married then." As if a girl could *make* a boy do that without her daddy's shotgun. As if she *should* marry a boy who might be cruel or unfaithful or abusive just because they think being a single mother is worse. As if there is an EASY button and she is just too stupid or too stubborn to press it. No wonder the world looks at us like we don't love or **think**. It's not that I believe marriage is bad, but bad things can happen and be justified because a woman is married to the one who did them, or because she is scared of being a poor single mother with all its social

---

[85] Mark 10:14 & 16 (NIV)

stigma. And although marriage **should** be part of the solution, it is too often part of the problem. I would rather there be more single mothers with decent jobs than more marriages with secrets too heinous to tell. There are far too many that would protect marriage before they would protect these young women and children, and an even greater number who care more that things look good than if they are good. Apparently, it's okay if things are ugly on the inside as long as they are pretty on the outside. It makes me sad... and angry. But I'm not the one who matters. It's Him we should be seeking to please. And He makes it abundantly clear throughout His word that it is *the least* He loves, those without a protector. It is them He wants to reach, them He wants to know about His grace which knows no bounds, not them He seeks to condemn and abandon.

I know, I know... it's a messy business and you don't want to be bothered. Loving the shamed, serving them, let me guess, God called you to something different, right? God called you to share Christ with more important people, people you can play golf with, people with clout who have great jobs and even greater connections. Too often you are more passionate about frugality and fundraising than you are about love. You care more for your campus development projects than you do for the safety and security of those with no father, more for holding on to resources then filling needs. You are more involved with attaining power, influence, and esteem than helping the helpless. You preach the gospel and sound doctrine but look away as people suffer. You implore the importance of personal responsibility, the doctrine of endurance, the consequences of immorality, and the task of the church to spread the good news. Have you forgotten, that "knowledge puffs up, but love edifies?"[86] Have you forgotten He gave us a living well that won't run dry? Do you not remember the wise words of St. Francis of Assisi, "Always preach the gospel, and when necessary use words?" Love is the voice the human heart hears. Love. I know different people are given different gifts, called to different tasks, but a need of this size cannot be met by only a few. It needs, if not the involvement, at least the backing of God's people as a whole. This is more a problem of leadership having ill-placed priorities and ignoring needs they don't want to bother with more than anything else.

---

[86] 1 Corinthians 8:1 (NKJV)

Yet if the church is Christ's Body on Earth, all that the Earth can see Christ's Body doing is pointing out how wrong and messed up the culture is, oh, and watch you build big buildings and ignore suffering. They say to themselves, if that's Jesus, I don't want any part of Him. But that isn't Jesus at all! Jesus ate with sinners, fed hungry people, healed sick people, spoke truth to the greedy and arrogant, saved sinners, washed dirty feet, and beckoned little children to His side so he could... love. He didn't build any buildings; He fished, for men. Of course, He used love for bait, and they tasted His truth.

I know you congratulate yourselves for all the other things you're doing. But none of it comes close to how much of God's money you're spending on buildings, on things, when God's church is made up of His people, not His bricks. No matter how pretty or big or electronically equipped these places are, they can't save. He never said his followers should build buildings to bring Him glory. He said, *"Let your light so shine before men, that they see your good works and glorify your Father in heaven."*[87] Maybe instead of spending millions of dollars to build even bigger buildings with even better stuff, which He never said to do, maybe instead you could wash little feet, maybe you could bear another's burden, maybe you could even look after the fatherless, all of which our Savior *did* tell us to do. He said when we serve those with nothing, we serve Him. Maybe the energies of His Church, His Body, would be better spent doing what He would do, investing in the desires of His heart, the people who actually bear His image.

So, church, what if you showed the world you believe in life by removing a stumbling block from the lives of these young women and helped meet the needs of those little lives who deserve to live, so they actually *could* live? You already have nurseries equipped with toys and cribs and swings, and playgrounds with sandboxes. Why not provide childcare for single mothers while they work or go to school? You would be investing in the youth and in the culture, you would be an influence of good to those who are vulnerable to deceit and manipulation, you would be developing relationships where you can share God's love and truth. These are the things you say you seek, the things you believe His Kingdom includes. By meeting such a critical need, you speak a love that is truer than any words you could hope to compose. The labor,

---

[87] Matthew 5:16 (NKJV)

well, it could be supplied through a variety of means. Faith based government funds could be made available to assist with paying the wages of childcare workers. Trained volunteers could decrease labor costs, as well as provide an opportunity for parenting instruction to young women who would gladly receive and benefit from the help, and maybe, **maybe even some of those building funds could pay for building up babies instead of bricks.** By utilizing existing facilities, costs could be kept to a minimum, but the opportunities for outreach are only limited by the number of little people to love.

Again, this is just one idea to address a piece of this critical problem. Another option is working with a childcare center and paying the expenses so these young mothers can go to school and work and trust their child is well cared for. Maybe several churches could join together to provide childcare for many at a drastically reduced cost. Pregnancy centers are also in need of such cooperative efforts from those who believe in life enough to provide the resources to make living financially possible. Additionally, the affordable housing needs to be where these young women are so they can keep their lives, their hopes and dreams as intact as possible. Empty office parks could be rented and renovated to provide affordable housing and an opportunity to use part of the facilities as a storefront for the small businesses these women begin, giving them more time for their families and reducing the costs of running their businesses. God's people also need to open their homes to foster children and give them hope for a different future instead of turning their backs on neglect and abuse and teaching Nietzsche's "whatever doesn't kill you makes you stronger." God's people should take God's direction and remember His Word says, *"If a brother or sister is naked and destitute of daily food, and one of you says to them, 'Depart in peace, be warmed and filled,' but you do not give them the things which are needed for the body, what does it profit? Thus also, faith by itself, if it does not have works, is dead."*[88] Who knows how many more good ideas are in the minds of citizens right now? What's yours?

Sadly, one thing I have learned is this. Leaders will not lead this way, or take recommendations from stupid, single mothers. Nor will corporations lower prices and raise wages out of goodwill unless it is also in their interests. It will take good people doing good, competing

---

[88] James 2:15-17 (NKJV)

against the greedy, and fighting for the worker and a free, fair marketplace. It will take people doing what is good for all, not just themselves. It will be up to God's people to move God's Church to reach out to those who need His love and His help. This is a battle that cannot be won by a few, it needs the many. With prayer and perseverance, hands that help and heal, words that encourage, hearts of kindness and grace, homes that are opened, and opportunities that are given, "*she will be loved.*"[89]

One more thing...

I remember the story of a sleepy, grumpy William Booth (founder of the Salvation Army, who did more to protect the laboring poor of England from the ravages of industrialism than any government program) arriving at work one morning and asking what all those people were doing milling around outside. His son told him they were hungry. To which he replied, "Well then, FEED them!" and the first Salvation Army soup line was served. When William Booth died, Queen Victoria slipped into the back of the church and took her place by a woman in poor, simple, modest dress that the queen discovered had been saved from prostitution. As the coffin came by the woman stood up and placed flowers on it. As they were leaving the queen asked the woman, "What brought you to the service?" The woman replied, "Well, he cared for the likes of us."[90]

...

HEALTHCARE or HELPING PEOPLE STAY ALIVE AND WELL

"Ethics is nothing other than reverence for life"... "I have always held firmly to the thought that each of us can do a little to bring some portion of misery to an end."

– Albert Schweitzer

I would also like to mention some ideas about healthcare. I know there needs to be reform, digital medical records to eliminate tragic and costly errors, health-based care as opposed to disease-based care, and a host of other issues, including exercise and nutrition to ward off diseases, although these in particular should always be things to

---
[89] Maroon 5 *She Will Be Loved*
[90] <u>Jesus Freaks Vol. 2</u>; dc Talk; pp. 162-167

encourage not regulate. What does this have to do with abortion, right? Well, if you believe in life, you should believe in and therefore protect life at all ages and stages. You shouldn't demand children be born and then abandon them to sickness, starvation, and a slum existence. In order to keep kids and moms alive and well, contributing to society, they need to be protected from disease. Disease strikes the poor more than any other group. Why? Because they can only afford the cheapest foods and often not enough, which deprives their bodies of the nutrition they need to fight viruses, bacteria, and disease. Impoverished living conditions, the only ones they can afford with the measly fruit of their labor, are breeding grounds for sickness, for heartache. Poverty and disease are kin. Is it really acceptable to support a system that for reason of creating and hoarding wealth tells the poor they do not make enough money to be seen by a doctor, that they are not worth enough to be well? *There are not words for this wicked wrong!* So what do we do? This problem has many fronts. But as with most things, anytime you try to pull out one thing you find it is connected to... everything else. So here are a few thoughts.

Apparently, all those years when people grew their own food was a good idea. They usually cared for the land because it was their life, so the food was full of good things. The good food kept them healthy, full, alive, not dependent on the value someone else placed on their labor to buy their daily bread. When lands have been raped for profit, soils have been depleted, and people have starved. Just look at our own history to see the human suffering resulting from the Dust Bowl and the immigration of the starving poor fleeing the Potato Famine. When people lose their land, they lose their independence. They become the slaves of those who control all the capital, which in our society is corporate America. They are slaves for someone else's profit. Now we have grocery stores full of food staples from corporations who are profiting not only from food monopolies but from subsidies, despite the severe deficiency in nutritional value on the shelves. Corn, found in everything from cereal, ketchup, dressing, bread, and beyond as high-fructose corn syrup, is so well subsidized it is the equivalent of $9 a gallon.[91] Many farmers feel forced to grow corn because it is the only thing they know will guarantee them a profit. Maybe there shouldn't be

---

[91] Food Fight: The Citizen's Guide to a Food and Farm Bill, Daniel Imhoff; 2007.

a subsidy on corn and other crops, maybe that would lower prices, allow for more competition, allow the land to grow other foods and heal, and even allow people to eat better, live better, prevent illness, and save money. A fight for food is a fight for the living. But it is people alone who can challenge and change the way things are. They have to stop buying junk so it doesn't sell, so corporations won't make it. They have to grow their own food if they can, or buy from local, healthy farms and farmers' markets. They have to find a way to buy back the land, make it grow again, and find their sufficiency in what they grow and trade with their own hands. People can trade food, churches can use their land to sponsor community gardens, fruit and nut trees can be planted instead of ornamental trees, people can need each other and seek what is good and what truly satisfies. Sounds heavenly, *"Ho! Everyone who thirsts, Come to the waters; And you have no money, Come buy and eat. Yes, come, buy wine and milk without money and without price... Let your soul delight in abundance. Incline your ear, and come to Me."*[92]

As far as having a healthcare system based on wellness and not disease, it's a noble idea, and it makes sense. But how do you make it happen? Trying to reduce expenses and the cost of living led me to rethink how our healthcare could be funded. It occurred to me that one industry is profiting extensively and yet it does more to prevent the treatment and health of people than anyone, health insurance companies—the ultimate oxymoron. The very organizations people give their money to in order to secure treatment are the very organizations which exist to **not** authorize or grant access or pay for treatment. Volumes could be written about humans who have died because they have been denied access to the treatments that would save their lives, not to mention the suffering, illnesses, and chronic conditions left untreated because somehow in the fine print, these people don't qualify. Only the people who are well and don't need a doctor qualify for one. Call me crazy, but if you give a company money for a service and they don't allow you to use the service, isn't this robbery? All they exist to do is collect our money and keep it. Why do we need them if they don't do the very thing they are paid to do? Eliminating one entire level of profit makers and health deniers is bound to lower costs. What if instead hospitals and doctors, those who actually desire to heal

---
[92] Isaiah 55:1,2b,3a (NKJV)

people, form medical groups and people could choose between these different groups which could offer different plans at competitive prices. This is still market-based and cost-efficient. Doctors and patients would need to maintain the freedom to choose the group that did the best job offering, not withholding treatment, and there could be competition between the groups, who could offer the best care at the best price. Nutritionists and gym memberships could be included in the different plans, which would make people feel like they were actually receiving something for the money they pay each month, but also improve their health and therefore decrease medical costs. Again, this is just the bones of one idea, and maybe this could be the spark for someone else with a greater imagination and vision. This is what I know. There are many more battles to tackle, many more wrongs to right. But things can't continue to exist as they are. Because in a country so wealthy, there are far too many who can't afford to be alive.

...

CONSTITUTIONAL AMENDMENT

Our posterity, those tiny, precious human beings not yet born but endowed like us with certain unalienable rights, need the protection of those rights secured for all of us in the Constitution. The Due Process Clause in the 14th Amendment states: "No State shall make or enforce any law which shall abridge the privileges or immunities of citizens of the United States; nor shall any State deprive any person of life, liberty, or property, without due process of law; nor deny to any person within its jurisdiction the equal protection of the laws." That is the protection all human beings need at all times for the simple reason that we are always human at every single stage of our lives and these rights are for those *endowed* with humanity, not for humans who can *do* certain things. Yet until there is an Amendment which defines and claims that all human beings at all stages of development should have these rights and their protections, there will be others who will fight to exclude them and kill them for reasons that have nothing to do with whether or not they are a human being. This is why a Personhood Amendment is critical to protecting all people both now and in the future so that we never define people by what they can or can't do, by how much they are or aren't wanted, or by how much they will cost the rest of us.

The other important measure is an Amendment which defines and limits the powers of the courts. If they are going to use the power of judicial review, then they should at least, in a positive grant system of government such as ours, have the expressed consent of the people to use such authority. Until the courts have a specific guideline and limit to how far their power reaches, we can expect the courts to continue to expand their power. If history teaches, it most certainly confirms that "power tends to corrupt, absolute power corrupts absolutely."[93]

So it is in our best interest and in the interests of those too small, too weak, and too poor to struggle for those securities which would protect so many, even if the struggle is a long, difficult, and costly one. For in securing those rights we protect all human beings no matter the circumstances and prevent injustice, and this is an effort, an endeavor worthy of human beings who call themselves free and brave.

...

A PLACE TO MOURN, A PLACE TO REMEMBER

How do you honor and recognize the death of 50 million innocent children in this country? How do you do it in a way that heals instead of condemns? For so long I have wished there was a place for people to go who have experienced abortion, a place for people to recognize and remember, a place to acknowledge this great wrong and weep over each life. So for a long time I have had a dream, a dream of a large beautiful field of tiny lambs, each lamb recognizing each day that killing innocent human beings has been legal in our country. But these tiny headstones are not just monuments to these children, they would be a place for their parents to come and grieve, mourn, and heal. A place where these parents could kneel in front of the lamb that marked that day their child died. This would be a place that would have people present who have walked this road and understand this very particular pain. This would be a place where there were people who know how to counsel these broken hearts, and a place where people will point to the One who has borne it all so those who mourn can know they are forgiven, a place with arms open wide in love and mercy.

What can wash away my sins?
Nothing but the blood of Jesus

---

[93] Lord Acton, English Historian and Moralist, written in a letter to Bishop Mandell Creighton, 1887.

> *What can make me whole again?*
> *Nothing but the blood of Jesus*
> *Oh! precious is the flow*
> *That makes me white as snow*
> *No other fount I know*
> *Nothing but the blood of Jesus*[94]

"Therefore I say to you, her sins, which are many, are forgiven, for she loved much. But to whom little is forgiven, the same loves little." [95]

...

"No one could make a greater mistake than he who did nothing because he could only do a little."[96]

Even though I am only a mom, this hasn't stopped me from looking at my world, looking at my friends, their children, and their struggles and seeing what could be if some things were different. This is why I have been audacious and bold enough to suggest new solutions to old problems, but I also realize this is only a beginning. Once we change what we chase after to what truly lasts, what truly matters, we will begin to see the lasting effect we long for. I believe we can make a difference simply by seeking what is good for people, instead of what is good for me or you only. God speed to you as we each seek with His help what He delights, and through His power make things new… "*old things have passed away; behold all things have become new.*"[97]

Then sings my soul, my Savior God to Thee
How great thou art, How great thou art![98]

---

[94] Words and Music, Robert Lowry, 1876
[95] Luke 7:47 (NKJV)
[96] Edmund Burke, English Statesman
[97] 2 Corinthians 5:17
[98] Words by Carl Gustaf Boberg, music old Swedish folk tune, translated by Stuart K. Hine

SOURCES

The Holy Bible- *New King James Version and New International Version*

Uncle Tom's Cabin, Harriet Beecher Stowe; Borders Classics; J.W. Edwards, Inc. 2006; ISBN 13: 9787-1-58726-366-8.

Anti-Abortionist At Large: How to Argue Intelligently About Abortion and Live to Tell About It, Raymond Dennehy; Trafford Publishing, 2002; ISBN: 1-55369-380-9.

The Girls Who Went Away: The Hidden History of Women Who Surrendered Children For Adoption in the Decades Preceding Roe v. Wade, Ann Fessler; Penguin Press, 2006; ISBN: 1-59420-094-7.

The Feminine Mystique, Betty Friedan; W.W. Norton, 1997; ISBN: 0393040496.

From Conception to Birth: A Life Unfolds, Alexander Tsiaras, Text by Barry Werth; Doubleday, a division of Random House, 2002; ISBN: 0-385-50318-0.

Should the Baby Live?, Helga Kuhse and Peter Singer; (preface) Oxford: Oxford University Press, 1985.

Handbook on Abortion, Dr. J.C. & Mrs. Wilke; Cincinnati: Hayes Publishing Company, Inc.; 1971.

Abortion: A Woman's Right to Know booklet developed by the Georgia Department of Human Resources to comply with the Georgia "Woman's Right to Know Act" of 2005.

Night, Elie Wiesel, Translated by Marion Wiesel; Hill and Wang, 1972, 1985; Translation copyright, 2006; ISBN-13: 978-0374-50001-6.

Jane Eyre, Charlotte Brontë; Oxford University Press, 1969, 1999; ISBN: 0-19-210042-4.

The Grapes of Wrath, John Steinbeck; Penguin Books, 2006; ISBN: 0143039431.

The Long Winter, Laura Ingalls Wilder; Harper Collins Publishers, New York, NY, 1971; ISBN:0-06-026460-8.

A Tree Grows in Brooklyn, Betty Smith; Harper Perennial Modern Classics, 2006; ISBN: 0061120073.

The Boy in the Striped Pajamas, John Boyne; David Fickling Books, A Division of Random House, Inc., 2006; ISBN-13: 978-0-385-75106-3.

The Diary of a Young Girl: the Definitive Edition, Anne Frank; edited by Frank Otto and Mirjam Pressler; Doubleday, Division of Random House; 1991, 2001; ISBN: 0-385-47378-8.

Mere Christianity, C.S. Lewis, original copyright, 1952, C.S. Lewis Pte. Ltd.; Harper Collins Edition, 2001; ISBN: 0-00-065292-6.

The Weight of Glory and Other Addresses, C.S. Lewis, excerpt originally published in *Theology*, 1941, original compilation and copyright, 1949, C.S. Lewis Pte. Ltd.; Harper Collins Edition, 2001; ISBN: 0-06-065320-5.

The Voyage of the Dawn Trader, C.S. Lewis, C.S. Lewis Pte. Ltd.; copyright 1952.

The Last Battle, C.S. Lewis, C.S. Lewis Pte. Ltd.; copyright 1956.

A History of the Supreme Court, Bernard Schwartz; Oxford University Press, 1993; ISBN: 0-19-508099-8.

Let Justice Roll Down, John Perkins; GL Publiscations,1976; Family Christian Press, 2001; ISBN: 1-930871-66-X.

King Leopold's Ghost: A Story of Greed, Terror, and Heroism in Colonial Africa , Adam Hochschild; First Mariner Books Edition, 1999; ISBN-13: 978-0-395- 75924-0

First Things: An Inquiry Into The First Principles of Morals and Justice, Hadley Arkes; Princeton, NJ: Princeton University Press, 1986

A Journey Through the Life of William Wilberforce, Kevin Belmonte; Day One Publications, 2006; ISBN13: 978-0-89221-671-0.

Jesus Freaks, Vol.2: Stories of Revolutionaries Who Changed Their World Fearing God Not Man, d.c. Talk; Bethany House Publishers, 2002; ISBN: 0-7642-2746-7.

The Nazi Doctors: *Medical Killing and the Psychology of Genocide*, Robert J. Lifton; (New York,1986).

By Trust Betrayed: Patients, Physicians, and the License to Kill in the Third Reich; Hugh C. Gallagher; (New York, 1990). Christian Pross & Gotz Aly; The Value of the Human Being: Medicine in Germany, 1918-1945 (Berlin, 1991).

Abortion Practice, Warren Hern; J.B. Lippincott Company, 1984.

In Necessity and Sorrow: Life and Death Inside an Abortion Clinic. Dr. Magda Denes; Basic Books, Inc. New York, 1976.

Food Fight: The Citizen's Guide to a Food and Farm Bill; Daniel Imhoff and Michael Pollan; 2007.

Woman's Body, Woman's Right: A Social History of Birth Control in America, Linda Gordon; New York: Grossman Publishers, 1976.

"Dilation and Extraction for Late Second Trimester Abortions", Dr. Martin Haskell, paper published 1992; interviewed by AMA News in 1993; interviewed on procedure and reported in Dayton Daily News; Dec 10, 1989.

20/20 Investigation; Chief Correspondent Chris Wallace; aired March 8, 2000

A Walk Through an Abortion Clinic, Carol Everett; ALL About Issues magazine Aug-Sept 1991.

When is the Violence Real? Sept/Oct 1994; Celebrate Life.

Abortion and the New Disability Cleansing, Gregg Cunningham, Esq.; National Review, November 10,1997.

The Serious Health Decision Women Aren't Talking About. Until Now; Liz Welch; Glamour Magazine: March 2009.

Fetal Psychology; Janet L. Hopson; Psychology Today; Sep/Oct 98

Is the Fetus Human?: The Abortion Conflict: What it Does to One Doctor; Dudley Clendinen, New York Times Magazine, August 11, 1985.

The Abortionist, Leo Wang; Berkeley Medical Journal, Spring 1995 Edition.

The First Ache, Annie Murphy Paul; New York Times Magazine, February 10, 2008.

The Eugenic Value of Birth Control Propaganda, Margaret Sanger; <u>Birth Control Review</u>, October 1921.

The United States Constitution & The Declaration of Independence (Thomas Jefferson)

<u>Common Sense</u>, Thomas Paine, 1976.

The OYEZ Project. *U.S. Supreme Court Media*

Georgia Right to Life Education Department

United States Holocaust Museum and Teacher Resource Center (www.ushmm.org/research)

"*Meet the Abortion Providers*"; Film 1989, produced by The Pro-Life Action League

"*Precious Unborn Human Persons*", Gregory Koukl; published by Stand to Reason.

"*Hard Truth*"; produced by American Portrait Films.

Hearing on H.R. 4292, the "Born Alive Infant Protection Act of 2000"

Transcript House Commerce Subcommittee, March 9, 2000

Center for Responsive Politics/ OpenSecrets.org (information gathered in March 2009)

Sojourner Truth Speech (www.kyphilom.com/www/truth/html)

Susan B. Anthony List (www.sba-list.org)

Feminists for Life (www.feministsforlife.org)

Georgia Division of Public Health (OASIS)

Alan Guttmacher Institute (www.guttmacher.org)
Center for Bioethical Reform (www.AbortionNO.org)

Abortion Facts.com